THE CACTUS AIR FORCE

- Brings to vivid life the nightmare world of Pacific warfare—a world of impenetrable jungles, treacherous weather and vast, uncharted ocean.

- Tells the stories of real men—men like Indian Joe Bauer, Swede Larsen and the legendary Joe Sailer—performing true feats of heroism. Includes photographs and a complete appendix of squadrons and pilots.

- Explores the unique role played by the courageous coastwatchers, often the only source of information on Japanese movements.

- Describes in exciting detail two important carrier battles—the Eastern Solomons and Santa Cruz.

THE BANTAM WAR BOOK SERIES

This is a series of books about a world on fire.

These carefully chosen volumes cover the full dramatic sweep of World War II. Many are eyewitness accounts by the men who fought in this global conflict in which the future of the civilized world hung in balance. Fighter pilots, tank commanders and infantry commanders, among others, recount exploits of individual courage in the midst of the large-scale terrors of war. They present portraits of brave men and true stories of gallantry and cowardice in action, moving sagas of survival and tragedies of untimely death. Some of the stories are told from the enemy viewpoint to give the reader an immediate sense of the incredible life and death struggle of both sides of the battle.

Through these books we begin to discover what it was like to be there, a participant in an epic war for freedom.

Each of the books in the Bantam War Book series contains a dramatic color painting and illustrations specially commissioned for each title to give the reader a deeper understanding of the roles played by the men and machines of World War II.

THE CACTUS
AIR FORCE

THOMAS G. MILLER, JR.

Foreword by
Lt. General James M. Gavin, U.S.A. (Ret.)

THE CACTUS AIR FORCE

*A Bantam Book / published by arrangement with
Harper & Row, Publishers, Inc.*

PRINTING HISTORY

*Harper & Row edition published August 1969
2 printings through September 1969
Bantam edition / June 1981*

*Illustrations by Greg Beecham and Tom Beecham.
Maps by Alan McKnight.*

In Loving Memory
T. G. M. III
1951–1968

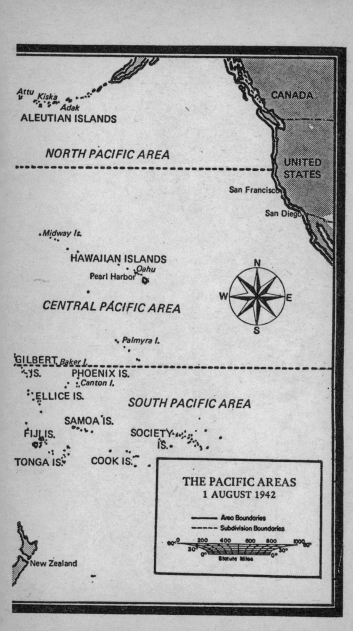

THE PACIFIC AREAS
1 AUGUST 1942

CONTENTS

FOREWORD
by Lt. Gen. James M. Gavin, U.S.A. (Ret.)

World War II was the first truly world war, and its global character and unprecedented violence were unique. American soldiers, sailors, airmen, and Marines were deployed all around the world, massing from time to time to make a decisive effort in what were to become some of the greatest battles in man's history. The names of Guadalcanal, Midway, and Normandy can still bring chills of apprehension to those who survived them. Finally, the total violence was capped by man's most awesome technical achievement, the atomic bomb over Hiroshima.

There has been no war in which such masses of ships, aircraft, and men have been committed to decisive action. To many historians, Midway is now in the category of one of the great, decisive battles of the world. The Battle of Normandy also has a special niche in history. And to those of us who fought through Europe, our memories of the cold, gray, winter days of the Ardennes will always be vivid. But all of the later triumphs would not even have been possible if we had not won our first offensive campaign of all: the Battle of Guadalcanal.

It is about the battle of Guadalcanal that Thomas G. Miller, Jr., has written, and written well. The commitment to Guadalcanal was known by the code name "Cactus." And so the small but courageous air force that supported the 1st Marine Division at Guadalcanal was known as the Cactus Air Force.

Veterans of those days between Pearl Harbor and our first physical engagement with the enemy remember all too well the anxiety, the frustrations, and the impatience of delay.

We were far from ready for war when the Japanese struck at Pearl Harbor, and months were to pass before any commitment could be made to battle. But finally, the Navy and Marine strategists decided that we should seize the island of Guadalcanal with its partially finished Japanese airfield. It was a risk, as indeed all battles are. But this was a particularly deadly risk because it would mean committing the 1st Marine Division, with what small air force could be scraped up, to the seizure of an island deep in the flanks of the Japanese southward thrust in the Pacific area. It was estimated that there was approximately a division of Japanese troops on the island protecting the construction crews, and they had a capability of reinforcing the island rapidly. Whether or not the reinforcements could be stopped depended upon the Navy and the Cactus Air Force. After the reinforcements made it ashore, which some of them did, then it was up to the 1st Marine Division to destroy them. Hence there was an intense interdependence between the Division and its air support. Neither would be able to survive without the other.

The venture was a gambit, the opening move in the Pacific War, and it was a gamble. The Japanese finally realized that the outcome of the battle depended upon the destruction of the Cactus Air Force. Incidentally, it began with thirty-one planes, none of which had a performance capability to match that of the Japanese planes. In fact, the Army Air Force plane, the P-400, could not fly above 15,000 feet and hence could not even reach intercepting altitudes. But, by bravery and skillful piloting, assisted by an intelligence net unique in history, the Cactus Air Force was able to keep the upper hand. In desperation the Japanese made an all-out effort, including many severe naval bombardments of the field. On October 13, 1942, for example, 918 14-inch naval shells, plus many of smaller caliber, destroyed most of the planes and practically all of the fuel, and inflicted many casualties on the pilots in their foxholes. but Cactus Air Force survived and went on to turn back every effort of the Japanese to reinforce their beleaguered troops.

In summary, it was air power—from which we perhaps expected too much in the 1940's—at its very best. Mr. Miller's account of Cactus Air Force's survival and triumph is intensely interesting and well documented. He has made an exhaustive study of Japanese sources and documents. His account of the desperate efforts of the Japanese to destroy

P-400

Cactus Air Force and the 1st Marine Division is vividly done. A rated Navy pilot of Korean War vintage, he knew a number of the participants, and his vignettes of them at Henderson Field during the critical days of its struggle are gripping and colorful. The whole is held together by fine writing. It is good history, and when one finishes reading it, one realizes that it was the dedication and extraordinary courage of that young generation of Americans that made the victory at Guadalcanal possible. And in doing so they made all the other victories that followed possible.

PREFACE

In the midsummer of the disastrous year 1942, a division of United States Marines landed on Japanese-held Guadalcanal in the Solomon Islands and captured it. This was the first territorial reverse that the overweeningly proud Japanese ever had suffered, and they determined to recapture the island. From mid-August to mid-November they attempted four progressively more powerful and dangerous combined offensives to wrest the island from the Americans. All four failed disastrously. Although Marine, and later Army, infantrymen and Navy ships took a prominent part in these four battles, the decisive role was played by a few score Marine, Navy, and Army pilots and their aircraft flying from Henderson Field on Guadalcanal.

Because Guadalcanal was referred to by its Navy code name "Cactus" in all contemporary correspondence, this brotherhood of airmen called itself "The Cactus Air Force." Always outnumbered in the air, rarely possessing more than a handful of dive and torpedo bombers to protect an island under virtual blockade, often only a hairbreadth away from grounding through lack of gasoline or defeat by attrition, the Cactus Air Force held on. It inflicted losses out of proportion to its size and to those it suffered. It exerted a decisive influence on the Guadalcanal campaign, an influence not completely understood or appreciated by any of the later historians. The Japanese Navy, much of its offensive power already severely crippled at the Battle of Midway, lost almost all of its best surviving pilots trying vainly to overcome American air power on Guadalcanal, and with it much of its ability to defend its stolen empire. The Guadalcanal campaign ensured that the United States would not lose the Pacific war.

This book tries to tell the story of the men of Henderson Field. Although it discusses the background of the campaign and occasionally touches lightly on land and sea actions, it does not pretend to be any more than a history of the Cactus Air Force during the three critical months when its fate and that of Guadalcanal hung in the balance. On only two occasions does it venture into detail on other matters. In late August and again in late October the carriers of the Japanese Combined Fleet intervened in the Guadalcanal campaign. The resulting sea-air battles were an integral part of the struggle for air supremacy over the southern Solomons, and therefore are a proper part of the chronicle of the Cactus Air Force.

I am greatly obliged to a large number of people who have made this book possible. Rear Admiral E. M. Eller, USN (Ret.), the Director of Naval History, extended, in addition to his approval and best wishes, the invaluable assistance of his efficient organization. Dr. Dean C. Allard and his excellent staff in the Classified Archives Branch of the Office of Naval History were particularly helpful; Mrs. Mildred Mayeux and Mr. B. F. Cavalcante cheerfully helped to track down many an obscure war diary and action report. In the Marine Corps Historical Branch, Mr. Rowland P. Gill and his predecessor, Mr. D. M. O'Quinlevan, and their staff were cooperative far beyond the requirements of courtesy or their positions.

The personal papers and reminiscences of several participants in the Guadalcanal campaign have been of invaluable assistance in the preparation of this narrative. Chief among these was Lieutenant General L. E. Woods, USMC (Ret.), who was the chief of staff of the Cactus Air Force from September to November, 1942, and actually commanded it during the climactic Battle for Guadalcanal in mid-November. Others were Rear Admiral Louis J. Kirn, USN; Brigadier General Jack R. Cram, USMC (Ret.); Colonel A. L. Nehf, USMC; and Mr. R. R. Witte, Contemporary interviews with Lieutenant Commander J. R. Cobb, USN; Captain J. J. Foss, USMC, Lieutenant Commander H. H. Larsen, USN; Lieutenant Colonel R. C. Mangrum, USMC; and Major J. L. Smith, USMC, were outstanding primary sources for information and observations that somehow did not find their way into the histories.

My friends Adrian Van Wyen of the office of the Chief

of Naval Operations and Lee Pearson of the Naval Air Systems Command gave me valuable advice on specific points as well as the more general benefit of their years of experience in naval aviation history.

I am particularly indebted to professor E. B. Potter of the U.S. Naval Academy, a most distinguished naval historian, for taking the time to criticize parts of the manuscript. His advice—as it was also to a young midshipman twenty years before—was kindly, direct and helpful.

A. E. Ferko called to my attention and loaned material of which I was unaware.

Dr. Douglas H. Robinson and Mr. M. M. Henkels, both friends and critics, did me the favor of reading the manuscript in its formative stages.

Finally, my thanks to Melanie McDonald and Pamela Morton for typing and re-typing that must have seemed endless.

I wish to acknowledge the permission given by Little, Brown to quote from Admiral Samuel Eliot Morison's *U.S. Naval Operations in World War II*, Volume V, *The Struggle for Guadalcanal;* by Houghton Mifflin to quote from *The Island* by Herbert Merillat; and by Harper & Row to quote from *Devilbirds* by J. A. DeChant.

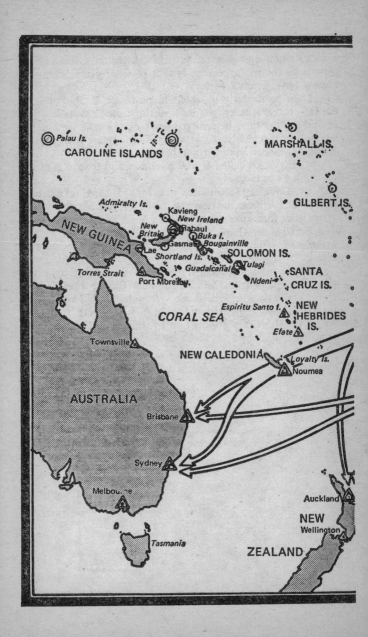

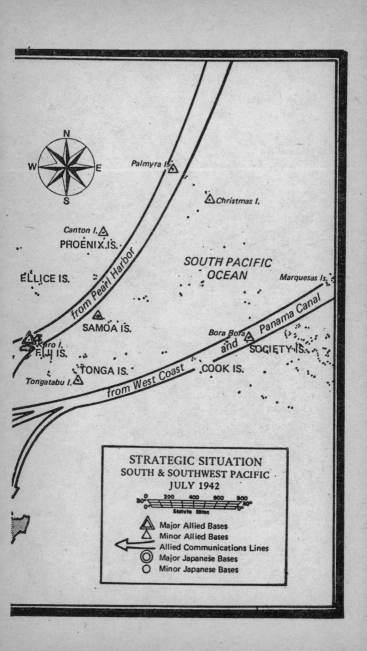

STRATEGIC SITUATION
SOUTH & SOUTHWEST PACIFIC
JULY 1942

Major Allied Bases
Minor Allied Bases
Allied Communications Lines
Major Japanese Bases
Minor Japanese Bases

1
INTO GUADALCANAL
August 7–9

Early in the morning of August 7, 1942, the Japanese radio station at Tulagi in the Solomon Islands sent an urgent message to the major Japanese air base at Rabaul: "A large force of ships of unknown number and types is entering the sound. What can these ships be?" The answer came not from Rabaul but from the ships themselves. Gunfire from cruisers and destroyers and bombing and strafing attacks by carrier-based planes tore at Japanese troops, many of whom were from noncombat labor battalions. Into what had been unchallenged waters an American invasion task force, including the carriers *Saratoga, Enterprise,* and *Wasp,* had sailed. Soon two regiments of United States Marines were landing on Guadalcanal, across what was destined to be named Ironbottom Sound from Tulagi, driving the defenders into the jungle. In Tulagi Harbor, all sixteen seaplanes of the Yokohama Air Group lay wrecked by strafing attacks. Their pilots died fighting alongside the soldiers who fiercely opposed four Marine battalions which had fought their way ashore on Tulagi and two small adjacent islands.

Within hours, Rear Admiral Sadayoshi Yamada, commanding the 25th Air Flotilla at Rabaul, responded with speed and decision unusual in senior Japanese officers. Though his forces were far below combat operating strength and he lacked intelligence about American targets, Admiral Yamada canceled a previously planned attack on the American base at Rabi, New Guinea, and had his pilots rebriefed to hit the troop transports assembled off Guadalcanal. At 0930, with the invasion still in its early stages, twenty-seven medium

1

bombers, seventeen fighters, and nine dive bombers lifted
from the Rabaul airfields, grouped into formation, and set out
for Guadalcanal.

An hour later, they passed over Buin, on the south coast
of Bougainville Island. Below, from his hiding place in the
south coastal mountains, a bespectacled forty-year-old Australian ex-planter, Paul Mason, spotted them and radioed Rear
Admiral Kelly Turner, commander of the South Pacific Amphibious Force: "Forty bombers headed yours." The Japanese were still two hours from their target, so the American
ships were able to prepare for the attack. The *Saratoga* and
Enterprise turned into the wind and launched their fighter
combat air patrols (CAPs in Navy terminology), which
climbed to attack altitude. As the stubby Grumman F4Fs
maneuvered upward, Yamada's planes kept their course for
Guadalcanal. The first of the dogfights that would rage for
months in the Solomons skies was shaping up.

The focus of combat would be the bombers, and the
Imperial Japanese Navy operated one of the best twin-
engined medium bombers in the world, the Mitsubishi Type
One (in the American code designation system called Betty).* A trifle bulbous, with a large fat fuselage studded with
protuberances, the Betty was nevertheless nearly as fast
cruising at altitude as was the Grumman F4F flying at
maximum speed. It was not only a high-level bomber but a
torpedo plane as well, and in that capacity had helped to sink
the British battleships *Prince of Wales* and *Repulse* in a single
day off the Malayan coast. The plane had an enormous range,
but that was a mixed blessing, for its great fuel supply was
made possible by two 600-gallon gas tanks located in the
roots of the wings between each engine nacelle and the
fuselage. Since to armor them would reduce their capacity by
almost half, the tanks were totally unprotected. A hit in either
one would blow up the plane, killing the seven-man crew.
This fatal weakness had contributed to the loss of nearly half
the Bettys in operation during the six months after December
7, 1941. Officially the "Type-One Bomber," to the Japanese
flyers it was sometimes known as the "Type-One Lighter."

The dive bombers in Admiral Yamada's counterattack
were Aichi 99s, or Vals, as the Americans called them. The

---

*This system, although not adopted until a year after the period covered
by this book, is nevertheless used hereafter for convenience.

Val was single-engined, with an oddly tapered low wing that gave it exceptional maneuverability for so large an aircraft, even with its anachronistic fixed landing gear. Speedier than the American Navy's Douglas SBD dive bomber, which had a retractable gear, the Val was so lethal a weapon that early in the war it was obtaining up to 80 per cent hits on moving ships under practice conditions. In April, 1942, eighty Vals sank two British heavy cruisers in a matter of minutes, with every bomb dropped scoring either a direct hit or a damaging near miss.

Protecting the bombers was the outstanding aircraft of the imperial Navy, the Mitsubishi Zero, or Zeke. Rather than a mere copy of western aircraft, as wartime propaganda maintained, the Zeke was the result of the efforts of a brilliant design team and of specifications so demanding that the firm of Mitsubishi had no competition for the contract. Briefly, the Navy wanted a carrier-based fighter that would equal in speed and exceed in maneuverability and range any foreign opponent likely to be flying before 1942. In 1937 the plane was completed: elegant, low-winged, weighing only 5,500 pounds. The Grumman F4F outweighed the Zeke by a third and its Pratt and Whitney Twin Wasp engine delivered 1,200 horse power compared to the Zeke's 875, but the Zeke, with its light weight and large wing area, could outclimb and outmaneuver the Grumman and even the crack British fighter of Battle of Britain fame, the Hawker Hurricane. With the help of a belly gas tank, the Zeke could remain airborne for nearly twelve hours and had almost twice the combat radius of the Grumman.

As did the Betty, the Zeke paid for its range and lightness: for the pilot there was no protective armor plating; for the gas tanks there was no leak-proofing. And while the extra belly gas tanks gave the Zeke an advantage in range over the F4F, they reduced the Zeke's speed and maneuverability. All the Zekes flying from Rabaul to Guadalcanal had to carry belly tanks, thus reducing their advantage over the Grummans and making them more vulnerable. Should an opponent get into position actually to fire at a Zeke, some well-placed shots could destroy the Japanese plane. However, during the first six months of the Pacific war, surprisingly few Allied pilots were able to do so. With only two slow-firing cannon of low muzzle velocity and two rifle-caliber machine guns, the Zeke remained dominant.

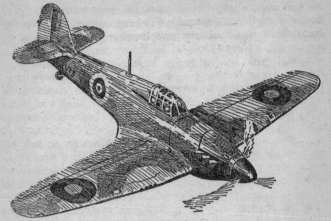

Hawker Hurricane

Japan's naval pilots were among the best and most rigorously trained in the world. Training for Japanese naval aviation included doing somersault dives from a high diving board to the ground, supporting oneself by one arm from the top of an iron pole for ten minutes, swimming under water for a minimum of one and a half minutes, and wrestling in matches where defeat meant automatic expulsion. Japan's ace enlisted pilot, Saburo Sakai, competed for entrance to the training program with 1,500 others—only he and 69 other men graduated. Typically, two-thirds of each class washed out. In a land where the concept of the Samurai, the faithful hereditary warrior, still gripped the imagination, and the Navy was considered the premier service, these skilled and proud aviators were all considered heroes. Their numbers were kept small, so that it became incumbent upon these elite flyers to survive, in spite of the vulnerability of their planes, if air superiority was to remain in Japan's control.

American flyers were also well trained and proud, but lacked the combat experience the Japanese had been gaining since the invasion of China. Their first-line naval fighter in 1942, the Grumman F4F-4 Wildcat, was not a superior aircraft by mid-1942 standards. It was almost 50 miles per hour slower at combat altitude than the Zeke, and had a rate of climb only 80 per cent of that of its antagonist. Being

2,500 pounds heavier, it had a much shorter range and was much less maneuverable than the Zeke. Its peculiar narrow-tracked landing gear made it look rather like a knock-kneed bumblebee on the ground. Like any airplane, it had its crotchets. For example, its retractable landing gear had to be cranked up and down manually; one of the characteristics of the F4F, in fact, was an undulating flight path after take-off as the cranking motion of the pilot's right hand was transmitted through his body and left hand to the sensitive control stick. Also, it was almost impossible to trim the controls so that the plane might "fly itself." And frequently, on landing, one or another landing-gear shock-absorber strut would collapse; in itself, this was harmless, but pilots would instinctively try to compensate for the resulting tilt of the aircraft by tapping brake on the high side, at which point the little Grumman, with its narrow wheelbase, would whip into a ground loop. This same landing gear made it hard to taxi on the ground in a cross wind and increased the tendency to swerve on take-off.

Such deficiencies were outweighed, however, by excellent features. The F4F's armament of six 50-caliber machine guns was far superior to the Zeke's fire power. If the Grumman was heavy because of its exceedingly rugged construction, including armor plate and self-sealing gas tanks (Navy and Marine pilots referred to the manufacturer as the "Grumman Iron Works"), it was still far more likely than the Zeke to survive battle damage and bring its pilot home.

Now, at early afternoon on August 7, the Grummans circled at attack altitude, waiting to sight Yamada's Bettys. At 1315 the radar of the cruiser *Chicago* picked up the inbound bombers, and five minutes later the Japanese formation was sighted over Savo Island, a sinister volcanic cone that loomed from the sea ten miles north of Cape Esperance, the northern tip of Guadalcanal.

The Japanese were met first by a four-plane division from *Enterprise*'s Fighting Squadron Six, which shot down two of the Bettys without loss. A few minutes later, another six F4Fs from the same squadron sighted the enemy formation, which by now had dropped its bombs harmlessly into the sea and was heading back to Rabaul. The *Enterprise* fighters sent another Betty flaming into the water north of Savo, but three of the six F4Fs were shot down by Saburo Sakai in the course of a sharp dogfight. At almost the same time, two divisions from *Saratoga's* Fighting Five, totaling eight F4Fs, intercepted the Japanese and damaged two more Bettys so badly that they had to ditch in the sea on their way back to Rabaul. However, five of the *Saratoga* pilots were shot down and only one was recovered. All were downed by another of the Japanese Navy's star fighter pilots, Hiroyoshi Nishizawa, who eventually would be Japan's greatest ace.

This day gave the enemy fighter pilots pause. It was the first time they had encountered either the Grumman F4F or U.S. Navy pilots. Two of the Zekes had been shot down, as well as five of the bombers they were supposed to be protecting, and two more fighters had been damaged. Lieutenant Commander Nakajima, the Air Group commander, barely survived his initial experience with the sophisticated fighter tactics of the Americans, and Sakai was almost killed when he mistook two divisions of TBFs (American torpedo planes) on a bombing mission for F4Fs and was badly shot up by the concentrated fire of eight 50-caliber rear-turret guns. Almost blinded and only half conscious, Sakai managed to fly his riddled plane back to Rabaul, but he was out of the war for almost two years.

The Vals followed the Bettys in by an hour. Just as they were diving on the destroyer *Mugford,* they were jumped by an eight-plane CAP from Fighting Five; those who escaped the *Saratoga's* pilots were then worked over by two divisions from *Enterprise.* The victory claims of the American pilots totaled almost twice as many Vals as were present, but the actual count was good enough. Six of them were shot down outright and the remaining three ditched on the way home. The destroyer was hit but not badly hurt. Not one of the bombers made it back to Rabaul.

The Japanese attacks on the 7th were ineffective and cost them fourteen bombers and two Zekes destroyed. Although they justified this by extravagant claims of American losses, the actual count was eight F4Fs and one SBD (whose daring pilot attacked a group of Zekes and was shot down by Sakai and killed).

By the evening of August 7 all the initial objectives on Guadalcanal had been secured by the marines against little opposition. Only Tulagi remained in enemy hands. But the Japanese had no intention of letting the challenge pass. Vice-Admiral Gunichi Mikawa, leading seven cruisers and a destroyer of the Eighth Fleet, left Rabaul the afternoon of the

7th with orders to proceed to Guadalcanal. The Misawa Air Group, then based on Tinian in the Mariana Islands, was ordered to fly down to Rabaul immediately. Nine of the group's thirty-six Bettys arrived at Rabaul late on the afternoon of the 7th, partially replacing Yamada's bomber losses.

The Japanese mounted a maximum effort on the morning of August 8. Twenty-three bombers, with fighter escort, took off armed with torpedoes, their target the still-unloading American transports. Once again they were spotted early. Australian Jack Read reported them as they roared over the northern coast of Bougainville, and Turner's force was alerted. However, the American air-search radars did not detect the approaching Bettys until they passed over the eastern tip of Florida Island, only five minutes from the transports. The Combat Air Patrol, therefore, was not able to attack the Japanese in strength. Three of Fighting Six's F4Fs, patrolling high overhead, saw the bombers beginning their run on Turner's ships and dove on them, shooting four of the Bettys and a Zeke into the water. By the time the last of the five planes had been splashed, the remainder were heading straight into the waiting American formation. The ships' antiaircraft gunners shot down thirteen in less than two minutes, and skillful maneuvering by Admiral Turner restricted the damage to a single torpedo hit on the destroyer *Jarvis*. Some of the Japanese fighter escort followed the Bettys and made strafing runs on the American ships, and one of them, fatally hit by an antiaircraft shell, crashed flaming into the transport *George F. Elliott*. The burning ship was abandoned by her crew and later sunk. The cost to the 25th Air Flotilla was prohibitive: eighteen of the twenty-three Bettys were lost, in addition to two Zekes. Admiral Yamada could not afford to risk such losses again, even though seventeen more bombers of the Misawa Air Group arrived at Rabaul during the day. For the 9th, therefore, he planned to restrict his remaining aircraft to search missions and decided not to attack unless American carriers or battleships were sighted.

As of early afternoon on August 8, things had gone very well for the Americans. Stiff Japanese opposition on Tulagi had been overcome, all the Marines' initial objectives there and on Guadalcanal had been secured, the enemy's air attacks had been repulsed with minor losses, and there seemed little further to worry about except getting the transports unloaded. However, before the next morning the situation would change catastrophically.

The first setback was the news—discovered accidentally by Admiral Turner, in charge of the landing force—that Admiral Fletcher proposed to withdraw his carriers that night. In a dispatch to Admiral Ghormley, commander of the invasion force, Fletcher cited as his reasons for leaving the large number of Japanese bombers and torpedo planes in the area, the loss in combat or operational accidents of twenty-one of his ninety-nine fighters, and low fuel supply. In actual fact he had been heading south for twelve hours before formally requesting permission to do so, his available fighters exceeded the total number of surviving aircraft in the Japanese 25th Air Flotilla by a considerable margin, and the fuel shortage was simply fictitious. Fletcher had been the senior U.S. officer present at the Battle of the Coral Sea, where *Lexington* was lost, and at Midway, where his flagship *Yorktown* was sunk. More likely, his primary concern was not to protect the expeditionary force of which he was the commander but rather to keep from losing another carrier.

The second blow followed quickly. Admiral Mikawa, although sighted by American reconnaissance aircraft, was not recognized as a threat to the transports and cruisers off Guadalcanal. When he steamed into Ironbottom Sound shortly before 0100 on August 9, he found five American and Australian heavy cruisers, unready for combat, steaming slowly to and fro north and south of Savo Island. In a lightning gunfire and torpedo attack the Japanese sank the American *Quincy, Vincennes,* and *Astoria* and the Australian *Canberra* and damaged the *Chicago,* escaping without loss. Fortunately, Mikawa felt that this fantastic success was enough and did not attack the transports.

Even prior to this disaster, Kelly Turner had decided that he had to withdraw the transports. Fletcher's desertion left him no choice. The loss of virtually all his covering force could only accelerate his leaving. Turner kept his ships in the harbor through the daylight hours of the 9th, unloading as much as he could, and then they sailed away leaving 19,000 Marines ashore with only limited supplies of food and ammunition and no heavy equipment. The islands on which the Americans were virtually marooned lay in waters now controlled by the enemy. Their air and surface ship protection—that which survived—was fleeing southward. It was the greatest humiliation in the Navy's history, greater even than Pearl Harbor; the Americans knew the Japanese were coming and should have been ready.

"Betty"

Japanese air power contributed nothing to the American debacle except the threat posed by its existence. But it did write a short footnote to history on August 9. Admiral Yamada's search planes mistook some of the single-funneled American destroyers for British *Warspite*-class battleships. An attack group of sixteen Bettys was launched and that afternoon found the crippled *Jarvis* slowly making her way unescorted to New Caledonia. In a lonely, savage battle the little destroyer was torpedoed repeatedly and sunk with all hands. Before the men of the *Jarvis* died, they shot down two of the Japanese bombers and damaged another four. With this brief, murderous skirmish came an end, not only to a valiant ship, but, until it could be replenished weeks later, to Japanese air power in the South Pacific. In three days the 25th Air Flotilla lost twenty-four twin-engine bombers, three-quarters of its original strength, as well as nine dive bombers, four fighters, and sixteen seaplanes. Until the bombers, particularly, could be replaced, enemy air strength would be in no position to endanger the abandoned Marines on Guadalcanal. They therefore had some precious days to get their supplies dispersed from their vulnerable dumps on the beach, complete the captured airstrip, and build a defense perimeter around it.

2

SOLOMON'S ISLES
February 18–August 6, 1942

That the Marines on Guadalcanal should hold their beachhead and subsequently conquer the island was of the utmost importance in the prosecution of the war. Since the beginning of the conflict, moves and countermoves by the Japanese and Allies had raised the value of the Solomons area enormously. At stake were the fate of Australia and New Zealand and the ability of the United States to maintain a strong presence in that part of the world. Neither Japan nor America could afford to lose the islands and control of the seas surrounding them.

The rapid crumbling of the Philippines and the Far Eastern empires of Great Britain and the Netherlands during the first six months of 1942 had left the United States with no option but to fling as many men, ships, and aircraft as could be spared into the defense of Australia and New Zealand. The first task was to build up enough strength to hold the Antipodes against the apparently irresistible irruption of Japan into the South Seas. Eventually they would serve as bases from which the march back would be started. Supplying Australia and New Zealand therefore became a major American preoccupation during early 1942.

From Pearl Harbor, the ship routes to the great ports of Brisbane and Sydney crossed the Equator near Christmas Island, passed north of Samoa and through the Fijis and New Caledonia, thence to Australia. Major U.S. bases were established in Samoa, on Koro in the Fiji Islands, and at Nouméa, New Caledonia.

The Japanese thrust south did not yet endanger these

bases and the vital supply routes they protected, but the emergence of such a threat became clear when the Japanese occupied and garrisoned Rabaul, the major port and city of New Britain, a large island east of New Guinea, and Kavieng on the island of New Ireland, 130 miles north of Rabaul. From Rabaul three successive island chains ran southeast, pointing directly at the Pearl Harbor–Australia ship route. From northwest to southeast they were, respectively, the Solomons, the Santa Cruz Islands, and the New Hebrides.

The Americans started moving into this no-man's-land in March, when they garrisoned the island of Efate in the New Hebrides. In May they began another airfield on Espiritu Santo, but that same month the Japanese seized the island of Tulagi, capital of the Solomons. These islands, optimistically named for King Solomon by treasure-seeking Spanish explorers, by mid-1942 were almost certain to become an area of battle.

From a distance the Solomons are beautiful, green islands set in the blue sea framed by huge white clouds. From close up they are eerie, darkly oppressive, an area of sometimes frightening natural violence much as was all earth in its primitive youth. The islands form two parallel chains, separated by a long, wide passage which had no name until 1942. The northernmost line of islands is comprised of Buka, long, mountainous Bougainville, Choiseul, Santa Isabel, and Malaita. The southern group includes Vella Lavella, Kolombangara, New Georgia, the Russells, Florida, Guadalcanal, San Cristobal, and Rennell. Of volcanic origin, the islands are large, and most of them have high mountainous interiors and malarial coastal plains. Their highlands and lowlands are overgrown with thick tropical rain forests, and the islands stink of rotting, insect-infested vegetation. This is a region of what meteorologists call "convergence," where different air masses constantly flow together from opposite directions. The line of their meeting, the Intertropical Front, is marked by almost continuously present low rain clouds interspersed with towering cumulus buildups that can extend upward to 40,000 feet or more. According to the climatologists, November through March is the rainy season and the other seven months of the year the "dry" season, although this distinction was lost on those who served in the Solomons. The heat and humidity are so high that local thunderstorms break over the mountains almost every day, yielding torrential showers and

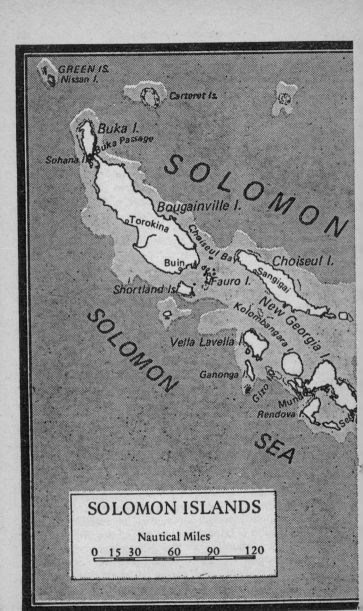

GREEN IS.
Nissan I.

Carteret Is.

Buka I.
Buka Passage

Sohana I.

SOLOMON

Bougainville I.

Torokina

Choiseul Bay

Choiseul I.

Buin

Sangigai

Fauro I.

Shortland Is!

New Georgia

Kolombangara I.

Vella Lavella I.

SOLOMON

Ganonga

Gizo

Munda

Rendova

Sea

SEA

SOLOMON ISLANDS

Nautical Miles

0   15   30   60   90   120

PACIFIC OCEAN

ISLANDS

Ontong Java

Rekata Bay

Santa Isabel I.

THE SLOT

Vangunu I.

Gatukai I.

Russell Is.

Savo I.

Tunnibulli

Thousand
Ships Bay

Florida Is.

Tulagi

Lunga

Malaita I.

Guadalcanal I.

San Cristobal I.

leaving behind a thick, gooey black mud, the surface of which soon dries in the sun.

The decision to contest the Solomons was made by Ernest Joseph King, the tall, stern strategist who was commander in chief of the U.S. Fleet and Chief of Naval Operations. Admiral King's position in the Navy was unique in its history, and his enormously strong personality gave him complete dominance of the Joint Chiefs of Staff when it suited him to exercise it. Only George Marshall, the great Chief of Staff of the Army, was King's professional equal; King had no superior.

At the end of February, 1942, only a few days after Singapore fell to Japan, Admiral King first raised the possibility of an American offensive in the South Pacific. In a memorandum to General Marshall, he recommended establishing a series of bases from which United States forces eventually could advance through the New Hebrides, Solomons, and Bismarcks up to Rabaul. However, the agreed-upon Allied strategy of beating Germany first while holding Japan, and particularly the American landings in North Africa, which then were in the early stages of planning, naturally had the full support of the Army and Army Air Force, which would play the major roles in a predominantly land and air war. They were reluctant to sanction any but the most basic kind of defensive measures in the Pacific, and there was even talk in Washington of letting Australia and New Zealand go rather than divert American resources from Europe. King was absolutely opposed to such narrow-mindedness. In early March he wrote another memorandum, this time to President Roosevelt, the gist of which was contained in the sentence, "We cannot in honor let Australia and New Zealand down." Roosevelt agreed, and the Joint Chiefs reviewed American strategy again in mid-March, affirming the need to secure the Antipodes and the lines of communication between them and the United States.

The Japanese also had been thinking about the South Pacific. In the first flush of enthusiasm over their easy victories in the first five months of the war, they made plans to capture New Caledonia, Fiji, and Samoa. They also resolved to occupy the island and harbor of Tulagi, in the Solomons, as a seaplane base, and to take the American-Australian base of Port Moresby, New Guinea, by amphibious assault. A two-pronged expedition to accomplish these latter objectives left Rabaul in early May. The Pacific Fleet was, as usual, forewarned by its outstandingly efficient cryptographic unit, and two American carriers were waiting for the Japanese in the Coral Sea. They were too late to prevent the seizure of Tulagi, but the Port Moresby expedition suffered the loss of the small carrier (*Shoho*) that was providing its direct air support and the two large carriers (*Shokaku* and *Zuikaku*) furnishing distant support lost their air groups. The Battle of the Coral Sea was a tactical standoff, since the big U.S. carrier *Lexington* was lost, but it was a strategic defeat for the Japanese, their first of the war.

Late in May, the entire Japanese Combined Fleet headed eastward toward the island of Midway. Its nominal objective was the seizure of that American outpost at the end of the Hawaiian chain. Its actual objective, the long-sought goal of its commander in chief, Admiral Isoroku Yamamoto, was the destruction of the United States Pacific Fleet. In a masterful combination of accurate intelligence and interpretation, tactical skill, and sacrificial bravery on the part of many American pilots, the Pacific Fleet surprised and destroyed the four carriers that constituted the main striking force of the Combined Fleet. The balance of carrier air power in the Pacific changed suddenly and dramatically from complete Japanese superiority to precarious equilibrium. To Ernest King, this was a time of opportunity.

On June 25 King sent another memorandum to Marshall, proposing that advantage be taken of the post-Midway situation by capturing the Japanese seaplane base at Tulagi. Marshall agreed, but suggested that the offensive be commanded by MacArthur, whose Southwest Pacific Area boundary passed through the middle of the Solomons. King firmly refused on the logical grounds that *all* the forces were to be provided by the Pacific Fleet. The Joint Chiefs issued a directive on July 2 ordering Admiral Nimitz to "seize and occupy the Santa Cruz Islands, Tulagi, and adjacent positions." The operation was given the code name "Watchtower."

The man who was actually to carry out this directive was fifty-nine-year-old Vice-Admiral Robert Ghormley, who, under Nimitz, commanded the South Pacific area. (In navalese, his title was abbreviated "ComSoPac.") Ghormley had had a long, distinguished, and varied career in the Navy and was deemed to be a superior strategist. The admiral possessed outstanding ability as a diplomat and negotiator, and his most recent assignment had been as a special observer with the British Admiralty in London.

Scarcely had the JCS directive been issued when an American reconnaissance plane on routine patrol over the Solomon Islands on July 5 made a discovery that assigned to Watchtower a new urgency. The Japanese were beginning the construction of an airstrip on the island just to the south of Tulagi. This island was Guadalcanal.

The implications were grave. If the Japanese were to base their bombers on Guadalcanal instead of Rabaul, 560 miles to the northwest, they would be able to interdict American supply routes to Australia and provide air cover for operations against the New Hebrides and islands farther south. More immediately, having a nearby operational enemy air base against which to contend would greatly complicate the problem of landing in the Solomons.

The discovery of the Japanese airfield on Guadalcanal redirected attention from the Santa Cruz Islands to Guadalcanal and Tulagi. The JCS directive gave August 1—just a month off—as the target date for the operation. Ghormley was appalled at this precipitancy and, after a meeting with MacArthur in Australia, issued with him a joint recommendation that the operation be delayed until greater strength was available in the South Pacific to carry it out. MacArthur, who only three weeks previously had offered to take Rabaul itself, was perhaps not anxious to see an effort started in the Pacific that he did not command. Ghormley's reaction was that of an intelligent but conventional commander. Only King seemed to grasp the situation. In a reply to Ghormley and MacArthur on July 10, the admiral expressed one of the crucial decisions of the Pacific war. He said that he would sanction no delay in the execution of Operation Watchtower.

To carry out his orders, Ghormley was given forces that he considered adequate. The landing was to be made by the First Marine Division, three regiments of which were en route from Norfolk, Virginia, to Wellington, New Zealand. They were to be supported by the Pacific Fleet's surviving aircraft carriers, *Saratoga* and *Enterprise*, joined by the *Wasp.* The Marine commander was Major General A. A. Vandegrift, a quiet, gentlemanly Virginian who had been in the Corps since 1909. Vandegrift's principal characteristics were calmness under stress and stubbornness.

The senior naval commander on the scene was Vice-

Admiral Frank Jack Fletcher, who had commanded at battles of the Coral Sea and Midway until his flagship was disabled. In theory Fletcher was in tactical command of all aspects of the landing. In practice his concerns were confined to his three carriers and their supporting ships, organized into Task Force 61.

The transports that would actually land Vandegrift's division, and their screening and fire-support ships, were under the command of Rear Admiral Richmond Kelly Turner, the newly appointed Commander, Amphibious Force, South Pacific. Admiral Turner was a most interesting and complex person. He was highly intelligent, irascible, vastly capable, dogmatic, opinionated, and unable to delegate work. For this command he probably was one of the best choices that could have been made. Before him no one ever had run an amphibious force; indeed, the concept of such a force was less than ten years old. Turner personally and brilliantly worked out in detail every aspect of this highly complicated kind of operation, but he had to learn a few things first. Some of his learning was at the expense of quite a few Marines.

All the land-based aircraft in the South Pacific—Army, Navy, Marine, and some oddments of the Royal New Zealand Air Force—were placed under Rear Admiral John S. McCain, Commander Aircraft South Pacific ("ComAirSoPac"). By the end of July, McCain's command consisted of 291 aircraft of all types. Three Marine and three Army fighter squadrons represented ComAirSoPac's defensive strength. His offensive power was built around thirty-five Army B-17 bombers and a medium bomber group. Thirty-one Navy PBY flying

B-17

boats made up McCain's long-range reconnaissance capability. The rest of his force was mostly part of New Zealand's tiny air force, flying ancient British aircraft from the Fijis. Numerically, AirSoPac was larger than the Japanese 25th Air Flotilla at Rabaul. But the Japanese were concentrated, while the American aircraft were scattered across thousands of square miles of island-dotted ocean. Furthermore, the enemy could draw reinforcements from the whole of the Eleventh Air Fleet, which had six air flotillas defending the perimeter of his newly won South Seas empire. McCain had no such option available. His were all the planes there were.

The Japanese naval forces in the South Pacific had been organized into the Eighth Fleet in June. This fleet, commanded by Vice-Admiral Mikawa, included five heavy and three light cruisers. Japan's two surviving large carriers, five smaller ones, and all her twelve battleships were in home waters.

Their air strength in the South Pacific consisted of the 25th Air Flotilla of the Eleventh Air Fleet, commanded by Rear Admiral Sadayoshi Yamada. Most of Admiral Yamada's flotilla was based at Rabul, its efforts having been directed primarily against the American and Australian forces in New Guinea. His largest unit was the crack Tainan Air Group with a nominal strength of sixty Zeke fighters. This group had taken part in the invasion of the Philippines and the Netherlands East Indies, and had compiled an excellent combat record against American Army pilots in New Guinea. It included the three leading fighter aces of the Japanese Navy, Sakai, Nishizawa, and Toshio Ota. Offensive striking power in Rabaul was vested in the forty-eight Betty bombers of the fourth Air Group. The reconnaissance arm of the 25th Air Flotilla was the Yokohama Air Group, which operated a mixed force of four-engined Mavis flying boats and float Zeros. The Second Air Group also was based at Rabaul, attached directly to the Eighth Fleet to provide air support for its cruisers. This group consisted of sixteen of the clipped-wing, short-range Zeros (called Hamps) and eighteen Val dive bombers.

The Americans planning Watchtower realized it was risky, but after Midway Admiral King was in a mood to take risks. What was not widely foreseen, though, was the possibility of a prolonged battle of attrition in the Solomons. This kind of campaign was one the Americans were not well prepared to prosecute in the summer of 1942. Production of aircraft and warships and training the people to man them was a slow process, and all the new output was earmarked for the North African landings, scheduled for November. Even after Midway, the Pacific Fleet was outnumbered by the Japanese in every category of warship and had to rely on local superiority to win any battle. The enemy had 800 land-based naval aircraft guarding his "co-prosperity sphere," and the geography of the Pacific islands made it easy for him quickly to reinforce one area by flying in planes from another. Viewed in terms of relative air and naval power, as Ghormley and MacArthur acurately saw, the prospects for Watchtower were not brilliant.

However, the Americans had one thing throughout the war in the South Pacific which the Japanese never had. This was the coastwatcher organization, planned by the Australian Navy before the outbreak of hostilities and put into operation as a part of the Allied Intelligence Bureau in March 1942. The network was set up to convey intelligence of Japanese aircraft and ship movements as they were sighted by little groups of Australians or New Zealanders with a few natives, located on dozens of islands in the Bismarck and Solomons Archipelagoes. The men themselves were a conglomerate lot of peacetime planters and colonial administrators, some holding commissions in the reserve, some enlisted men, some civilians beyond retirement age, with bravery and fierce independence the only real common denominator. They and their simple radios performed the combined functions of strategic and tactical reconnaissance, intelligence, and early warning for which the skimpy American and Australian forces lacked the ships and aircraft.

It was apparent to the American planners that Japanese air attacks against Guadalcanal, once occupied, would come from the bases at Rabaul and Kavieng. The direct air route from Rabaul to Guadalcanal passed over Buin on the south coast of Bougainville; that from Kavieng passed over Buka Passage, which separates Bougainville from its northern neighbor, Buka. Each of these vital locations already had a coastwatcher in place by June. Jack Read oversaw Buka Passage from Porapora Hill at the extreme northern tip of Bougainville, and Paul Mason surveyed Buin and the Shortlands from Malabita Hill, high in the mountainous southern part of the island. Read was a wiry, dark-haired, tense colonial administrator who had lived in New Guinea for twelve years, and who thoroughly understood the islands and the ways of their Melanesian inhabitants. Mason had been a planter on Bougainville before the war and was resolved to stay on his island. He was taciturn and calm, and a self-taught radio expert.

In the southern Solomons, too, the coastwatchers were established. McFarlan, Hay, and Andressen—a naval intelligence officer, a planter, and a miner—were installed in a comfortable camp 4,000 feet up in the mountains of Guadalcanal. Martin Clemens, the prewar District Officer on the island was located forty miles east of Lunga Point at Aola. Rhoades was stationed on the western end of Guadalcanal at a plantation which he had managed in peacetime. On the sinister volcanic cone of Savo, a sick, frail old storekeeper named Schroeder kept his watch. A New Zealander, D. G. Kennedy of Segi on New Georgia, was at the village; Sexton and Marchant on Malaita; Josselyn, Keenan, and, later, Firth on Vella Lavella; Evans on Kolombangara; and Horton on Rendova. Far to the south on pestilential Vanikoro, a lone woman, Mrs. Boye, operated a radio station which acted as a link between the Solomons and the New Hebrides.

The weeks before the landing were frantic. Vandergrift's men worked night and day to unload their transports in Wellington and reload their equipment on other transports that would carry them into battle. An intelligence team hastily gathered all available information on the Solomons in general and Tulagi and Guadalcanal in particular. Since the 7th Marine Regiment of the First Division was in Samoa, the division was to be brought up to strength by loaning it the 2nd Regiment, based at San Diego. Most of the major warships of the expeditionary force were in Pearl Harbor. Although the landings finally had to be delayed a week, until August 7, all the planning was done in enough time for the ships to sail. In the middle of the afternoon of July 26, just a little more than three weeks after the issuance of the JCS directive that originated Watchtower, scores of warships and transports from Pearl Harbor, Wellington, Sydney, and Nouméa all met south of the Fiji Islands.

From July 28 to 31 a dress rehearsal of the operation was held in the Fijis. It did not go well, but there was no time for more practice. The ships then headed for the Solomons, luckily sheltered from Japanese air reconnaissance by bad weather, and by nightfall on August 6 the leading cruiser of Turner's amphibious force was sixty miles from Cape Esperance, Guadalcanal. A few hours later the decisive campaign of the Pacific war began as the ships approached Tulagi and the air action got under way.

3

THE AMERICANS
DIG IN
April 10–20

While General Vandegrift's riflemen hastened to consolidate their positions around the unfinished airfield on Guadalcanal, the men and airplanes soon to make its name legendary were on their way across the Pacific. It had taken guts to propose Marine Air Group 23 as Guadalcanal's air garrison. To be sure, the first idea of the planners was to send only the bomber elements of MAG-23 to the island, and to use the fighter squadrons to relieve two that already were in the South Pacific for service as Guadalcanal's air defense. However, Admiral McCain pointed out that neither of these squadrons—Marine Fighting 212 at Efate and Marine Observation 251 on New Caledonia—was any more trained than those of Air Group 23, and recommended that they be left where they were for the time being. Thus, MAG-23 was "selected" somewhat offhandedly for what was obviously going to be rough duty.

Marine Air Group 23 had been formed on the 1st of May at Ewa Field and was training on the island of Oahu when it was selected to go to Guadalcanal. MAG-23 consisted of two fighter squadrons, Marine Fighting 223 and 224, and two dive-bomber outfits, Marine Scout Bombing 231 and 232. The fighter squadrons had been equipped with a few old Brewster F2A "Buffaloes," long since obsolete, in which they had been training the ten or so pilots they each had. The dive-bomber organizations were similarly undermanned, and were flying SBD-2s, aircraft recently phased out of Navy squadrons in favor of the newer SBD-3.

Things changed fast for MAG-23 when Admiral Nimitz decided that it should support the Guadalcanal landing. In early July the squadron commanders were told that their outfits were to participate in a "special mission"—of unspecified nature—and were the immediate recipients of an embarrassment of riches. The slow Brewsters vanished overnight and were replaced by a full complement of twenty new Grumman F4F-4s. Each of the fighter squadrons was brought up to strength in pilots, but these came from two different sources. VMF-223 got mostly new second lieutenants just out of the training command, their total flying experience limited to basic and advanced trainers. VMF-224 got some of these, too, but also a number of survivors of Marine Fighting 221, which had been virtually wiped out at the Battle of Midway. These survivors had been given forty-eight hours' leave in Honolulu after the battle and then reassigned, some to 223, most to 224. This cavalier treatment following on their nightmarish experiences at Midway made some of them less than ideal additions to squadrons about to go into combat. Others more than rose to the occasion, finding unsuspected personal resources to resist almost unbearable pressures.

The skipper of 223 was a dark, saturnine Captain named John Lucian Smith, who had become a Marine artillery officer after graduation from the University of Oklahoma, and then became a dive-bomber pilot after going through flight training. He had been in a fighter squadron only a few short months when he found himself commanding one. Now in four weeks he had to transform a bunch of just-graduated student aviators, most of whom never had flown anything but trainers, into combat-ready fighter pilots. MAG-23 was to go to Guadalcanal in two parts. The forward echelon, VMF-223 and VMSB-232, was to sail from Pearl Harbor on August 2. The other two squadrons were to follow two weeks later.

Major Richard Mangrum, handsome mustachioed commander of Marine Bombing 232, had a similar problem. On the 10th of July his squadron had ten pilots just out of flight school and enough SBDs to bring the total aircraft strength up to twelve, two-thirds what it ought to have been. Not one of Mangrum's pilots ever had flown an aircraft more advanced than the SNJ trainer, and none had ever even dropped a bomb.

Both squadron commanders simply flew the tails off

their young charges in the three or four weeks that followed.
In John Smith's words:

> ... We all had to qualify on an aircraft carrier,
> which we did. We spent as much time as we could
> flying on Saturdays and Sundays and every other
> day, doing gunnery and dummy runs and anything
> that would help to give people quick experience or
> quick training ... it was the first experience that
> I've ever had trying to train anybody, but it seemed
> to me that gunnery was the most important thing.
> ... So we concentrated on gunnery more than any-
> thing else, which was a good thing after we found
> out where we were going.

Mangrum, too, flew his pilots from dawn to dusk. Pearl
Harbor was not well suited to dive-bomber training; there
was not much real estate available on which to set up a
practice target, and much of what there was was too mountainous. Nevertheless, the young pilots somehow learned
enough in three weeks to make them more dangerous to the
enemy than to themselves.

While MAG-23's pilots and ground crews sweated in
Hawaii, the men they were to support were already on their
way to the Solomons. Then, five days before the landings,
Smith's and Mangrum's squadrons loaded their pilots and
aircraft on the little aircraft carrier *Long Island* and their
ground crews and equipment on the transport *William Ward
Burrows* and sailed from Pearl Harbor. The ships had been at
sea for a week when news of the Savo Island disaster was
received. It was clear that plans were going to be changed,
and *Long Island*'s captain put into Suva, in the Fijis, on the
13th to await further orders.

The two weeks after the disastrous start of Operation
Watchtower had turned into a race between Japanese and
American efforts to get aircraft into the South Pacific and
find bases for them. The ace in the hole for the Americans
was their possession of Guadalcanal with its partially completed airfield; their secret weapon was Vandegrift's 1st Engineer Battalion. Using captured Japanese steamrollers, gaso-
line-powered locomotives, dump trucks, and shovels, these
men worked day and night to finish the Guadalcanal airstrip,

which still had a large hole in the middle of the runway and too many trees too near its approach end. Vandegrift told Ghormley on August 8 that he would have 2,600 feet of the strip in operating condition in two days and 3,800 feet within a week. This was very close to what the Marines actually achieved. On August 12, Admiral McCain's aide, Lieutenant William Sampson, made the first landing on the airfield in a BPY-5A amphibian, and pronounced it to be in excellent condition and suitable for fighter operations. Under the circumstances, this opinion required a basically optimistic outlook. The field was raw, unfinished, muddy from the rains that drenched Guadalcanal daily, and there still were too many trees at the end.

Meanwhile a change in the plans for the airstrip's eventual occupants was under consideration, suggested by the *Long Island*'s captain, who learned of his passengers' limited training on the way to Suva and advised Admiral Ghormley accordingly. Ghormley passed the problem on to Admiral McCain, who felt a sense of urgency about getting aircraft into Guadalcanal. He worked out a solution overnight. A dozen of Smith's greenest fighter pilots would be replaced temporarily by an equivalent number of trained men from Efate-based VMF-212. Thus reinforced, Fighting 223 would continue on to Guadalcanal, while its fledglings went into further training at Efate. Ghormley approved this suggestion the next day and McCain sent two old destroyers converted into fast transports up to Guadalcanal from Espiritu Santo carrying aviation gas, lubricating oil, bombs, ammunition—and a letter to Vandegrift telling him his planes would be arriving on the 18th or 19th.

On the Japanese side, direction of the air effort had been taken over personally by Vice-Admiral Nishizo Tsukahara, commander of the Eleventh Air Fleet, who arrived in Rabaul on the 9th. It was a frustrating initiation for the one-armed admiral, who found himself on the morning of August 11 with only twenty-two bombers and seventeen fighters in condition to fly, and who was not to receive any aircraft reinforcements for the next ten days. Tsukahara's few available planes flew reconnaissance missions over Guadalcanal every day the weather permitted, from the 12th to the 19th.

In the military sense, the Japanese reconnaissance flights over the island were niggling little things. They would not even have been noticed were not the Marines so keenly aware

that they had been abandoned and were completely without
air cover. It was galling for them to look at the empty
airstrip, and ominous to see the increasing insolence displayed
by the enemy aircraft when they came over. On the 11th six
Zekes reconnoitered the island and strafed the airfield. The
next day three Bettys came down from Rabaul and circled
overhead. On the 14th three more flew over, leisurely photo-
graphing the field, while the Marines' few 90-millimeter
antiaircraft guns banged away fruitlessly. Two days later
another reconnaissance was made, and the planes dropped
supplies to Japanese troops hiding in the jungle. Eight planes
came down on the 18th and, for the first of many times,
bombed the airfield. This time the antiaircraft gunners were
more skillful, and five of the eight Bettys were damaged.

The Marines were uneasy and jumpy. For the first few
days they fired at any odd sound in the jungle, and one night
a noisy fire fight raged between Marines dug in on different
sides of the field. They were shelled occasionally by a submarine which was sent down to establish contact with the
scattered Japanese troops. A destroyer disembarked 200 sailors of a naval landing force in broad daylight on the 16th,
and the beachhead was shelled by destroyers during the
nights of the 17th, 18th, and 19th. Dysentery raged through
the entire division, further weakening men already enervated
by the heat and humidity. The Marines had gone onto
reduced rations on the 12th, and only a huge stock of
captured Japanese canned food made their two meals a day
possible. All these things they could have borne had they felt
anyone cared what happened to them. But for ten days,
almost without exception, the only ships and aircraft they saw
were Japanese. Admiral McCain summed up the obvious
remedy in a letter to Vandegrift: "The best and proper solution of course is to get fighters and SBD's onto your field."

At long last the day came. On the afternoon of August
20, the *Long Island*, which had sailed from Efate two days
previously, arrived off the southern tip of San Cristobal, 190
miles from Guadalcanal. There the clumsy-looking carrier
swung into the southeast trade wind blowing across the Coral
Sea and prepared to launch her aircraft.

Long Island's 400-foot flight deck was too short for the
heavily laden aircraft to make a normal "deck run" take-off,
and they had to be catapulted off, one by one. The F4Fs and
SBDs, blue on top, light gray on the bottom, lined up, propel-

lers shiny wavering disks, waiting for their turn to be fastened to the carrier's single catapult.

Only a handful of the pilots of Smith's and Mangrum's squadrons ever had been catapulted from a ship. This was a complex procedure and somewhat unnerving even to experienced pilots. Each aircraft in succession taxied to the forward port side of the flight deck, controlled minutely by the signals of a director gesticulating like an orchestra conductor, who kept it exactly on white approach lines painted on the deck. Having finally jolted into the correct position amid alternate blasts of power and taps on right or left brake, the plane was attached by a stout wire bridle to a hook that projected from a powerful hydraulic piston through a long thin slot in the deck which ran a hundred feet or so up to the bow. Once the tension was taken up on the bridle, the catapult officer waved two fingers over his head in a circle. This was a signal to the pilot to run up to full power and check the engine for proper operation. When the pilot had hastily surveyed his instruments, he saluted the catapult officer and braced his head against his headrest. Then there was a sudden surge of flattening acceleration, a noisy rush, and the pilot found himself just above the sea, clawing for air speed and altitude.

One by one the nineteen F4Fs and twelve SBDs were shot off the little carrier as she waddled at full speed through the white-capped sea. The aircraft circled the ship climbing, joining up by twos and threes into a larger formation. Then, in a gently undulating mass, the thirty-one planes passed over the ship for the last time and disappeared beyond the cloud-studded horizon into history.

4

STORM FROM
THE NORTH
August 20–24

Around 1600 on the 20th, the Marines on Guadalcanal heard the sound of a large formation of aircraft. Wearily they reached for helmets and started toward trenches or foxholes. For almost two weeks now, the only aircraft they had seen or heard had been Japanese. The sound grew louder, and then twelve unmistakable SBDs roared over the field, followed by nineteen F4Fs. "A shout of relief and welcome went up from every Marine on the island," wrote one of them later. The first man to land was Major Mangrum; when he had taxied up to a parking space and climbed out of the cockpit, General Vandegrift stepped forward and wrung his hand fervently.

The Marine flyers, pleased but a little puzzled by being greeted as heroes, were more interested in the field from which they would be flying. Just a few days before it had been named for Major Lofton Henderson, killed at Midway. It was about 3,500 feet long and 150 feet wide, and covered with gravel. The strip lay in the middle of a cleared field, mostly surrounded by the coconut palms of the Lever brothers' plantation. It ran approximately east and west, with the west end just short of the Lunga River and the east end pointing toward the mouth of the Ilu River, about a mile away. Revetments, or parking places, for each plane had been prepared around the airstrip by Lieutenant Colonel Charles Hayes (inevitably called "Fog"), the C.O. of VMO-251, who had been sent up from Espiritu Santo on August 9 for temporary duty to prepare the field for MAG-23. These positions were properly dispersed, but, as the pilots would discover the next day, the terrain of the roughly bulldozed field was so poor that it was very difficult to taxi the planes out to their revetments and almost impossible to get them in. On this first evening, however, the tropical sunset came early, and so, after 1730, the airmen were driven off to the tents among the coconut palms where they would live—some of them—for the next six weeks.

About 0200 the next morning, the newly arrived flyers were awakened by the roar of artillery and small-arms fire. They didn't know what it was all about—"we thought it was just a Fourth of July celebration and went on back to sleep," said John Smith afterward. The men of the 1st Marines only a mile away at the mouth of the Ilu River got little sleep, however; they were fighting an attempt by 900 men of an "advanced echelon" of the Japanese 28th Infantry to rush right through the perimeter around the field.

While the ground fighting on the perimeter continued, the Marine pilots looked around the field the next morning and found that 140 sailors from an obscure Navy unit called CUB-1 were to fill in as their ground crews—their own were still aboard ship. All the fueling had to be accomplished by using hand pumps stuck directly into standard 55-gallon gasoline drums. Rearming of the SBD's had to be done by laboriously manhandling 500-pound and 1,000-pound bombs since there were no bomb-handling trucks, bomb carts, or bomb hoists on the island. The enlisted men of CUB-1 had had something less than four months' service and had to be constantly and minutely supervised by their commanding officer, Ensign George Polk. However, the men were intelligent and willing to work, and young Polk was a very good man. Colonel Hayes had been given the job of field operations officer. Routine morning and evening searches for the SBDs and a combat air patrol were established.

The newly arrived pilots did not spend their first day idle; several of them flew some observation and strafing missions in support of the infantrymen, who by midafternoon had virtually wiped out the attacking Japanese, and Smith's squadron mounted continuous fighter patrols. About noon a division of four F4Fs led by Smith and an experienced enlisted pilot Sergeant Johnny Lindley had a brief skirmish with four Zekes between Lunga Point and Savo Island. None

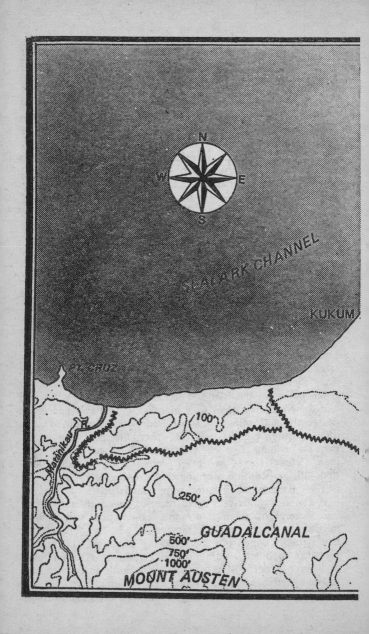

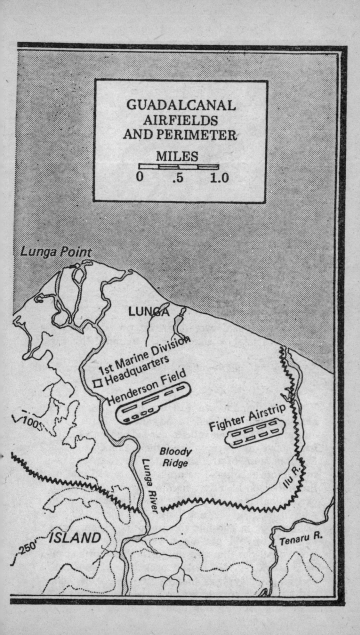

GUADALCANAL
AIRFIELDS
AND PERIMETER

MILES

0   .5   1.0

Lunga Point

LUNGA

1st Marine Division
Headquarters
Henderson Field

100

Fighter Airstrip

Bloody
Ridge

Lunga River

Ilu R.

ISLAND

250

Tenaru R.

F4F

of the four pilots had ever flown in combat, and the two wingmen had a total of sixteen days' training with Fighting 223.

The division was flying at 14,000 feet when, in Smith's words:

> We were flying down just south of Savo Island heading toward Russell Island, and six Zeros came on to us about a half mile to our side and about 500 feet above us. I recognized them immediately as Zeros because of the silhouettes I'd seen, and we turned into them, and naturally they turned into us. From then on it's pretty hard to say what happened except that the plane I was shooting at pulled up with his belly to me, and I shot him fairly well and went on by, only to find there were two other Zeros on my tail; so I got out toward the field.... We later found out that this one plane had crashed off Savo Island.... We looked back over Savo Island and as [Lindley] was missing we joined up again and went back to help him.... They got on our tail again and shot up our planes a little more.... It

was easy to disengage from them. Just head[ed] for the field ... and they went off, because they were just as scared of us as we were of them.

Lindley glided in for a dead-stick landing at Henderson Field, his oil tank shattered and his wheels up. His plane was a complete loss, a "strike" in the parlance of naval aviation.

This inconclusive exchange told neither side much about the other. That knowledge would come in the next few weeks. One thing it did do, however. The four pilots had encountered the dread Zeke and had been duly shot up, but their planes had brought them back. "After that," said Smith, "our pilots had a great deal of confidence in the Grumman."

Late in the afternoon of the 22nd, the first reinforcements arrived for the Marine flyers, five Bell P-400's (export versions of the P-39 Airacobra) of the Army Air Force's 67th Fighter Squadron, Captain Dale Brannon commanding. The other two flights of Brannon's squadron were due a day after him, but were ordered to wait at Espiritu Santo because of the condition of Henderson Field. A calm in the action enabled the senior commanders to turn their attention to the critical problem of supplying Guadalcanal. Fighting 223 already was out of oxygen bottles, and Vandegrift radioed Admiral McCain that he had had to suspend fighter patrols until they could be replenished. McCain already had urged— in a dispatch sent the day Mangrum's and Smith's squadrons arrived—that the transport *William Ward Burrows,* loaded with essential ground equipment and personnel, be sent to the island without delay.

Thus began the struggle to maintain an air base in Guadalcanal. Every day for the next three months saw some crisis arise as fast as a previous one was overcome. The most frequently recurring crisis was the shortage of some critical item of supply or equipment needed to keep the planes flying. The story of Henderson Field must be told not only in terms of combat but of continuous desperate efforts to give the isolated airmen what they had to have to keep the Japanese from recapturing the island.

The American landing on Guadalcanal elicited a much stronger reaction from the Japanese Navy than from the Army. The latter service thought that it could recapture the island with a minimum commitment of man power, and appeared far more interested in capturing Port Moresby in New Guinea than in the sideshow in the Solomons, which the Navy appeared to have well in hand anyway. The Navy on its part did little to discourage the Army's feeling that Guadalcanal was a naval affair. It had never told its sister service that most of its carriers had been lost at Midway.

It was the memory of Midway that shaped Admiral Yamamoto's response. He decided to concentrate the entire strength of the Combined Fleet in the Solomons, apparently feeling that nothing less than an all-out effort could overcome the American carrier task forces. If this was his estimate, he was far more realistic than the soldiers. But then, he was the only Japanese commander in centuries who had known defeat in battle, and this perhaps had sharpened his perception of reality.

The Second Fleet of Vice-Admiral Nobutake Kondo— one battleship, five heavy cruisers, a destroyer squadron, and the seaplane tender *Chitose*— sortied from the Inland Sea on August 11, bound for Truk. Vice-Admiral Chuichi Nagumo, commanding the Third Fleet, followed him on the 16th with the only two large carriers the Japanese had left. *Shokaku* and *Zuikaku*, plus the small, old light carrier *Ryujo*, two battleships, and a destroyer squadron. A heavy-cruiser division and a destroyer squadron that had been in the Indian Ocean also headed east for the rendezvous at Truk. And on the 17th the great Yamamoto left the beautiful green islands of his homeland forever, to sail south in the gigantic fleet flagship *Yamato*.

While the naval strength of Japan converged on its major Central Pacific operating base, Vice-Admiral Tsukahara went ahead with efforts to reinforce the scattered Guadalcanal garrison. On August 17, part of the Navy's 5th Sasebo Special Naval Landing Force was put ashore at Tassafaronga without opposition. The next night the 900-man advance group of Colonel Ichiki's 28th Infantry landed at Taivu Point. Tsukahara's plan was to embark the major elements of these two forces in two transports and land them on Guadalcanal on the 21st. The overconfident Ichiki, though, impatient of delay, actually started his suicidal lunge at the Marine perimeter on the 20th, and it was this attack that greeted the newly arrived airmen that night.

Earlier that day Tsukahara's scouting planes had sighted Fletcher's three carriers west of the Santa Cruz Islands. As a result Tsukahara postponed the landing originally scheduled for the 21st until the 24th, when the Combined Fleet then nearing Truk would be in position to support it in strength.

Fletcher's Task Force 61, which had been passively patrolling south of the Solomons since 9 August, included, besides the three aircraft carriers, one battleship, seven cruisers, and eighteen destroyers. Its real strength, however, lay in the 256 aircraft, organized into three air groups, that were based on the carriers.

The air groups of *Saratoga* and *Enterprise* consisted largely of squadrons that had fought at Midway, many on other carriers, reequipped with new aircraft and their depleted ranks filled with replacement pilots. Like all the carrier air groups in the Pacific during 1942, they had been hastily flung together from the remnants of others that had been broken up.

Saratoga's air group commander (CAG, pronounced as spelled) was Commander H. D. (Don) Felt, a short, aggressive pilot of long experience in carrier squadrons who had commanded *Lexington*'s dive bombers at the Coral Sea. Lieutenant Commander Maxwell Leslie was the *Enterprise*'s CAG. He too was a most experienced pilot and had commanded *Yorktown*'s VB-5 at Midway. Fletcher's third carrier, *Wasp*, had a well-trained but not combat-tested air group commanded by a stern New Englander, Commander Wallace Beakley.

At dawn on August 23 the Japanese Combined Fleet was creeping down like a dark shadow from the north, its presence only suspected by the Americans. As was typical of all Japanese fleet dispositions, it was divided into several separate groups—five in this case. Its striking power reposed in the Carrier Force of Vice-Admiral Nagumo, *Shokaku, Zuikaku,* and *Ryujo.* A few miles ahead of the carriers was the Vanguard Force of two battleships and three heavy cruisers. Far in advance of the carriers steamed the Support Force of six cruisers and the seaplane tender *Chitose* under the command of Vice-Admiral Kondo. To the west of Nagumo and Kondo, near Ontong Java, was the Transport Group, consisting of the transport *Kinryu Maru* and four old converted destroyers, escorted by Rear Admiral Raizo Tanaka and his Destroyer Squadron 2. Yamamoto himself was at sea in the *Yamato,* but remained near Truk.

Yamamoto's tactical plan was basically the same that the

Japanese had used at the Battle of the Coral Sea, back in May. The little *Ryujo* was to be detached and used to attack Henderson Field, but its primary mission was to be detected and itself attacked. With only two large carriers left in the Combined Fleet, it was essential that the American carrier planes be kept away from them until their own air groups had been launched. Yamamoto proposed to sacrifice *Ryujo* in order to get Fletcher's aircraft committed to it as their target.

That same dawn, August 23, Fletcher's carriers were seventy miles east of Malaita, just turning into the southeast trade wind to launch the morning search. Far to the south McCain's PBYs, too, lumbered into the air on their long daily searches from Espiritu Santo and Graciosa Bay, Ndeni. *Enterprise* was Fletcher's duty carrier that day, and hence was responsible for Task Force 61's air searches. Her early morning search was launched at 0630, and within an hour a Japanese submarine was sighted on the surface, steering south at high speed. Fifty minutes later at 0815, a second submarine was sighted, also heading south on the surface. These sightings were very important, for the Japanese normally preceded fleet movements with a line of scouting submarines. At 0950 one of the PBYs from Ndeni found Tanaka's transport force steaming toward Guadalcanal and reported its composition fairly accurately. This report, when eventually received by Fletcher early that afternoon, decided him to launch *Saratoga's* air group to attack the small Japanese force.

The PBY's contact report also reached General Vandegrift on the afternoon of the 23rd. It worried him deeply. The prospect of heavy ground reinforcements for the Japanese was chilling to him, isolated as he was in a tactical no-man's-land. He had no choice but to commit his tiny air force to an attack on the enemy transports. Both Fletcher and Vandegrift thus independently decided in midafternoon to mount attacks on the transport force. Unknown to both of them, however, Rear Admiral Tanaka had been ordered to reverse his course to the north so that he would not be caught, unsupported, by Fletcher's planes. The PBY still shadowing him despite almost constant rain picked up Tanaka's change of course about 1300, and then lost him in the bad weather. A relief PBY crashed taking off from Graciosa Bay, and the transports were thus uncovered for many hours. Either the PBY failed to send a message to her tender, *Mackinac*, back at Ndeni, or it did not get through. At any rate, *Mackinac* did not find out about Tanaka's turn until the patrol plane returned, and Fletcher and Vandegrift did not hear about it until after midnight on the 24th.

Don Felt led *Saratoga*'s air group—thirty-one SBDs and six TBFs—down the old giant's flight deck at 1410. Because the reported distance of the transport force—275 miles—was well in excess of the maximum radius of the F4Fs, the attack was to be made without fighter escort. About an hour after take-off, they ran into a solid weather front with large and frequent rain squalls. They went through on instruments and emerged into a clear area at the time they should have sighted Tanaka. There was nothing to be seen, of course. The Japanese were now way north. Felt turned westward for a last look, then, in obedience to his orders, took the air group into Guadalcanal, since it would otherwise arrive back at the *Saratoga* after dark.

The Marine flyers left Henderson Field at 1630, as the *Saratoga* air group was approaching the estimated position of the transport force. Major Mangrum had a total of nine SBDs, escorted by twelve of Smith's F4Fs. Vandergrift stood silently in front of the Japanese-built control tower known as the "Pagoda," watching the handful of planes take off and disappear. For all he knew he was seeing them off for the last time. Hardly had Mangrum's small attack group vanished from sight when there arrived another reminder of the shoestring existence of Cactus Air Force—Admiral McCain's own PBY-5A amphibian carrying all the oxygen bottles that could be crammed in the airplane.

Less than an hour out on their missions, the Marines ran into the vicious squall line encountered by Don Felt's group. Less experienced than Felt's pilots and undoubtedly finding the front rougher going near the high hot islands than *Saratoga*'s people did over open ocean, the Marines turned back. When they arrived at the field and went to the Pagoda for their debriefing, they found a stricken Vandegrift pacing back and forth, waiting. The pilots were most upset at their failure. The kindly general tried hard to calm them, but his strained face showed his own distress. The Japanese transports, as far as anyone on the island knew, were due at midnight.

Saratoga's air group arrived over Henderson Field about 1830, just as the tropical night was falling, and for the next thirty minutes they landed on the strange field with the aid of a jury-rigged lighting system that included jeep headlights and flashlights. The pilots, Felt wrote, "were distracted somewhat by occasional machine gun tracer fire streaming astern from either Japanese snipers or doubting Marines." The planes were dispersed as well as the condition of the field permitted, and the pilots repaired to the Marine tents to eat their emergency rations and scrounge a little coffee. The men of CUB-1 refueled the aircraft by hand through the long night.

The night dragged slowly on the pilots and gunners, none of whom were accustomed to the sultry heat and jungle noises. To the Navy men, used to the comforts of life on a carrier, but now sitting or lying in blacked-out tents under the palm trees, hearing weird calls and occasional shots, feeling the enveloping air of crisis settling over the island, it was like some nightmare world. About 0200 a Japanese destroyer briefly bombarded the island, doing no damage except to the frayed nerves of the already-sleepless Americans.

Thanks to the night-long work of Ensign Polk and his men of CUB-1, all of the planes were gassed and armed by dawn on the 24th. Felt held his air group in readiness while Mangrum's morning searches looked for the Japanese transports. They found nothing, and Vandegrift having finally received the delayed report of Tanaka's reversal, it was considered safe to release *Saratoga*'s aircraft. The group, less two SBDs delayed by engine trouble, arrived back at the ship at 1130. They left behind them twenty-seven 1,000-pound bombs for Mangrum's squadron. These were the only heavy bombs on the island.

Dawn on the 24th found Fletcher's Task Force 61 with one less carrier. Having received a dispatch from the usually accurate CINCPAC Intelligence locating all Japanese carriers north of Truk, he had detached *Wasp* at 1800 on the 23rd to refuel far down south. This decision, unfortunate in retrospect, and not readily defensible in the absence of up-to-date information about the movements of the Japanese transport force, deprived him of a third of his striking power just before a battle. What was more, until Felt returned late in the morning with most of the *Saratoga* air group, Fletcher had only *Enterprise* to handle both search and attack missions. The dawn search was flown off at 0630, twenty-three SBDs searching through leaden skies and intermittent rain almost the complete semicircle from west to east out to 200 miles.

Their search was uneventful, except for the sighting of another surfaced submarine, further indication of the existence of an advanced scouting line preceding a major fleet movement.

Admiral Nagumo, commanding the Japanese carrier force, was 360 miles north of Fletcher at 0600. Two hours previously he had detached the decoy carrier *Ryujo,* escorted by the heavy cruiser *Tone* and two destroyers, to make an air attack on Henderson Field, and to draw Fletcher's air groups. Admiral Tanaka, once again heading south toward Guadalcanal with his transports, saw her speeding, hull down, across the eastern horizon a little after noon, heading for her destiny, a destiny which had been assured two and a half hours before, when a Ndeni-based PBY sighted her.

The PBY's contact report to the *Mackinac* was picked up by the *Enterprise* and immediately reported to Fletcher in *Saratoga* at 1017. At 1158, the *Saratoga* heard the shadowing PBY repeating its contact report to the *Mackinac*. Fletcher was indignant over the previous day's fruitless mission by the *Saratoga* air group, which he properly blamed on poor reporting by the patrol plane. Now he simply refused to believe the report of *Ryujo*'s sighting. Finally at 1216, after hearing the second message from the PBY shadowing her, he reluctantly ordered Commander Task Force 16 (Rear Admiral Kinkaid in *Enterprise*) to launch a search to verify the contact.

While Fletcher was reading the PBY's contact report and making his decision at least to investigate it, his air strength was being restored. Felt and the *Saratoga* air group, tired and red eyed, started to land back aboard at 1130.

The Japanese in turn were probing the American carrier force. At 1222 *Saratoga*'s air-search radar picked up an unknown aircraft, and Lieutenant David Richardson, leading a division of four F4Fs on Combat Air Patrol, was vectored out to investigate. In the spare, staccato exchange between "Scarlet Base," *Sara*'s radio voice call, and Dave Richardson's division, "Scarlet 7," can be found something of the tenseness and sudden exhilaration of air combat:

> "Scarlet 7, Scarlet Base. Vector 260, Buster."
> "Scarlet 7, Scarlet Base. Bogey ahead 15."
> "Wilco."

"On the port bow, Dave."

"Up or down? . . . Tallyho, one Kawanishi. Repeat, one Kawanishi. Follow me."

"Go below the clouds, go below the clouds, Hank."

"Below you. I see him."

"Box him in, box him in."

"A little to the right and down, to the west of you. I'm going in now."

"In the clouds. I got him, Hank. Bingo!"

"Nice going, Dave."

"Boy, look at him burn!"

Shortly before 1300, *Enterprise* sounded flight quarters in preparation for launching the search that Fletcher had ordered so reluctantly. On the flight deck her planes were gassed and armed for the mission, and spotted aft in the order they were to take off. Down below in the ready rooms, the pilots and air gunners were assigned the sectors—narrow wedges 250 miles long—that they were to search, and worked out their compass headings and times to turn to new courses. Then, from the metal-voiced loudspeakers: "Pilots, man your planes."

The pilots, each assisted by his plane captain, the mechanic who took care of the plane he was to fly that day, climbed into their cockpits and busied themselves with dozens of routine tasks, accompanied by gentle metallic clinkings. Put the navigation plotting board on the floor of the cockpit for a minute to get it out of the way. Buckle on the seat-pack parachute, arms through the shoulder straps, thigh straps next, then buckle the chest strap. Then the safety belt and shoulder harness, making sure that the latter could be unlocked, permitting all the switches and handles in the cockpit to be reached, and also locked, holding the pilot firmly in his seat. Then the cockpit checkoff list.

Enterprise's 20,000 tons of steel, 794 feet long, turned slowly around into the wind, signal flags flying, the red and white "fox" flat at the dip. In the signal book it meant, "I am conducting flight operations." Presumably the flag would lay to rest any doubts that an observer might have about what was going on. Then an authoritative bullhorn from "Pri Fly," the flight officer's glassed-in post on the bridge:

"Check for loose gear about the deck.

"Stand clear of propellers.

"Start engines."

Forty puffs of black smoke appeared simultaneously from as many aircraft as the starter cartridges fired. The propellers, impelled by the gases of the exploding cartridges, began to turn over slowly. Mixture controls went into full rich, then magneto switches were turned on. Slow, rhythmically flailing propeller blades moved jerkily faster, then became shining silver disks. For a moment or two the engines warmed up, then the pilots ran them up to 1,800 rpm to check their magnetos. Then, urged by a yellow-jumpered figure, the first F4F taxied slowly forward out of the pack of planes clustered aft, accompanied by two plane handlers carrying wooden chocks.

At 1305 the flight-deck officer saw a green flag replace a red one outside of Pri Fly, held up a tiny checkered flag to the F4F pilot, then began to revolve it rapidly over his head. The Grumman went to full throttle, brakes held on and elevators full up. Suddenly the flight-deck officer dropped dramatically to one knee, pointing at the bow with the flag that he had been waving. The pilot released his brakes, his tail wheel rose from the deck, and with a crackling roar he was off.

One by one, emerging from the mass of aircraft and whirling propellers, the F4Fs taxied up in single file abreast of the island and were launched. Sixteen fighters of VF-6, led by the squadron C.O., Lieutenant Lou Bauer, were to fly combat air patrol over the *Enterprise* while SBDs and TBFs went out on the search. When the F4Fs were gone, the ship began to send off the bigger planes, eight from Bombing Six and seven each from Scouting Five and Torpedo Three. They formed up in pairs and flew out on the first leg of their searches, each sector shaped like a segment of a Japanese folding fan.

Less than fifteen minutes after the *Enterprise*'s search was off, *Saratoga*'s radar picked up another bogey—a blip that did not automatically identify itself as an American aircraft. Lieutenant Dick Gray's division of the ship's CAP vectored out to investigate, found, and shot down another big four-engined Kawanishi flying boat only seven miles away from the task force. The Japanese were still keeping in contact. However, as was the case with the Americans, there apparently were no direct communications between the patrol seaplanes and the fleet that needed their reports of sightings. Admiral Nagumo never received any information from the two Kawanishis before they were shot down by *Saratoga*'s combat air patrol. *Shokaku*'s and *Zuikaku*'s striking groups thus remained on their decks, ignorant of the position of the American carriers.

Ryujo, however, had launched her tiny attack force at 1300, just a few minutes before the *Enterprise* sent off her search. Six torpedo planes carrying bombs, escorted by fifteen Zekes, headed toward Guadalcanal to attack Henderson Field. At 1350 the *Ryujo* air group was picked up by *Saratoga*'s air-search radar at a range of 100 miles. This contact finally convinced Admiral Fletcher that the PBY reports of a Japanese carrier were correct. He ordered *Sara* to launch her air group to attack the *Ryujo*.

In the meantime, Fighting 223 on Guadalcanal, alerted

"Zeke"

either by *Saratoga* or by one of the coastwatchers as *Ryujo*'s air group passed over Malaita, scrambled at 1420 and had most of its Grummans airborne long before the Japanese reached the beleaguered island. They came in toward Guadalcanal at the suicidally low altitude of 9,000 feet and fared accordingly. Fourteen F4Fs caught them flatfooted between Malaita and Florida and shot down all the torpedo planes. the Zekes put up a good fight, though, and three young American lieutenants did not return from the flight. Lantern-jawed Captain Marion Carl, one of the great American aces of World War II, started his impressive list of victories by shooting down two torpedo planes and a Zeke.

Perhaps eight Zekes survived the fight. The old *Ryujo* had done her best. Now she was that most useless of warships, an aircraft carrier without aircraft, waiting for certain death.

At 1415, only twenty-five minutes after *Ryujo*'s aircraft en route to Guadalcanal appeared on the *Saratoga*'s radar scope, Don Felt's weary air group began to take off again from *Sara*. The SBDs and TBFs, launched one after the other with the rapidity that placed American carrier operations in a class by themselves, circled over the ship, the long line of single aircraft quickly grouping into sections, divisions, and squadrons.

Almost at the same time a Japanese float observation seaplane was spotted by a division of the *Enterprise* CAP. Before it was shot down it managed to radio the carrier's position back to Nagumo. At last the Japanese admiral had a target.

The sighting of *Enterprise* by the Japanese coincided within minutes with the location of *Ryujo* by a two-plane team of the *Enterprise* search group. Their contact reports were picked up by the *Saratoga* but never penetrated the roar of radio interference to reach their own carrier. Within the next few minutes several more of the American search planes were in contact with both *Ryujo* and the Vanguard Force.

The most important sighting of the day, if only Fletcher had been able to act on it, was made a little before 1530. Lieutenant Ray Davis and his wingman, Ensign R. C. Shaw, located a force of Japanese ships and started to attack a cruiser when they sighted a big carrier behind it, and then another. They climbed and circled for an attack from up sun, while Davis sent an electrifying contact report: "Two large CV decks full, 4 CA, 6 CL, 8 DD, latitude 05-45 south, longitude 162-10 east, course 120, speed 25."

They had found Nagumo.

At 1545 the two SBDs dove from 14,000 feet on the nearest carrier, the *Shokaku*. Each dropping a single 500-pound bomb from 2,000 feet and pulled out low and fast toward the east. Davis' bomb hit just off the big carrier's starboard beam and Shaw's on the starboard quarter. The two bombs caused some damage and casualties. The two SBDs escaped unscathed. But this was the only damage done to Nagumo's big carriers during the battle.

With Davis' attack on the *Shokaku*, the American carrier forces' search aircraft had done their job. Unfortunately, Fletcher apparently never found out about it, and had little striking power to follow up the contacts even if he had.

5

BATTLE OF THE
EASTERN SOLOMONS
August 24

Don Felt's *Saratoga* air group, twenty-nine SBDs and seven TBFs, had to go 216 miles west of the *Sara*, roughly an hour and a half away to reach the *Ryujo* force. Felt had with him thirteen SBDs from Lieutenant Commander DeWitt Shumway's Bombing Three and fifteen from Scouting Three led by Lieutenant Commander Lou Kirn. Bruce Harwood led Torpedo Eight.

After forty minutes at low altitude the formation began to climb slowly into the almost cloudless blue sky. On the way, Felt picked up a contact report from a B-17 placing the Japanese farther to the north than first reported, and he altered course accordingly. This turned out to be incorrect, and when contact was not made the formation turned westward back toward the original position. About this time, the crackle of static in the CAG's earphones abruptly faded. His radio receiver was out of order, which meant he could be heard but could not hear. Felt dropped back alongside Lou Kirn's SBD and signaled to him with a tap on the helmet followed by a pointing index finger that he, Kirn, was now leading the air group. A few minutes later, 1605 to be exact, *Ryujo* and her escorts were sighted.

Ryujo had been running west at 20 knots since she launched her attack on Guadalcanal, heading toward a prearranged rendezvous with the returning aircraft. She had another nine Zekes aboard, but had been distinctly leisurely about launching any of them to fly combat air patrol. Finally, after *Enterprise* search planes and B-17s had been seen

45

several times, the old carrier did launch three of her fighters, which then pursued the shadowing TBFs. The remaining six Zeros were starting up their engines on her flight deck when the *Saratoga* air group was sighted.

Felt's planes were between 14,000 and 15,000 feet, the sky over the Japanese ships dotted with scattered clouds, the four wakes standing out as white lines on the calm blue sea. It was an ideal setup for an air attack. Felt broke radio silence to order it: he directed Kirn's squadron and one division of Shumway's plus five of the TBFs to the carrier, and the second division of Bombing Three and the remaining section of torpedo planes to attack the *Tone*. The air group turned away toward the north, and the SBDs split up, VS-3 to attack from a northwesterly direction, VB-3 from the northeast. It took almost fifteen minutes for the planes to reach their attack position after the Japanese were first sighted, and Lou Kirn didn't push over into his dive until 1620. Just before he did so, *Ryujo* swung around into the wind and began launching the rest of her fighters. By then it was far too late.

The combat role of an air group commander was mainly that of tactical director. It was up to him to judge the progress of the attacks he had ordered, reinforce unsuccessful ones, and redirect his aircraft onto new targets. Felt circled overhead, therefore, rather than make an attack himself, while he waited to see how things went.

They did not go very well to start with. As the CAG watched with growing displeasure, the first ten SBDs scored only near misses on the carrier, which circled clockwise at frantic high speed that appeared oddly slow-motion from 15,000 feet. Felt then broadcast a cancellation of his original attack plan and redirected everyone onto the *Ryujo*. When he thought that all the bombers had made their dives—and still had scored no hits—he too throttled back, nosed up, opened his SBD's swiss-cheese-like dive flaps and rolled over into a near-vertical plunge on the carrier. His attack was worthy of a veteran dive-bomber pilot: the 1,000-pounder hit almost directly in the center of *Ryujo*'s flight deck.

Actually, Don Felt's was not, as he had thought, the last SBD to attack the carrier. The radio transmission reassigning VB-3's second division from *Tone* to *Ryujo* had caught them just starting their dives on the cruiser. They pulled out at high altitude, reformed, and then started down on the new target just about the time the air group commander's bomb hit her.

Of the seven SBDs, three scored direct hits and four near misses, and the *Ryujo* was doomed.

While the SBDs distracted the Japanese antiaircraft gunners, Bruce Harwood's five TBFs were waiting for their chance at the carrier. They split, two and three, to attack the carrier on each bow, bettering their chances of getting a torpedo or two into her no matter which way she turned. The ship was burning furiously and the torpedo pilots had to break off their attack three times before the smoke cleared sufficiently for them to see her. At length the *Ryujo* was clear and the five big Grummans bored stolidly in on her, flying at the maximum speed 200 feet off the water. The carrier's three Zekes attacked, but the TBFs paid no attention. Between 800 and 900 yards away from the carrier, their torpedoes dropped into the sea and the pilots banked away, "jinking" to avoid antiaircraft. They were able to see one large fire raging on the ship's hangar deck and many other small ones. Then one of the torpedoes hit, and *Ryujo* slowly began to lose way. Miles away, over the horizon, Rear Admiral Tanaka saw "a gigantic pillar of smoke and flame" and knew that she was gone. Actually, she hung on until after dark, when a destroyer took off 300 survivors, and then rolled over and sank.

In twos and threes Felt's air group rendezvoused after their attack and headed back toward their ship, unscathed. After missing the Coral Sea and Midway, the mighty old *Saratoga* finally had struck at the Japanese Navy.

While the *Saratoga* air group was delivering its attack and the *Enterprise* afternoon search was coming back, the Japanese, too, were on their way. Nagumo had launched his first attack group at 1537, just a little over an hour after the search plan told him where the Americans were. Typically of Japanese carrier aviation tactics, he split his strength. The first launch included only six fighters and nine dive bombers from the *Zuikaku* plus another group from the *Shokaku*. We do not know exactly how large the *Shokaku* contribution was, since that carrier's war diary for August was lost, but the number of Japanese planes encountered by American pilots during the battle suggests that the total strength of the Japanese attack was about thirty-six dive bombers and nine torpedo planes, escorted by perhaps twenty-seven fighters. Obviously, most of these aircraft must have come from the *Shokaku*.

From the time that Felt departed with his air group, Fletcher was prepared for an attack, and also for a strike against a second Japanese carrier should one be sighted. From 1430 the *Enterprise* had ready an attack group of eleven SBDs and seven TBFs. A sizable CAP from both carriers was kept constantly in the air, and the invisible beams of the ships' air-search radars rotated ceaselessly, groping out a hundred miles beyond the horizon.

If it had not turned into such a beautiful day, the Japanese might never have found Fletcher at all. By 1630 the weather near the two American carriers was clear, the ceiling unlimited with only scattered fair-weather cumulus clouds here or there in the sky. As is usually the case after the passage of a weather front, the visibility was exceptional. One pilot from the *Enterprise*'s Combat Air Patrol reported being able to see the task force from a distance of eighty miles.

At 1632, *Enterprise*'s and *Saratoga*'s radars simultaneously picked up a large body of aircraft eighty-eight miles northwest of the *Enterprise*. Then, almost immediately, the blip vanished from the radar scopes. This disappearance had a special significance. In the radars of that era, each beam consisted of a number of "lobes" of electromagnetic energy separated by voids where no energy penetrated. When a target flew into one of these null areas, it vanished, reappearing when it again encountered a lobe. By matching the range of a target and the length of time it was in a null with the known pattern of a particular radar beam, it was possible to arrive at a fair estimate of the plane's altitude, which was most important for fighter pilots to know. It was vital that the slow-climbing, relatively unmaneuverable, but fast-diving F4F start an attack on Japanese aircraft with an altitude advantage in order to even the odds.

The *Enterprise* fighter director officer, Lieutenant Commander Leonard Dow, had assumed fighter direction for both task forces just before the Japanese raid showed up, and thus was responsible for putting the *Enterprise* and *Saratoga* fighters in the right places at the right times.

The Japanese were in the null for seventeen minutes. During this time, *Enterprise* and *Saratoga* scrambled all available fighters and broadcast a warning to *Enterprise*'s incoming search planes to stay clear of the task force while attack was pending. (Some of the search plane pilots did not hear this transmission, to their later sorrow and to the inconvenience of the defending fighter pilots.)

At 1649 the unidentified aircraft reappeared on the carriers' radar scopes at a range of forty-four miles. Using their "fade charts," the ships' radar officers estimated the altitude of the unknown (properly presumed to be enemy) at 12,000 feet, and the CAP was so advised. At this time there were thirty-eight fighters in the air over the two American task forces, more than enough to keep the Japanese aircraft at a distance if properly handled.

Dow had two four-plane divisions over the carriers at altitudes between 10,000 and 15,000 feet, and a third over the *Enterprise* at 2,000 feet. Another two divisions were circling at 15,000 feet forty miles north of the *Enterprise*. The other four divisions, sixteen F4Fs from *Enterprise,* were given a "vector" (a compass course to steer) to intercept the raid almost the instant it reappeared. Besides the thirty-eight fighters that Dow had airborne, eight more were just completing gassing and arming on the *Saratoga*'s flight deck, and seven were part of the *Enterprise* striking group that had been standing by most of the afternoon.

When the incoming raid was detected, Fletcher decided to launch all *Enterprise*'s remaining SBDs and TBFs on another strike against the Japanese. This would clear the decks of both carriers for fighter operations and also fling a final bolt at the enemy. The departure of the *Enterprise* group freed her remaining seven F4Fs for the defense of the task force. They took off at 1653, and Dow assigned them to orbit the carriers at 15,000 feet.

At 1655 the men in the Combat Information Centers of the two carriers were watching the luminous green spike that marked the Japanese raid on the radar scopes coming closer and closer. Twenty miles away, "Red 2," a division of Fighting Six led by Lieutenant Albert Vorse, was clawing for altitude as it headed out on Dow's vector. Suddenly Vorse saw them—thirty-six Val dive bombers in two groups, ahead and high above, with shepherding Zekes above and below. From Vorse's altitude of 8,000 feet, the fighter director's estimate of 12,000 for the Japanese at first looked correct, but for only a minute. It rapidly became clear that the enemy attack group was at 16,000 feet, much higher than the American fighters that were supposed to intercept them.

Achi "Val"

Now the situation became chaotic. With fifty-three fighter pilots all using the same radio frequency, even the most stringent discipline could not have prevented extreme difficulty with communications. The discipline was lacking. The fighter pilots, most of them inexperienced, caught at a tactical disadvantage and preoccupied with their own immediate problems to the exclusion of any other thoughts, all began talking at once. Some of the messages were vital "tallyho" reports, giving the particulars of enemy numbers and altitude. Others were less consequential. The net effect was to make it impossible for Dow to even understand the tactical situation, much less control it. It immediately became a pilot's battle. The ships below could hear only a crazy quilt of radio transmissions:

"Don't let them get away, Lou."

"Let's go to high [supercharger], here they come, Hank."

"Barney, just above me. Hey, Scope, on our right, get in back of them, let's go get them, get up there."

"Zero right above us, Scope."

"I don't see them."

"Many bogeys approaching west of us."

"I see them, I'm getting altitude."

"Knock off the chatter about the belly tanks and get in there."

"Those squadrons are ready to attack."

"Hank, they're attacking the *Enterprise*."

They were indeed attacking the *Enterprise*. The large force of American fighters, caught well below the Japanese dive bombers, struggled to catch up with them, thwarted by their lower altitudes and by attacking Zekes. Most of them didn't make it before the Vals pushed over into their dives on the twisting carrier.

Vorse first sighted the Japanese, and his division was jumped by Zekes as they strained through 10,000 feet. Red 2 fought them indecisively until they reached 20,000 feet, when the Japanese fighters turned away. The four F4Fs then dove on the Vals, which had just let down to 12,000, preparatory to pushing over on the *Enterprise*. The Americans were intercepted by four more Zekes. Vorse and his wingman, Dick Loesch, got one of them; Sumrall, a warrant Machinist, shot down a second. Ensign F. R. Register, Sumrall's wingman, executed a wingover—a very steep climb with a reversal of direction at the top—and caught a Zeke, the pilot of which bailed out without a parachute at 6,000 feet. With another wingover, Register got a second one, which burst into flames. Almost out of gas after their long climb and combat, Vorse's three division mates just made it back to the *Saratoga*. He himself ran out on final approach, ditched just astern of *Sara*, and was picked up by a destroyer.

Lieutenant Hayden Jensen of the *Saratoga*'s Fighting Five led one of the few divisions to intercept the Japanese bombers before they started their attack on the *Enterprise*. He and Ensign J. M. Kleinman and Lieutenant (j.g.) C. B. Starkes caught the second group of nine Vals—the enemy had formed a column of four nine-plane Vs—about fifteen miles east of the carrier at 16,000 feet. Jensen was credited with three of the dive bombers and his two wingmen with two apiece. Starkes also shot a Zeke off his division leader's tail.

Another warrant officer, Machinist Don Runyan of Fighting Six, caught one of the other groups of Vals when they were almost over the *Enterprise*. He and his division had climbed to 18,000 and attacked from an excellent position out of the sun. Runyan, a veteran fighter pilot, did most of the work with assists from his three teammates, Naval Aviation Pilot H. S. Packard and Ensigns Reed and Shoemaker. Runyan made a high-side run on one Val, which exploded. He recovered from his run and climbed back up-sun for a second attack. He dove steeply onto the tail of a second Val, and it burst into flames. As Runyan climbed back up for a third attack, a Zeke dove on him from above. It made the mistake of diving in front of him, and Runyan, nosing over, set it on fire with a short burst. He then attacked a third dive bomber from underneath, and it too fell burning three miles into the Pacific.

Another of Fighting Six's divisions, led by Machinist D. C. Barnes, caught the Japanese just as they pushed over into their dives. Barnes's wingman, Ensign R. A. M. Dibb, shot down a Val at 14,000 feet, was chased right down to the water by a Zeke, and there, recovering, shot down another dive bomber after its pullout. Gunner C. E. Brewer, the second section leader of the division, followed the Vals down in their dives, claiming two plus a Zeke. His wingman, Ensign D. M. Johnson, downed another Val, but was thoroughly shot up in return by its rear gunner. His left aileron connecting rod, radio antenna, and Pitot tube were shot away, and he had several bullets in his wings as well as one through his propeller.

And so it went. The Japanese dive bombers had a hard time of it, although their escorting fighters were able to keep perhaps one-quarter of the *Enterprise* and *Saratoga* fighters occupied. Despite the hideous confusion on the radio and the opposition of the Zekes, eighteen F4Fs intercepted the Vals and, of the thirty-six in the Japanese attack group, only about half actually completed their dives on the twisting *Enterprise*. Of these, three scored direct hits on the carrier, killing seventy-four men, wounding ninety-five, and temporarily disabling her steering gear so that she careered through her screen at 24 knots, out of control. However, three hits from thirty-six dive bombers was not much of a score. *Shokaku* and *Zuikaku* had not been in combat since the Battle of the Coral Sea in May, and they showed it.

The nine enemy torpedo bombers might have determined the outcome of the battle had they attacked in coordination with the Vals. As things turned out, the Kates never attacked at all. Ensign G. W. Brooks's division of fighters from the *Enterprise* caught them forty miles northwest of the fleet, flying only fifty feet off the water. Brooks shot down two of them as the formation frantically "S"-turned back and forth, and his mates took care of four more. The remaining three torpedo planes escaped.

The Japanese attack was over in a matter of a few minutes, although scattered skirmishes between the F4Fs and the retiring Vals and Zeros continued for a little longer. At 1721 another large flight of aircraft showed up fifty miles to the west on the carriers' radar scopes. Within five minutes they were also sighted by the *Saratoga* air group, homeward bound from its attack on the *Ryujo*. It was Nagumo's second attack group. Evidently they did not sight the American planes. While the radar officers on the carriers tensely watched their scopes, the glowing spikes showing the Japanese aircraft began to recede. The enemy was flying on by, heading south. After a while they turned northwest. The Japanese had shot their bolt for the day.

The final episode of the Battle of the Eastern Solomons (as it came to be called by the Americans) was the attempted second attack by the *Enterprise* and *Saratoga* dive and torpedo bombers. The *Enterprise* attack group included eleven SBDs of Bombing Six and Scouting Five, seven TBFs of Torpedo Three, and the CAG. They began launching just a matter of minutes before the Japanese attack on their ship. The dive bombers, led by Lieutenant Turner Caldwell, C.O. of VS-5, started off at 1640, followed by the TBFs. Lieutenant R. H. Konig led the TBFs. The last aircraft off was the TBF of the Air Group commander, Max Leslie. The *Enterprise* Air Group was still trying to rendezvous when the Japanese dive bombers appeared overhead. The sky filled suddenly with planes and antiaircraft bursts, and the two squadrons made off toward their target, leaving Leslie to follow as best he could.

Caldwell flew high, while Konig's TBFs stayed low. In the confusion of launching just as an attack was being mounted on their carrier, the two squadrons never rendezvoused, and headed toward their target independently. Leslie never sighted either squadron. After being fired at and hit by the *North Carolina*'s five-inch antiaircraft guns, he had a brief brush with a Val. To top things off, he found that his

TBF

radio was not operating properly and he was unable to communicate with his squadrons. The *Enterprise* air group flew scattered and uncoordinated into the gathering darkness.

Saratoga, too, had had a reserve striking group on deck, five TBFs of Torpedo Eight and two SBDs of Scouting Three. However, its launch was uniquely disorganized. The pilots and crewmen assigned to these aircraft manned them casually about 1630, thinking they were only to taxi them forward to clear the flight deck for a fighter recovery. They had no briefing, no chartboards, and no flight gear. Hardly had they started engines, however, when a sailor came running out to the flight deck and held up a chalkboard instructing them to take off and rendezvous with the *Enterprise* attack group. As the last of Torpedo Eight's pilots, Chief Aviation Pilot Red Doggett, was taxiing into take-off position, his commanding officer suddenly appeared on the wing outside his cockpit motioning him out. The skipper, Lieutenant Harold Larsen, kibitzing down in *Saratoga*'s Air Plot, had gotten wind of the last-minute decision to launch the tiny strike and dashed up to the flight deck with his helmet, goggles, and chartboard. It was an act typical of the conscientious "Swede" Larsen: he would not have his squadron go helter-skelter into danger if he could do something about it.

There is something of a mystery about the selection of their target. *Saratoga*'s narrative of the battle records the receipt of Ray Davis' report sent about 1530, when he sighted *Shokaku* and *Zuikaku*. Presumably, Admiral Fletcher therefore would or should have known about the presence of the two big Japanese carriers. But the target given to Max Leslie was the *Ryujo* ,which already had been attacked. If the attack order came from Fletcher, it would be inconceivable that he would have ignored two big carriers to attack one small one for the second time. We can only conclude that Davis' report either was not received or, for some reason, was never passed on to the admiral. For whatever reason, the tiny *Enterprise* and *Saratoga* striking group was sent to attack the wrong target.

Swede Larsen's five TBFs from *Saratoga*'s Torpedo Eight met Bob Elder and his wingman, Gordon, flying Bombing Three's two SBDs, forty minutes after departing from overhead the carrier. Half an hour later, they sighted through the clouds a force they estimated as a battleship, five cruisers, and six destroyers. Actually it was the Japanese Support Force of Vice-Admiral Kondo, and their ship count was pretty accurate except that the "Battleship" was really the seaplane tender *Chitose*.

The two dive bombers attacked first, Elder and Gordon pushing over from 12,500 feet into very heavy antiaircraft from Kondo's cruisers. Elder's 1,000-pounder landed in the water just along the port side of the big *Chitose,* and Gordon's missed narrowly to starboard. The SBDs, totally unsupported, badly damaged the seaplane tender. She turned back to Truk, listing progressively more seriously as she flooded. However, her crew, working furiously, saved her. When she arrived at Truk four days later, her thirty-degree list had been corrected and she was able to make 16 knots.

Larsen's torpedo planes did not see the *Chitose* and, instead, attacked Kondo's five heavy cruisers. None of their fish hit, although Bob Elder thought one had. In the heavy antiaircraft fire and the dimming light the five TBFs had great difficulty in joining up. Ensign John Taurman briefly found three others, lost them again, and was suddenly alone in the darkness. Without a chartboard it was hopeless to try to navigate to the *Saratoga* at night. Taurman ditched off a San Cristobal beach and swam ashore with his crewmen. Ensign E. L. Fayle, similarly lost, landed near a small island and he and his crew took to their life raft. Larsen and the other two made it back to the *Sara* and landed safely aboard about 2200.

About 1850, Max Leslie, chasing the *Enterprise* air group, saw the hoped-for illumination from the full moon gradually disappearing behind a layer of low, broken clouds and realized that it was going to be very difficult to locate the Japanese that night. Still in only intermittent radio contact with his squadrons, he ordered them to attack and return at their discretion. He received no reply, but fifteen minutes later heard Konig report sighting the target. He ordered Torpedo Three to attack.

Konig's six remaining TBFs (one had developed engine trouble after take-off and returned) deployed for attack and bored in low and fast toward the feathery wakes that marked ships moving through the dusk. As they grew nearer, the white "wakes" suddenly became recognizable as tiny surf-beaten islets. Torpedo Three was making its run, not on Japanese ships, but on lonely Roncador Reef.

The frustrated Konig wisely ordered his pilots to jettison their torpedoes to reduce their gas consumption, and the TBFs started on a long night flight to their carrier. Max Leslie, who had arrived over Roncador Reef just about the time Torpedo Three was attacking it, elected to do the same thing. It was not until 2200 that they got back. One TBF landed aboard the *Enterprise*, but a second crashed on deck, closing it. Konig's remaining four landed on the *Saratoga* with from four to forty gallons of gas remaining. The *Enterprise*'s air group commander, who had not sighted any of his group since take-off, finally landed aboard the *Sara* just half an hour before midnight, after over six hours of fruitless search.

Turner Caldwell led his flight sixty miles beyond the point where they had expected to find the Japanese. They sighted nothing—from their altitude, not even Roncador Reef. They were then almost 300 miles away from the *Enterprise*, and even if they had been sure of locating their carrier in the darkness they barely had enough gas remaining to make it back. Caldwell elected to head for his alternate, which was Guadalcanal. The SBDs dropped their bombs in the water and headed toward the island. It was a decision that helped greatly to hold that island in the days ahead.

Henderson Field, alerted by Caldwell on the radio, had lighted a few flare pots to mark the strip. It is never easy to land at night even on a familiar field, and these Navy pilots had never seen Henderson Field, which was dimly lit and surrounded by jungle. Nevertheless, although the first two SBDs landed downwind, they all made it in without mishap.

So ended the Battle of the Eastern Solomons for the American flyers. John Taurman and his crew waited for rescue on San Cristobal. Frenchy Fayle and his crew bobbed in their liferaft in the Coral Sea. At Henderson Field, Caldwell's pilots and gunners lay down for the night in the only beds the Marines could give them—canvas stretchers.

East of the islands, the opposing carrier forces were retiring from the scene of their brief encounter. Fletcher withdrew to the south to refuel and rendezvous with the *Wasp*. Nagumo turned back toward Truk, while Kondo ran toward Fletcher's last reported position with battleships and cruisers. By midnight he too turned back.

Technically, it was an American victory. The *Ryujo* was sunk, while *Enterprise* was only damaged. Japanese air losses somewhat exceeded American. The Marine and Navy claims totaled over seventy. It is impossible to tell now what the actual losses were, since the records of the Japanese carriers involved did not survive the war. Subtraction of known naval air losses for the rest of August, 1942, from those recorded for the entire month presumably gives the losses for August 24. These figures lead to an estimate that seven Zekes and six Kates were lost from the *Ryujo* and fourteen Zekes plus eight Vals and Kates from *Shokaku* and *Zuikaku*.

However, the carrier battle decided nothing. Yamamoto's strength remained virtually the same. Despite the damage to *Enterprise,* so did Fletcher's. Perhaps its most important outcome was to provide a reinforcement, in the form of Caldwell's flight, for Mangrum's under-strength dive-bomber squadron on Guadalcanal. Furthermore, the now-retiring carriers and their escorts were only part of the fleet deployed by Yamamoto. There was still Rear Admiral Tanaka with his transports—and the troops they carried.

6

CACTUS ON
A SHOESTRING
August 25–31

The only offensive capability against ships possessed by the Americans on Guadalcanal reposed in the handful of dive bombers from the Marine squadron and the *Enterprise*. It was a nominal capability at best. The aircraft themselves were limited in performance, and half of the pilots had only the sketchiest training and no combat experience whatsoever. Dick Mangrum had only twelve SBDs and eighteen pilots, although his allowance was eighteen and forty, respectively. Much of the offensive burden during the days to come inevitably would have to be borne by Turner Caldwell and his pilots.

Caldwell was a scholarly professional, his style very low key, but he was a squadron commander of unusual effectiveness. Without driving or haranguing his pilots, he was able to extract their utmost abilities, a quality particularly valuable on Guadalcanal in 1942. His ten pilots all had combat experience and possessed the special skill and confidence in their flying ability that carrier pilots should have. Caldwell's executive officer was Roger Woodhull, a lieutenant, who was also "exec" of Scouting Five. The other nine pilots came from Caldwell's own squadron and from Bombing Six: Elmer Liffner, Walter Coolbaugh, Hal Buell, Elmer Conzett, Lloyd Barker, Walter Brown, Buck Manford, Gill Guillory, and Christian Fink. While the Marine squadron was picking up its skill and experience in combat, it was pretty much up to these eleven pilots to provide expertise in dive bombing.

The SBD was an airplane much beloved by those who

58

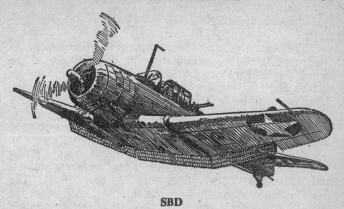

SBD

flew it. The product of a company that prided itself on "never having built a bad airplane," it was as rugged and dependable as its more famous distant relative, the DC-3. But it was a five-year-old aircraft and had performance deficiencies that made life a little harder for the Cactus pilots. With a 1,000-pound bomb slung underneath the fuselage, the SBD-3 had a cruising speed of 130 knots (the pilot's handbook claimed 174 knots), and a maximum rate of climb of 450 feet per minute (the Douglas handbook said 1,350 feet per minute). Small wonder that its pilots sardonically called it the "Speedy Three." But it was heavily armed and a good steady platform for dive bombing that brought its pilots back, and pilots appreciate that.

The Marine and Navy flyers were reminded only ten minutes after midnight on August 25 that the "victory" of the previous day in the Battle of the Eastern Solomons was an incomplete one. Five Japanese destroyers shelled the strip for two hours. At 0230, Major Mangrum and Lieutenants Iverson and Baldinus went out to attack the enemy ships, but all of their bombs missed. An hour and a half later, Roger Woodhull, Coolbaugh, and Brown took off to continue the harassment of the destroyers, which then were passing through Indispensable Strait. Again the SBDs' bombs missed, and Brown, lost in the predawn darkness, ditched off the coast of Malaita. At 0600 a third attack force of eight SBDs was sent out to intercept another Japanese force, which had been located by a PBY, and at 0830 the Japanese were sighted.

The enemy force was Tanaka's reinforcement convoy, its landings delayed by uncertainty over the outcome of the carrier battle. Tanaka's flag flew in the light cruiser *Jintsu,* and he had four old destroyers to escort three troop transports; he had just been joined by the five destroyers which had shelled the field, and was signaling his orders for course, speed, and force formation when the dive bombers plunged out of the clouds above him.

Mangrum's force included Lieutenants Lawrence Baldinus, Hise, Thomas, and McAllister from his own squadron, and Turner Caldwell with Chris Fink and Lloyd Barker. The five Marines dove on *Jintsu,* while the Navy men chose the largest of the three transports, *Kinryu Maru.* Mangrum's bomb failed to release; as Tanaka watched from his bridge, Hise, Thomas, and McAllister scored three successive near misses, then Baldinus got a direct hit on the cruiser's forecastle. The bomb exploded between the two forward 5.5-inch gun mounts, spraying the deck with splinters and knocking the admiral unconscious. Caldwell missed the *Kinryu Maru,* but Fink, corkscrewing down behind him, hit the big transport amidships and set it on fire. The eight SBDs were formed up and on the way back to Guadalcanal before the Japanese had collected their wits. The aircraft had scarcely rendezvoused, though, before Mangrum's wingman signaled to him that his bomb had not released. Turning the lead over to Caldwell, Mangrum went back alone and near-missed one of the small transports. He noted also that *Kinryu Maru* was burning furiously, but missed seeing *Jintsu,* which was already on its way back to Truk. Fink's hit had been most fortunate; not only was the *Kinryu Maru* carrying the entire 1,000-man Yokosuka Fifth Special Naval Landing Force, but the fire started by his bomb cooked off her ammunition, and the resulting explosions left her dead in the water and sinking. As the destroyer *Mutsuki* lay alongside taking on survivors, a flight of B-17s from Espiritu Santo rumbled overhead. A stationary target was one the big planes could handle excellently well; three bombs hit the luckless destroyer and she sank almost instantly. Her commander was hauled out of the water to observe, with admirable Oriental calm, that even B-17s had to hit something now and then.

So ended the first major Japanese effort to land reinforcements on Guadalcanal, defeated by eight dive bombers. Admiral Tanaka, his forebodings of disaster come true, returned to Rabaul on his own initiative, sporadically harassed by conflicting orders from his various superiors to land or not land the remaining three hundred troops. It was not to be the last time that the destroyer squadron commander would be frustrated by the handful of planes and pilots that comprised Cactus' air force—or by his countrymen's appalling lapses of military judgment.

Mangrum's planes did not take long to return to Guadalcanal, but were effectively grounded by the primitive fueling and arming facilities at the field. While the sailors of CUB-1 sweated and manhandled fuel drums, bombs, and cans of machine-gun ammunition into place for the next two hours, the exhausted pilots, most of them up all night, caught what rest they could. At 1100, one of the New Georgia coastwatchers reported twenty-one Bettys passing high over the island, heading toward Guadalcanal. They were less than an hour away. The threat of the Japanese convoy, plus that of the forthcoming raid, posed an almost impossible dilemma to the overworked CUB. By hand they completed bombing and gassing nine SBDs, but they could not work fast enough to get Smith's Grummans into the air in time to intercept the Bettys, which wheeled over in their customary tight formation at 1155. From 27,000 feet, the Japanese bombers dropped a tight pattern of over forty bombs, centered about the conspicuous Pagoda. All but three of the American aircraft had been scrambled, however, and the result was only minor damage to the runway and dispersal areas. The runway was patched up in time to handle the returning planes. The afternoon and night of the 25th were quiet and most of the pilots were able to get some of the rest that they had missed for the past five days.

Vandegrift, with time now to think about it, became deeply concerned by the rate of loss that had been suffered by the two Marine squadrons in their first five days on the island, and by the implications of this attrition for the future. Of John Smith's original nineteen F4Fs, three had been shot down, one was destroyed on a test flight, one was a complete strike after a crash landing, and three were under repair awaiting parts. Nine of Mangrum's twelve SBDs remained operational; one had crashed and two others were down for lack of spare parts. That afternoon, the worried general sent the first of a long series of dispatches to ComSoPac outlining his needs for parts and more aircraft. It ended: "Present rate attrition aircraft Cactus makes imperative present numbers be augmented earliest date. Recommended rear echelon MAG-23 arriving Samoa late August be sent Cactus with spare aircraft earliest practicable date. Urgently need oxygen replacement bottles filled."

The next day Smith's underequipped squadron sent four of its borrowed VMF-212 pilots back to Espiritu Santo on a departing Army B-17. During the morning the Grummans were prepared for the expected noon air raid. Kennedy, the New Georgia coastwatcher, saw the sixteen Bettys going over the island at 1124, and every flyable aircraft was off Henderson Field within twelve minutes. VMF-223 climbed for altitude in three four-plane divisions, and was comfortably situated by the time the Japanese bombers arrived. These were the first enemy bombers the new pilots had ever intercepted and they were enchanted by the beautiful target presented by the impeccable Japanese V formation three-quarters of a mile across. As the captain said later, "They wanted to shoot them all down. They did a lot of *general* shooting ... and didn't get any bombers at all." Actually, three bombers were shot down and all but two damaged, but this was almost entirely because of the individual expertise of Smith, Rivers Morrell, Marion Carl, Tex Hamilton, a visiting warrant offiicer, and Captain Loren Everton, both of whom were on temporary duty from VMF-212. Roy Corry was shot down, the only Marine casualty, and the rest of the chastened youngsters returned to the field. The Japanese, despite their losses, were not prevented from carrying out the mission. They dropped almost fifty bombs, of which a few were large and the remainder mixed incendiaries and fragmentation. Splinter damage was done to the dispersed aircraft and the field radio station, and 2,000 gallons of precious aviation gas set on fire. To complete the confusion, the huge fire cooked off two of the 1000-pounders bequeathed by Don Felt's air group three days before. Not a particularly good show, but the green fighter pilots would have ample opportunity to learn their business better.

By the evening of the 26th, eleven F4Fs and nine SBDs remained of the nineteen F4Fs and twelve SBDs that had landed six days before. Their opponents, over 500 miles away in Rabaul and Kavieng, were at a low ebb too. Only nineteen

Zekes and twenty-nine Bettys were operational in the Eleventh Air Fleet, and one of the Japanese accounts of the campaign stated, with resignation, that "reinforcements were sluggish."

The night was another quiet one, and an attempted Japanese raid the next morning was frustrated by bad weather. A B-17 came in while the air raid alert was still in effect and delivered three of Smith's pilots who, being least trained of all, had been temporarily exchanged for some of VMF-212's more experienced men. Now they had been sent up to Guadalcanal to pit their 275 hours of flying time against the veterans of the Tainan Air Group. Following closely on the B-17 came fourteen Army P-400s, the remainder of Dale Brannon's 67th Pursuit Squadron urgently sent for by Vandegrift. Unfortunately these aircraft, as would shortly be discovered, lacked any capability whatsoever for air combat.

Bad weather kept the Japanese away from the field for the third night in a row, and also prevented eighteen Bettys which set out from Rabaul on an important raid the morning of the 28th from getting through to Guadalcanal. Having decided after the disaster to their convoy on the 25th that it was safer to land troops at night from fast destroyers, the Japanese dispatched four of them from Truk carrying an advanced echelon of the second major land reinforcement to be sent to Guadalcanal, Major General Kawaguchi's 35th Brigade. The Bettys which failed to get through on the 28th were supposed to provide air cover for the destroyers.

The Japanese destroyers found themselves only seventy miles from Guadalcanal at 1700 on the 28th. There the evening patrol of two SBDs found them too, attacked them ineffectually, but reported their position accurately. Within half an hour, eleven SBDs had taken off from Cactus to strike the enemy. This group fell on the Japanese just before sunset. Turner Caldwell's five planes dove first. "Never miss 'em" Chris Fink hit the lead ship *Asagiri* directly amidships with a 1000-pounder, and Caldwell hit the *Shirakumo* with a second. The *Asagiri* exploded and sank, carrying down with her the division commander, Captain Yuzo Arita. *Shirakumo*, heavily damaged, was taken in tow by the undamaged *Amagiri*. *Yugiri* was "moderately" damaged, but was in a yard under repair until mid-January of 1943. The cost of this second consecutive defeat of an enemy landing by the Guadalcanal flyers was one SBD: Lieutenant Oliver Mitchell and his gunner Schackman, both Marines, their plane downed by antiaircraft as they tried to strafe the *Amagiri*. Mangrum and Caldwell were back at the field just after sunset. Behind them the surviving Japanese crawled north like crippled water bugs. The perceptive, realistic Tanaka saw exactly why this had happened: "This made it more obvious than ever what sheer recklessness it was to attempt a landing operation against strong resistance without preliminary neutralization of enemy air power."

What Tanaka saw so clearly in the last week of August, 1942, was not yet so clear to most of his colleagues, nor, perhaps, was it entirely obvious to ComSoPac or Vandegrift's hard-pressed Marines. The best defense of the island was the handful of Marine, Navy, and Army aircraft—which very shortly began to call itself the "Cactus Air Force"—flying from the primitive little airstrip rather grandiloquently called Henderson Field. It was their pilots who had the only chance of defeating the almost daily Japanese efforts to put more men ashore on Guadalcanal, and the entire campaign hereafter would turn around control of the Guadalcanal airstrip. Henceforth the Japanese would spare no effort to eliminate it, and the Americans none to save it.

On the following day, August 29, the Japanese launched two bombing attacks against the airfield, and this time neither was stopped by weather. The first was a small hit-and-run affair by three bombers early in the morning. The second came just before noon, delivered by eighteen Bettys which were advertised well in advance by the coastwatchers. John Smith's ten F4Fs and Brannon's fourteen P-400s were in the air and waiting when they arrived. But despite all the warning, the Japanese dropped their bombs before the Grummans found them. (The P-400s could not even climb to the altitude at which the combat took place.) The Marines struck after the bombs were dropped and claimed four bombers and four fighters. The Japanese records do not mention the loss of any aircraft in this attack, but this is not necessarily significant. For some reason—perhaps lack of time—the day-to-day accounts of Japanese attacks on Guadalcanal between August 29 and September 14 do not mention any losses, although the monthly operational summaries of the several air groups involved show that ten Bettys and twelve Zekes actually were shot down during this period.

The day further eroded Guadalcanal's available fighter strength; one of the F4Fs was so badly shot up that it was stripped for spare parts, and two others, damaged by bombs, were total losses. Vandegrift's feelings about the rapid shrinking of his tiny air force began to approach desperation. In a dispatch which went out to Ghormley early the next morning, he asked:

F4Fs are the only planes here which can operate against hostile craft at altitudes at which they approach. Only eight effective F4Fs at present. Fourteen P-400s in commission. This steady deterioration of fighter strength is alarming. Cannot additional planes be sent at once?

Just before the day's air raid, the transport U.S.S. *William Ward Burrows* arrived off Lunga Point and started to unload the ground personnel of the two Marine squadrons. After ten days of making do with the willing but green sailors of CUB-1, the Marines had their own mechanics, linemen, and ordnance men. Just in time, too. When the planes first arrived on the island, most of them were brand new. About all they required in the way of maintenance was gas and oil, which was about all the young CUBs were capable of doing. Now, after a week and a half of combat flying and operating from the alternately (or simultaneously) mud-caked and dust-swept airstrip, their state of repair was beginning to verge on the precarious. Mangrum, who had virtually adopted Caldwell's flight into his own squadron, assigned Marine plane captains to take care of the Navy SBDs. The *Enterprise* pilots had, of course, flown in with no supporting personnel whatever. The *Burrows* got underway at 1630, her unloading incomplete, to seek the greater security of Tulagi during the night. There she promptly ran aground.

During the day, the Americans caught sight of what they thought were five Japanese cruisers—actually seven destroyers—on their way down from the Shortlands. It was feared that they would sink the stranded transport and shell the island, and all available SBDs were launched shortly after midnight to find and attack them. Despite the clear night and full moon, the bomber pilots could not find the Japanese. The enemy destroyer division commander heard and saw the aircraft, however. After hurriedly disembarking 750 troops off Taivu Point, he fled incontinently back to the Shortlands in complete and flagrant disregard of his orders to attack American ships. Upon his arrival, the enraged Tanaka relieved him on the spot. However, the success of landing troops by destroyer encouraged the Japanese Navy to plan more such operations—code-named "Rat" landings by the Japanese.

Major General Kawaguchi, however, was not satisfied with the "Rat" tactics. Because of the success which his brigade had enjoyed with landing barge transport in the East Indies earlier in the year, he was anxious to adopt this method for reinforcing Guadalcanal. Tanaka recognized the dangers of using such slow and vulnerable craft when neither command of the sea nor of the air was consistently held by the Japanese. However, the Army was adamant. The Navy agreed to "study" the matter further, and landing craft began to be collected on the northern tip of Santa Isabel in anticipation of their eventual use.

The Marines heard from the coastwatcher Paul Mason at 0930 the next morning, August 30, the usual message about Japanese aircraft headed south. This time, however, Mason reported a large group of single-engine planes, rather than the customary Bettys. What he saw were eighteen of the Hamps—clipped-wing Zeros—from the Third Fleet carrier units that had been sent forward to Buka two days previously, crack pilots from the *Shokaku*'s and *Zuikaku*'s fighter squadrons. At 1100, as the fighters swept over New Georgia, Kennedy called in his report, always the signal for the alerted Cactus fighter pilots to take off.

Five minutes later, John Smith's F4F lifted its tail high and snarled down the runway, followed by the remaining seven serviceable Grummans. After them came seven of Dale Brannon's P-400s. The Army squadron commander, impatient with the passive role forced on him by the ceiling deficiencies of the Bells, volunteered to come along to the fight anyway. The shorthanded Smith naturally agreed. Another four P-400s had gone off earlier in the morning and were circling on low patrol over the grounded *William Ward Burrows*. Every one of the nineteen flyable fighter planes on Guadalcanal was airborne.

The F4Fs climbed only to 15,000 feet, in deference to the Army pilots' lack of oxygen equipment, Smith leading the first division, Rivers Morrell leading the second. They stayed in a wide, slow turn between Cape Esperance and Savo; the fast P-400s, unable to slow down enough to stay with the tubby little Marine fighters, held their position in the formation by riding on the outside of the turn. For forty minutes the fighters waited and looked apprehensively at the weather. A solid front, its clouds towering up to 40,000 feet, extended between Guadalcanal and Florida, moving slowly northwestward up Sealark Channel.

Suddenly Smith saw the seven Army "peashooters" peel off and plunge down toward Tulagi in a long olive-drab column. He had not heard Brannon call to him that enemy fighters were attacking the *Burrows'* fighter cover. But after one quick look he didn't need any explanation. He turned his F4Fs as quickly as possible to come down on the Japanese out of the sun, ordering his pilots to choose one enemy and not to change targets on the way down. Then the blue and gray Grummans rolled into their dives. They were upon the preoccupied Japanese like a swarm of bees: eight of the Hamps were shot out of their formation on that first pass.

When Smith pulled up to gain altitude for another run, he "was still just as scared as the Japs were." The first thing he saw was his wingman, Willis Lees, with a Hamp on his tail. The captain shot the Japanese off, and Lees fled for a cloud. Smith was just beginning to think this an excellent idea, when another Japanese came up underneath him. Smith made a head-on pass at his opponent and blew him up by putting a burst from all six guns right into his engine. Then he flashed into the protecting wall of cloud. The whole engagement was over in less than three minutes.

Even granting the exceptional circumstances of finding the enemy 3,000 feet below and already embroiled in combat, this fight was a sensational victory for the Cactus Air Force. Eight of the Hamps were shot down outright and two more, badly damaged, never returned to Buka. Four of Dale Brannon's badly outclassed P-400s were lost, although two pilots bailed out and later returned to the field. Two never came back. It was a bad mauling for the high-spirited young Army fighter pilots, all the more painful because they were acutely conscious that their country had equipped them with less than the best. The very high wing loading of the Bell made it fatally clumsy in combat. For the Grumman F4F-4, for Smith's tactics, and for Marine aviation, though, this defeat of a superior force of the very best Japanese pilots was a clear-cut triumph. But like so many of the triumphs of the summer of 1942, it was somehow transient.

The eight F4Fs returned without loss, but three of them were sufficiently damaged to be unfit for combat for a few days. Temporarily the Cactus Air Force was down to five fighter planes that could fly a mission, and the slaughter of *Shokaku*'s and *Zuikaku*'s fighters did not save the little old four-piper destroyer-transport *Colhoun* either. Eighteen Bettys appeared overhead a little after 1500 and sank the ship, one of many that ran supply missions to Cactus, with a beautiful pattern of bombs. Smith's five flyable Grummans were still being refueled and couldn't intercept. During the course of the day, the grounded *Burrows*' spare parts and supplies for VMF-223 and VMSB-232 were shipped across from Tulagi to Guadalcanal by a variety of small craft, but tons more were jettisoned in efforts to refloat the ship.

By far the most encouraging development on August 30 for the Americans on Guadalcanal was the arrival, during the alert that followed the sinking of the *Colhoun*, of thirty-one aircraft of the other two squadrons of MAG-23, led by Colonel William Wallace, group commander and veteran Marine aviator, with Major Robert Galer, commander of VMF-224, and Major Leo Smith of VMSB-231. The arrival of these aircraft—nineteen F4F's and twelve SBDs—was watched with intense interest and pleasure by Rear Admiral John Sidney McCain, Commander Air South Pacific, who had come up to visit Vandegrift for a couple of days and see for himself how the hard-pressed Cactus flyers were doing. A wiry, profane little Mississippian with very sharp features, a late comer to naval aviation (he graduated from Pensacola as a captain in his fifties), he grasped the essence of the American situation on Guadalcanal as fast as Tanaka had realized the problem facing the Japanese. In a dispatch sent early September 1, this uncommonly prescient admiral stated directly to Nimitz:

> Reinforcement 19 F4F-4, 12 SBD arrived just in
> time afternoon August 30. Pilots on Cactus very
> tired. Of 19 F4F-4 put in on August 20, 5 flyable,
> an attrition rate of 14 in 10 days. Cactus designed
> by enemy as major base, for which admirably locat-
> ed, and is making major effort to recapture, of
> which daily bombings are a part. Against enemy

power thus far shown 40 flyable high altitude fighters necessary to protect. P-400s no good at altitude and disheartening to the brave men who fly them. F4F more successful, due in part to belly tanks on Zeros, in part to cool maneuvering and expert gunnery. P-38s believed better, but 2 full squadrons

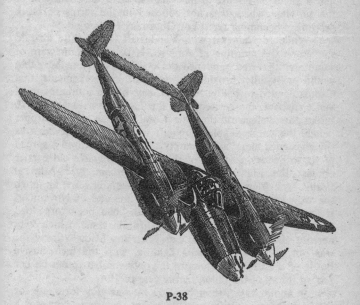

P-38

of P-38s or F4Fs in addition to present strength should be put into Cactus at once, with replacements in training to south. One of these types should be replacement and reinforcement planes for P-400 and P-39 pilots in the South Pacific, whose pilots are highly trained. The situation admits of no delay whatever. No help can or should be expected of carrier fighters unless based ashore. With substantially the reinforcement requested, Cactus can be a sinkhole for enemy air power and can be consolidated, expanded and exploited to enemy's mortal hurt. The reverse is true if we lose Cactus. If the reinforcement requested is not made available, Cactus cannot be supplied and hence cannot be held.

This was really laying it on the line. Such blunt forthrightness seldom survives the traditionally circumspect language of naval dispatches. It must have been both refreshing and a shock to Nimitz to have had so clear an exposition of the problem which was not couched in the terms of black pessimism becoming typical of Ghormley's messages.

While McCain sat with Vandegrift in his little air-raid shelter on the morning of August 31, they were unaware of something that had happened far to the south, something that would willy-nilly provide the aircraft reinforcements that Cactus needed so badly. At 0745, east of the southern tip of San Critsobal, the periscope of the Japanese submarine I-26 broke the surface of the blue Coral Sea. In it her skipper beheld the unmistakable silhouette of the U.S.S. *Saratoga* as she zigzagged along at a leisurely 13 knots. I-26 fired a spread of six torpedoes, and one of them hit the massive old carrier abreast the island, injuring, among others, Vice-Admiral Frank Jack Fletcher. The ship was not badly hurt, although she would be out of commission until the end of November. It was hard luck for the old *Sara:* she had been torpedoed once before in January off the California coast, which kept her out of the battles of the Coral Sea and Midway; now she was out of the Guadalcanal fighting, with the inconclusive Battle of the Eastern Solomons the only combat to put on her record for all of the bitter, heroic year of 1942.

In another way, though, I-26's hit was very fortunate for the Marines on Guadalcanal. It meant that there now was a trained carrier air group in the South Pacific without a carrier. With the situation developing as it was on Guadalcanal, it was inevitable that the precious pilots and planes eventually would be flung into the battle. The *Saratoga*'s skipper, "Duke" Ramsey, flew off thirty of his bomber and torpedo aircraft to Espiritu Santo on the afternoon of the 31st, and his fighter squadron to Efate on the second of September. To the air group, Ramsey sent a valedictory message from the departing *Sara:* "To VS-3, VF-5, VT-8. Your record of achievments is a matter of the greatest pride to us all and it is our fervent determination to rejoin you as expeditiously as humanly possible. In the meantime carry on as you have in the past. No one could ask more."

Admiral Nimitz, perhaps influenced in part by McCain's dispatch of the 31st, had resolved by September 2 that the carrier planes had to go to Guadalcanal. On that date, he sent a message to Admiral King in Washington:

> All aircraft that can be spared from *Enterprise* and *Saratoga* being transferred ComSoPac for use present campaign . . . employment carrier aircraft and pilots shore bases necessary because of lack of suitable Army type planes for Guadalcanal fighting, but such use carrier pilots most uneconomical from military viewpoint and our present shortage trained carrier air groups.

Emphasizing the remark made by Nimitz about the lack of suitable Army planes, Vandegrift told Ghormley on September 2: "P-400 entirely unsuitable for operations Cactus. Will not be employed further except in extreme emergencies."

The month of August, so hopefully begun, ended on notes of tragedy and apprehension. Three of Galer's newly arrived pilots were lost on their first flight because their oxygen masks leaked at high altitude; they became unconscious before they realized what was happening to them. And, despite the arrival of the other half of MAG-23, there were only twenty-six fighter planes and thirty dive bombers on Guadalcanal. On them rested the fate of 19,000 Marines.

7

TIME IN HELL
September 1–8

By the end of August the pattern within which the men of the Cactus Air Force would live and die for the next two and a half months had been set. It was a pattern unique in its hardship and terror. Out of it, as so often happens, came bravery, even glory.

To understand how men lived at Henderson Field one must first realize what a very small and exposed place it was. The airstrip itself about 3,800 feet long after enlargement by the Marines, ran northeast-southwest in the center of a grassy plain about a mile square. This plain was bounded on the south by ridges rising out of tangled jungle, on the north by Savo Sound, and on the other two sides by coconut groves. The First Marine Division was dug in around a perimeter that surrounded the airstrip on three sides—along the Ilu River on the west, the beach on the north, and, to the east, a line parallel to the Lunga River. To the South, where the jungle started, there was no well-defined line, only a group of outposts. From the middle of Henderson Field it was only about two and a half miles to the front lines in any direction except south. There the ridges, the jungle—and the enemy—were only half a mile away. The pilots, who had battles of their own to fight almost daily, were also involuntary participants in or nerve-rackingly close observers of every ground action.

The pilots and aircrewmen lived in tents in the strip of coconut grove between the field and the beach—"Mosquito Gulch," they called it. The tents had no flooring. Until there were enough cots, some of the flyers had to sleep on the ground on Japanese straw mats. The daily rains turned the ground into stinking black mud, into which cots and mats alike sank.

They had only flight suits or khakis to wear, whatever they had on when they arrived on the island. To shield their eyes from the bright tropical sun they were issued incongruously familiar baseball caps, dark blue for the pilots, red for mechanics. Clothes were rarely taken off because almost every night there was a raid by enemy aircraft, sent down "just to keep the enemy forces there disturbed" as a Japanese staff officer recorded after the war. These aircraft usually were Bettys from Rabaul or Kavieng at first; later, after the Japanese established a seaplane base at Rekata Bay, Santa Isabel, they were little two-place float biplanes. Their rickety-sounding engines were the nightly signal for the men of the Cactus Air Force to run from their tents to the nearby foxholes and slit trenches they had dug. For an hour or two, the enemy plane—called "Washing Machine Charlie" or "Louie the Louse"—flew back and forth overhead, dropping a small bomb every now and then. As much as any single factor, these night intruders were responsible for the pilot exhaustion that Admiral McCain had noted. As one of them wrote after the war, pilots were used to the sound of their own engines and guns. The sound of an enemy flying around in the darkness made them feel exposed and defenseless. The occasional eerie whistle of a falling bomb and the shattering crash and concussion of the explosion rubbed further on nerves already raw.

Food, such as there was, was prepared over open fires. Although the Marine cook who took care of all the flyers did his best, the only thing that was consistently good was the hot coffee—and even that occasionally tasted like creosote or kerosene as cooking utensils of ever more obscure origin were employed. The basic ingredients of meals were canned hash, Spam, sausage, captured Japanese rice, and dreadful dehydrated potatoes. Every effort was made to give the pilots three meals a day, but sometimes there wasn't enough food and sometimes they didn't have time to eat. Sometimes the pilots got so hungry they would kill one of the stray cows that wandered about the perimeter. This was unsafe from the viewpoint of food sanitation, but it was better than cold Spam and potatoes. Such a diet generated gas during digestion; at the reduced atmospheric pressure of high altitudes, this caused the pilots excruciating stomach cramps. Liquor—an after-battle necessity for most combat pilots—was nonexistent, except for the flight surgeons' emergency supplies. Cigarettes were whatever had been left by the Japanese.

Air combat is a relentless consumer of nervous energy. It is worse when the fighting is at high altitude. This means a debilitating couple of hours breathing pure oxygen, which dries out the nose and throat and burns the fuel of the body much faster than the familiar air of sea level. The physical fatigue of one or two flights a day, the climate, the poor diet, the emotional stress of frequent air combat, and, above all, the inability to sleep made nervous wrecks of the flight crews after about three weeks. Never before had flyers been forced to live under conditions approximating those of front-line infantry and fly combat, too. The infantryman can seek shelter in foxholes and solace in the physical presence of others. The pilot can find no such surcease. He is alone—dreadfully alone—when he flies, and his battles are terrifying affairs of singling out individuals for death and being singled out himself. Those who weren't wounded or didn't catch malaria were certain to be too shaky to fly within thirty days, and this was soon to be determined to be about the maximum permissible combat tour for pilots on Guadalcanal.

The evolution of battle in the air was far more satisfactory than the deadly squalor of life around the boundaries of Henderson Field. The great distance of their air bases from Guadalcanal forced an inflexible pattern of operations upon the Japanese. They had almost four hours to fly from Rabaul, and if they were not to take off at an unreasonably early time of the morning, they *had* to arrive over the island between 1130 and 1430. Between them and their objective were the coastwatchers. They were usually spotted shortly after takeoff by Reed or Mason on Bougainville; they were almost invariably picked up by Kennedy at Segi on New Georgia, forty-five minutes away from Henderson. On Guadalcanal, Lieutenant Hugh Mackenzie of the Royal Australian Navy was established, with an assistant and four Marine radio operators, in a damp and grubby former Japanese dugout on the northwest side of Henderson Field. From this obscure hole in the ground he continuously monitored the radio broadcasts of the entire coastwatcher network and passed word of incoming raids to nearby Marine headquarters by telephone. The radio dugout was even more miserable than most places on that foul island; when it rained, the water dripped through its decaying sandbags and coconut-palm logs and the radios could be kept dry only by covering them with raincoats. But without this rank cave and the organization it represented, the Marine fighter squadrons would have had an impossible job.

The *Burrows'* consignment of equipment had included an airsearch radar, and this was operating by the last day of August. At the altitudes at which they normally flew, the Bettys could be detected up to 125 miles away on this set. When air operations in the Pagoda got word either from Mackenzie or the radar that a raid was on the way, a Japanese Rising Sun flag was run up the flagpole in front of that building. The pilots, most of them sitting around the operations tent at the field waiting for the customary "Tojo time," would scramble all flyable aircraft at this signal. Other things being equal, the Marine fighters usually were at altitude waiting for the Japanese by the time they arrived.

Often, however, other things were not equal. The pilots and aircraft were dispersed as widely as the constricted perimeter permitted and there were almost no communications or ground transportation. On one occasion it took over thirty minutes to get the fighters airborne after an alert because there were no vehicles to take the pilots to their planes and no telephone to summon one. The crude revetments which sheltered the aircraft frequently became quagmires from which they could be extracted only by tractors.

It was in the field of fighter tactics that the Marines held an unequivocal and consistent advantage. Most of the credit for this must go to John Smith, although his tactics were based on the two-plane section and four-plane division developed by the Germans, refined by the United States Navy, and eventually adopted by almost every air force but the Japanese. The Marines normally were able to get a height advantage of 5,000 feet over the Bettys, and almost always made their interceptions with every available F4F. The type of attack Smitty preferred was the "overhead run." To get into the right position for this sometimes took ten or fifteen minutes, so slight a speed advantage did the little Grummans have over the Japanese. To do it, the F4Fs would climb ahead of and off to one side of the ponderous V formation always flown by the enemy bombers. When they were far enough ahead, they would turn sharply to a course exactly opposite that of the Bettys but far above them, almost simultaneously rolling over into inverted flight, then pulling through into a dive. When properly executed, this kind of run resulted in the fighter coming into the desired firing range of 1,000 feet at the same time that it was diving vertically down on its target, outside the train of any defending guns. It was the most complex of all the gunnery runs used by Navy and Marine pilots, needing intricate timing and rhythm which come only from long practice. But because it avoided defensive gunfire—a real consideration in fighting the Betty, which had a 20-millimeter cannon for a tail gun—and was almost impossible for an enemy to foil by maneuver, it was used whenever the Marine fighter pilots could get into the right position.

Smith trained his pilots to dive from right to left across the enemy V; with all friendly planes going in approximately the same direction, it was necessary only to take a little interval on the plane ahead to avoid any worries about colliding with someone else while concentrating on one's target. After the first attack, the F4Fs would pull out of their dives into climbing left turns, and look the situation over. If the Zekes had not shown up at this juncture, the Marines would make another attack on the bomber formation. If the Zekes did arrive and were in position to fight, the F4Fs would simply dive toward Henderson Field or into a nearby cloud. Inglorious sounding, perhaps, but thoroughly practical. The F4F was no match for a Zeke in a dogfight. Its assets were its high diving speed, rugged construction, and protection for pilot and gas tanks. The mission of the Marines was not single combat against enemy fighters, à la Guynemer or Bishop, but breaking up the bombing attack and living to break up tomorrow's bombing attack as well. This amounted to sophisticated hit-and-run tactics. They worked very well against an enemy who was always numerically superior, had better-performing aircraft, but had the burden of having to carry gasoline for an eight-hour round trip. The Zekes had to carry belly tanks in order to make these flights; they could not drop the tanks in combat, as fighters would normally do, or they would not have sufficient fuel to return to their base at Rabaul. Therefore, the Zeke could not maneuver at full throttle, because the resulting acceleration would rip their precious tanks right off them. Even with the tanks, they only had a few minutes of gas for fighting.

The air war over Guadalcanal looked pretty serious from the American viewpoint on September 1, 1942, but not too good from the headquarters of the Eleventh Air Fleet either. On that date, after three weeks of battle in the Solomons, Nishizo Tsukahara had two Air Flotillas, the 25th and 26th. However, instead of their nominal combined strength of 136 Bettys, 136 Zekes, 16 Vals, and 28 long-range flying boats, the total operational strength of the Japanese land-based units was 36 Bettys, 46 Zekes—of which 16 were too short-ranged to be able to reach Guadalcanal from Rabaul—6 Vals, and 10 patrol flying boats. The one-shot reinforcement of Zekes from *Shokaku*'s and *Zuikaku*'s fighter squadrons had been badly depleted by the costly and humiliating defeat for the carrier pilots on August 30. To top it all off, the Japanese bases, too, were subjected to daily bombings by the Army's Fifth Air Force in New Guinea, and this caused further attrition of their decreasing air strength.

The new month came in with the Japanese feverishly continuing their "Rat" landings. As the name suggests, this was entirely a nocturnal activity. The Navy's great historian, Rear Admiral Morison, sums up the situation at sea at that time as well as anyone ever will:

> A curious tactical situation had developed at Guadalcanal; a virtual exchange of sea mastery every twelve hours. The Americans ruled the waves from sunup to sundown; big ships discharged their cargoes, smaller ships dashed through the Sound, "Yippies" and landing craft ran errands between Lunga Point and Tulagi. But as the tropical twilight performed its quick fade-out and the pall of night fell on Ironbottom Sound, Allied ships cleared out like frightened children running home from a graveyard; transport and combat types steamed through Sealark Channel while small craft holed up in Tulagi Harbor or behind Gavutu. Then the Japanese took over. The "Tokyo Express" of troop destroyers and light cruisers dashed in to discharge soldiers or freight, and, departing, tossed a few shells in the Marines' direction.

The reason that the Japanese did not dare come in by daylight was not because of anything our largely nonexistent surface ships might have done to them, but for fear of the handful of SBDs that were the striking power of the tiny Cactus Air Force. The dive-bomber pilots tried to do something about the Express ("Tokyo Express" was a creation of some reporter; to those on the receiving end of these runs, they were the "Cactus Express."), going up to attack on the nights of September 1 and 2, but on each occasion ineffectually. Thus it was that Major General Kawaguchi and 1,000 men of his 35th Brigade were successfully landed by eight destroyers after midnight on the 1st, unmolested.

RD 4

An hour after sunset on September 3 an R4D transport plane came in from Espiritu Santo, landed in the glare of jeep headlights on the dark strip, and taxied over to the edge of the field. Out of the plane stepped a stocky, broad-shouldered Marine named Roy Geiger. He was a brigadier general, fifty-seven years old, and was the commanding general of Marine Air Wing One. He had spent twenty-five years waiting for that September night when he walked down the ladder from the door of the plane onto the black dust of Guadalcanal.

Roy Stanley Geiger was born in a little town in Florida

in 1885. He graduated from Stetson University in 1907 with a
law degree, and was admitted to the bar. Restlessness drove
him to enlist and then to seek a commission in the Marines,
and he graduated from the Parris Island "School of Applica-
tion" for officers in 1909 together with a fellow Southerner
named Archer Vandegrift. In 1916 the same restlessness
made him apply for flight training. He graduated from
Pensacola in 1917, the forty-ninth naval aviator, and only the
fifth Marine to fly. In 1918 he took over to France one of the
very first organized air squadrons in the Marine Corps. It
became the Seventh Squadron of the Northern Bombardment
Group, an ambitious but premature effort by the United
States Navy to attack the German submarine bases on the
Belgian coast with a strategic bombing force. Flying borrowed British aircraft, D.H.4s and D.H9.As, Geiger and his
young Marine reservists learned something of the problems of
flying slow and highly inflammable bombers on daylight
missions. After the war, Major Geiger commanded the Marine squadrons in Haiti, Santo Domingo, and Nicaragua, was
Director of Marine Corps Aviation, and graduated from both
the Army and Navy war colleges. As much as any man, he
made Marine aviation between the wars. Roy Geiger was a
Marine of the old breed, stern and unsparing of his demands
on his subordinates and himself. His face, chiseled into
classic, almost Roman lines under a thatch of white hair,
made him look cold and ruthless. He was. But he was also
one of the finest general officers that the Marine Corps ever
produced. In the next few weeks the flyers of Henderson
Field would have need of all of his qualities.

   With Geiger came his aide, Lieutenant Colonel J. C.
("Toby") Munn, and his chief of staff, a square-jawed
colonel named Louis Woods. This black-a-vised veteran of
twenty years in Marine aviation was to prove a tower of
strength in the days to come, both to Geiger and to the
Cactus Air Force.

   The little Air Wing staff set up shop and housekeeping in
the wooden projecting-roofed "Pagoda" constructed by the
Japanese on the edge of the airstrip. From there the two
veterans of Marine aviation surveyed a scene not noticeably
different from those at earlier airfields operated by the Corps
in Haiti, Santo Domingo, and Nicaragua. Only a thousand
feet of the airstrip was covered with the joined planks of
punched-out steel called Marston mat. This matting arrived

slowly on the beleaguered island, as did gasoline, bombs, and construction equipment. After a rain the normally dust-covered field became a swamp in which vehicles and planes were hopelessly mired. In the hot sun, though, it dried quickly. This aspect of the Guadalcanal climate helped to save the field and, therefore, the island. It was a little trying, though, for the men of the Cactus Air Force (as one of them put it) to stand up to one's ass in mud and simultaneously have dust blowing in one's eyes.

Geiger and Woods were determined to make their precarious command offensive-minded, and, largely because of bad weather which kept the Japanese bombers away during the first few days after their arrival, they were able to concentrate on bombing and attack missions. Their first target was Japanese landing barges hidden on Santa Isabel and little San Jorge Island across the sound by day, but whose build-up had been noticed and could only mean one thing: Japanese reinforcements were heading toward Guadalcanal by barge. The Marines did not know the precise timetable, but they knew the crossing from Santa Isabel to Guadalcanal was imminent. All during daylight hours on September 4, SBDs, F4Fs, and P-400s carried out bombing and strafing runs on every barge that could be spotted. Some damage was inflicted, but that night the remaining barges left their hiding places and started over to Guadalcanal. Most of them—fifteen barges carrying about 700 men—were still a few miles from Guadalcanal when the early morning air patrols from Cactus found them on September 5.

Dale Brannon and one of his pilots made pass after pass in the only two flyable P-400s over the weaving barges, firing 20-millimeter cannon and 50-caliber machine guns. In another twenty-five minutes they were joined by six F4Fs from VMF-224. Only one of the fifteen barges was sunk, but more than half of the seven hundred Japanese infantrymen they carried were killed. One F4F was downed by Japanese anti-aircraft fire.

Brannon's two planes returned later to attack the barges, now beached, but all eighteen of the remaining Grummans were sent up to intercept an incoming Japanese air raid reported on its way by the coastwatchers. The Bettys and Zekes arrived shortly before noon, and there was a brisk, brief, and, for the Marines, costly fight. Bob Galer and his wingman each got a Japanese plane, but two precious F4Fs and one pilot were lost, and another pilot, the experienced Rivers Morrell, was so badly wounded in the legs by the explosion of a 20-millimeter shell in his cockpit that he had to be evacuated. It was a discouraging setback for the Marine fliers, and a spiky introduction for Geiger and Woods.

Heavy weather on the 6th kept the Japanese bombers away, but it also led to the loss of two SBDs with their two-man crews who had taken part in an eleven-plane strike against ship and shore installations at Gizo Bay and were unable to find their way back. Sometimes these "lost" men found their way back. The phrase "walked in" had a special meaning for the Cactus pilots. It described in two words the good luck of an airman shot down who nevertheless made it back to his own lines. Thanks to their own ingenuity and to the Australian coastwatcher organization, quite a few pilots and gunners walked back in to Henderson Field. On September 6, a very special case of a "walk-in" turned up; an emaciated, dirty, and exhausted young-old man in a flight suit staggered into an outpost of the Eleventh Marines. He was Dick Amerine—Second Lieutenant Richard Amerine of VMF-224—who had been reported missing on the first mission of that squadron on August 31. He had jumped from his F4F when he recognized that his oxygen mask was leaking badly and had landed in a jungle in back of Cape Esperance. Starting back toward the Marine lines, he ran into Japanese troops. He found one of them asleep beside a trail. He killed him by beating his head in with a rock, and then took his pistol and shoes. Pilot's flight shoes were not made for jungle wear. In the next few days he killed two more soldiers with the butt of his pistol and shot a fourth. A one-time student of entomology, Amerine kept himself alive by the precarious expedient of identifying and eating nonpoisonous red ants and snails. It took him seven days to walk the thirty miles back from Cape Esperance.

On the afternoon of the 6th the first benefits of the *Saratoga*'s torpedoing accrued to the defenders of Guadalcanal. Six SBDs of Scouting Three arrived from Espiritu Santo shortly after 1600. These planes and crews from a Navy scouting squadron were sent up—nominally—to relieve the two Marine dive-bomber outfits of the chore of flying routine searches out of Henderson Field. Not only had this tied up aircraft which ought to have been available for attack missions, but the Marines were not well trained in overwater navigation, ship recognition, or the many other detailed skills which made a good scouting team out of a pilot, a radioman-gunner, and an SBD. The Navy men were. In the maelstrom of Guadalcanal, though, their specialization would soon vanish, overtaken by events. Within twenty-four hours, VS-3 crews would be flying attack missions indistinguishable from those carried out by Mangrum's and Leo Smith's Marines and Turner Caldwell's mixed bombing-scouting flight from *Enterprise*.

September 7 was a day of constant rain which kept the Japanese bombers away altogether and American air activity at a minimum. A B-17 led in four F4Fs from Espiritu, which were turned over to VMF-223. And the evening search by one of VS3's SBDs found enemy landing barges still lying off San Jorge and strafed them. By now this was flogging a dead horse. The last men of Kawaguchi's brigade had been landed on Guadalcanal during the night of the 6th and 7th, but by destroyers, not landing craft. The latter had been a highly unsuccessful experiment. From the initial American landings through the early morning of September 7, the Japanese landed some 5,200 men on the island; only 700 of these were put ashore by barge.

Still in utter ignorance of the actual Marine ground strength on Guadalcanal—close to 14,000 plus another 5,000 on Tulagi—Kawaguchi planned a highly complicated three-pronged attack on Henderson Field for September 13, supported by the Eleventh Air Fleet and the Second and Third Fleets, which had withdrawn to Truk on the 5th to refuel for the operation. Having sighted the convoy which was bringing the Seventh Marines from Samoa, the Japanese high command ordered an advance in the date of the attack. From Army headquarters in Rabaul, orders went out and finally caught up with Kawaguchi, who was floundering through the jungles of Guadalcanal. The attack must come on the night of the 12th.

A further flap was caused by the coincidence of an attack by Colonel Merritt Edson's Marine Raiders on the Japanese rear echelon at Taivu Point in the early morning of the 8th, simultaneous with the sighting of a couple of Navy transports which were coming in to unload off Lunga. The Japanese thought a major American landing was in progress, and ordered their entire remaining bomber strength out to attack it. The Bettys never got through the impenetrable wall of cloud and rain. But on this day the weather treated both sides with impartial malice.

The Cactus Air Force spent all day on the 8th supporting Edson's Raiders, who were happily wrecking the Japanese supply base at Taivu. Four P-400s, each loaded with a 300-pounder and a 100-pounder, accompanied two Marine SBDs off the rain-soaked field at 0635 that morning. They were back in less than an hour after dropping their bombs on enemy positions around Taivu and Tasimboko. The Army fighters were rearmed and another four of the 67th's pilots took them off again at 0835. The two SBDs came too, along with a third which had come up during the morning. All seven aircraft were back in forty minutes.

Then it started to rain in gray sheets that seemed almost solid, and Henderson Field shut down completely until just after noon. At 1205 Lieutenant Cook of 231 took off on his third mission of the day, and shortly afterward the 67th's four flyable P-400s got off the sodden field. Intermittent thunderstorms continued to soak the field during the afternoon, and by the time these aircraft returned it had been churned into six inches of mud. But the Raiders, now retreating from Taivu Point under heavy Japanese pressure, needed whatever support could be furnished, and at 1510 the 67th, then down to three planes, sent out another attack.

The pilot of the first of the three P-400s lowered half flaps to give his thin wing more lift, and ran his engine up to full throttle while standing on the brakes. The power began dragging the Bell through the slippery mud, even though its wheels were locked. Then the pilot let go his brakes and began wrestling it down the strip, thinking about the 300-pound bomb slung underneath. Somehow he staggered off the end of the runway.

The second man, Lieutenant V. L. Head, was not so lucky. He lurched and skidded down the strip, slowing sickeningly as he hit one pool of water after another, covering the plane with liquid mud. The torque of his big propellor almost pulled him sideways off the runway and he swerved and zigzagged desperately to stay on it. At the end of the strip, still lacking flying speed, Head yanked the P-400 off and tried to hang it on its propeller. It wouldn't hang. The little olive-drab fighter shuddered, stalled, and hit the ground, breaking into three pieces and simultaneously bursting into flames. The dazed Head unbuckled his safety belt and jumped through the fire. By some miracle his bomb did not go off.

Lieutenant Davis, at the far end of the runway, watched as his friend crashed, burned, and, for all he knew, died horribly. With only a moment's hesitation, he too gave his plane full throttle and started down the strip in turn. He made it, flying through the smoke and flame left by his predecessor.

For two hours these two P-400s covered the withdrawal of the Marines to the beach and their loading into landing boats. Their gas ran low and they switched to their reserve tanks, but they stayed until the last boat left at dusk. With only a fey minutes of gas remaining, they landed on the quagmire of Henderson in the failing light. Then they went off in search of the cook to see if he could scrape up something. Such were the men of the 67th Fighter Squadron.

At 1820 there was an air-raid alarm, and sixteen F4Fs of Smith's and Galer's squadrons scrambled. One of 224's planes crashed on take-off. The others were up for an hour as twilight turned into darkness, until it became obvious that the raid was not going to materialize. Eleven Japanese seaplanes from Rekata Bay had tried but were unable to find Henderson Field and bombed Tulagi instead. The fifteen Marine fighters returned to find that a thin ground fog lay over the strip. The landing turned into a complete shambles. Two of Smith's pilots ran into each other on the runway, completely wrecking both planes. Another of 223's fighters nosed over on landing in the mud, and this plane too was a total loss. One F4F of Galer's squadron also crashed on landing. None of the pilots were injured, but, of the sixteen fighters that had been in commission that morning, six had been lost and two others slightly damaged.

One of the pilots summed up this day in one sentence: "At this rate we can whip ourselves without any help from the Japs."

8

SEPTEMBER REMEMBER
September 9–14

By the second week in September the morale of the Cactus Air Force was beginning to ebb away. The pilots were sick and exhausted from the mental strain of a virtual blockade, three weeks of almost daily air fighting, the physical effects of the septic climate, and appalling living conditions. The flight surgeons, conscientiously doing their job, told Louis Woods that most of them were unfit to continue flying. "They've got to keep flying," barked the tough Marine veteran, "It's better to do that than get a Jap bayonet stuck in their ass!" Geiger and Woods, brought up in the iron-fisted tradition of the Corps, had no choice but to drive their pilots to their limits and beyond. There were no others to do the job.

Combat fatigue showed itself in several ways. The increasing accident rate was one, of course, exemplified at its worst by the fiasco on the 8th. Another was inability to concentrate on such simple tasks as reconnaissance: the SBDs flying search missions began to make elementary errors of identification and navigation. The last and most disquieting symptom, only displayed by a few, was reluctance to fight. The two Marine fighter squadrons had some pilots who had survived the massacre of VMF-221 by Zekes at midway. With exceptions, notably 223's Marion Carl and John Dobbin of 224, these pilots "were almost worthless," in the unsparing words of Bob Galer. The commander of Fighting 242 went on to say: "A percentage of these pilots could be said to avoid combat, while the majority would accept but not look for combat. . . . After a definite period a pilot who is undergoing daily alert periods and combat should be relieved before he is forced to request his relief from the Medical Department or before he is evacuated sick or wounded."

In spite of being almost constantly dazed with fatigue, the large majority of the Cactus pilots went up every day, accepting the weariness, the squalid and diseased existence, and the growing numerical superiority of the Japanese. They hated their job. They knew that in time it would kill them or take them off that horrible island emotionally or physically broken. But they did it because it had to be done.

On September 9 a new airstrip was ready for use on the island. It was located only 2,000 yards east of Henderson Field and was almost parallel to it. This strip, officially called Fighter One, was built by the 6th Seabees—the 6th Naval Construction Battalion—who had landed on Guadalcanal on September 1 and immediately started clearing a second strip inside the Marines' small perimeter. The fighter pilots called it "the cow pasture" because it was little more than a mown strip of Kunai grass. Since there was not enough Marston mat available to put a hard surface on it, it was reserved for the light fighter planes only. What mat there was went into building up the Henderson Field strip for the more heavily laden SBDs and, in due course, B-17s. The fighter squadrons used the new strip from mid-September onward, as long as its state permitted. Fighter One gave Geiger the chance to disperse his few aircraft somewhat; in days to come it would prove an increasingly important resource.

The wastage of men and planes continued on the 9th and 10th, both good flying days for that Southern Hemisphere spring. The Japanese came down from Rabaul and Kavieng each day with a large force of Bettys escorted by fighters as usual. On the 9th, still under the impression that a major American landing force was in the area, they wasted their bombs in an ineffectual attack on the miscellaenous shipping lying off the island. Sixteen F4Fs, eight from each of the two Marine fighter squadrons, scrambled at 1115. One of 224's pilots stalled and spun into the ground on takeoff, wiping out his plane, although without serious injury to himself. The Marines claimed five of the bombers and three Zekes. Marion Carl, twelve-plane ace of 223, and one of 224's pilots did not return from the flight. Clayton Canfield was shot down into Savo Sound, fortunately landing near a destroyer which picked him up. VMF-224's Moore made it back to the field wounded in both legs by a 20-millimeter shell which had exploded in his cockpit. Four more of Geiger's usable fighters were gone and another damaged, and three of his pilots were either wounded or missing.

The next day, after listening to the SBDs and P-400s go out on the early morning missions, the fighter pilots were scrambled at the now almost standard time of 1115. John Smith led four others of his squadron into a Japanese force of Bettys escorted by fifteen Zekes. The Americans claimed five victories, but 223's Zennith Pond was shot down. The balance of the day had gone against the enemy, but the two days had reduced Marine fighter strength by four pilots and five planes. By evening of September 10, only twelve F4Fs on Guadalcanal remained operational.

Against this meager force and the Marine division protecting the field the Japanese Army, overconfident as always, intended to launch a general attack the next day, September 11. They still did not understand that the Marines were on Guadalcanal in such strength, 14,000 men, which they proposed to assault with one 5,000-man brigade. Probably they would not have changed their minds if they had understood the situation. At any rate the attack of Kawaguchi's brigade was backed up by the Second and Third Fleets, which made up the major strength of Yamamoto's Combined Fleet, and by Tsukahara's Eleventh Air Fleet. Fortunately, Admiral Nimitz' customarily excellent intelligence section had the essentials of the enemy plan in hand almost as soon as the Japanese operating forces had. It was obvious that all available reinforcements must be flung onto the blockaded island as soon as possible. So the dry-docked *Saratoga*'s homeless aircraft were ordered on September 10 to proceed to Guadalcanal.

Henderson Field's fighters scrambled at 1210 on September 11, all twelve of them. The Japanese had sent down their usual raid, twenty-six Bettys with an escort of Zekes. Before they were intercepted, the bombers dropped their bombs along the eastern side of Henderson field, killing or wounding twenty-eight men and destroying a P-400 on the ground. Dale Brannon, commanding officer of the 67th, watched the Bettys' slow approach from the door of a cozy five-man dugout that he shared with four of his pilots and a couple of visiting Marines. "Here they come!" he yelled as he saw the bombs starting to fall, and dove into his shelter. While he was still suspended in midair, a 1,000-pound bomb exploded only five feet from the dugout and he, its other occupants and hundreds of pounds of sandbags, galvanized iron, and palm logs lazily rose twenty feet into a slow-turning pinwheel, then settled back to earth. Somehow they all lived, but the spirited Brannon had to be evacuated with the two worst injured of his pilots.

At 1330 the F4Fs came back triumphantly to Henderson Field, some full of holes, but all still flying except Bob Galer's. VMF-224's tough little C.O. had had a vicious dogfight with the Zekes, shooting down one after getting one of the bombers, but they had shot him up thoroughly in return. When his engine quit, he ditched his plane, riddled and smoking, off the beach and swam ashore. Smith's five aircraft had given the Bettys a good shellacking, Smith being credited with two—his twelfth and thirteenth victories—and three other pilots one each. Although the Japanese had the worst of the day's fighting, Geiger and Woods marked the increasing tempo of Red alerts and the decreasing number of fighter planes on Cactus. The two Marine squadrons were down to a total of eleven flyable aircraft on the afternoon of the 11th; Tsukahara had forty fighters capable of reaching Guadalcanal from Rabaul.

At this critical point, *Saratoga*'s homeless hawks flew up to the rescue. Twenty-four F4Fs of VF-5—Fighting Five—came in over Henderson Field at 1620 in a precise column of four-plane divisions and began the intricate, circling minuet of breaking up into a line of single aircraft following one close upon another into a landing.

The first of the Navy aircraft to land was flown by the squadron C.O., Lieutenant Commander LeRoy Simpler. A calm native of Delaware, Simpler had graduated from the Naval Academy in 1929, and was one of the few fighter pilots ever to have been based on an airship. He had been a member of the "hook-on" fighter detachments of the *Akon* and *Macon* back in the mid-thirties. Following him into their revetments came twenty-three experienced carrier fighter pilots, some from Lou Bauer's old Fighting Six, all veterans of the original Guadalcanal landings and the Battle of the Eastern Solomons. The Navy pilots weren't as good as they thought they were—at least not yet. But the arrival of this big, confident squadron with twice as many planes as the two Marine outfits put together gave a real boost to the Cactus Air Force's sagging morale.

The 12th of September started with a Red alert at 0800, which was a false alarm, and the fighters came back in half an hour. At 1100 another alert sounded, the real thing this time. John Smith led his squadron's five aircraft off, followed by 224 with six. Fighting Five sent up twenty F4Fs with their skipper leading.

The Bettys were sighted by Smith at 1142 and a few minutes later were visible from Henderson Field as they crawled across the cloudless blue sky, the shallow V of their formation looking like a silvery line. The Marine antiaircraft opened up, and appeared from the ground to be scoring, but the F4Fs were doing the shooting that counted. Smith's four-plane division was at 28,000 feet when they sighted the formation. They made an overhead run on the Japanese, 2,000 feet below them, just as the Bettys had dropped their bombs. Trowbridge got a Betty on the left side of the formation, and it pulled off and downward, trailing a thin plume of white smoke. He followed it and shot it down in flames. Seconds later, another bomber in the center of the V sprouted a tongue of flame which was almost instantly replaced by a thick cloud of black smoke; the plane nosed straight down, a wing pulled off, and then the other, fluttering in fragments behind the fuselage as it plummeted three miles down into the ground. Smith and Ken Frazier each shot two planes out of the formation on that single pass. The watchers far below saw six Bettys falling or leaving the formation simultaneously.

As the Bettys passed out to sea, ground observers watched Frazier dive on a straggler, and saw it first pull up into a stall, then dive almost vertically, pursued by the heavy F4F. Probably with a dead or dying pilot at the yoke, it pulled out of the dive and climbed steeply. Frazier's guns rattled again, just as the Betty stalled and spun into Tulagi Harbor, where it crashed in a huge puff of smoke and flame. The thousands of men on the island cheered madly. Slowly the Japanese formation disappeared to the northwest, the sound of its engines, which had filled sky and jungle, now dying away, the high-pitched drone interrupted by the sounds of diving Grummans and machine guns.

Once again the valiant remnant of Fighting 223 had borne the brunt of the day's combat and was officially credited with seven planes. Smith, Frazier, and Trowbridge were credited with two Bettys each, and Lees with a Zeke. VMF-224 was credited with three planes and VF-5 was credited with six. The newcomers suffered the only casualties: the squadron exec, Dave Richardson, came back wounded in the leg and was evacuated to Espiritu Santo; and a young ensign, C. E. Eichenberger, his plane damaged, was killed trying to make a dead-stick landing. Fighting Five had been introduced to the kind of fighting that the Marines had learned to handle so well, and found that they had something to learn too.

While the tense fighter pilots tried to unwind from the excitement of battle in air, another kind of drama was taking place on the ground. Rear Admirals Kelly Turner and John Sidney McCain flew in on an R4D from Espiritu Santo. Once the greetings were over and he was seated in Vandegrift's new command post, Turner silently handed the general a Navy message blank. On it was typed an estimate of the Guadalcanal situation prepared by Ghormley's staff. As Vandegrift read it, the blood drained from his normally ruddy Dutch face. It told him for the first time that the major strength of the Japanese fleet was concentrated at Truk, that their air strength at Rabaul and Kavieng was increasing, and that troops were being loaded aboard transports at Rabaul. A major Japanese effort to retake Guadalcanal within ten days was forecast. The report went on to enumerate American weaknesses in detail and concluded with the statement that Ghormley as ComSoPac could no longer support the Marines. Turner poured out three glasses of Scotch while Vandegrift's chief of staff, Colonel Gerald Thomas, read the estimate. When Thomas had put the dispatch in his shirt pocket, the three began to discuss what could be done about the situation which it described. Ghormley had, in effect, thrown up his hands. Now it was up to these three of his subordinates to see that the campaign continued despite his moral abdication. The outcome of the conference was an agreement that Turner could bring the Seventh Marines, the First Division's other infantry regiment, from the Fijis to Guadalcanal, which would provide Vandergrift with a much-needed reinforcement, and a joint message was sent to Ghormley strongly recommending this course of action.

The late-afternoon SBD searches by Scouting Three found the Solomons alive with Japanese warships. One plane located a cruiser and three destroyers forty miles from Rendova, another sighted a destroyer off Choiseul, and a third found two more destroyers off the northern tip of Santa Isabel. What the scouting planes had picked up was the advance guard of the Japanese fleet, closing in like a dark shadow from the north to support the imminent attack of Kawaguchi's brigade on Henderson Field. The cruiser—it was the *Tenryu*—and destroyers were a bombardment group on the way to Guadalcanal, and the pair of destroyers were heading for the PBY base at Graciosa Bay on Ndeni Island.

The *Tenryu* force was located twice more during the night, but nothing could be done to keep it away from the island. Louie the Louse dropped his green flares just before 10 o'clock and was closely followed by star shell, then bombardment ammunition from the Japanese 5.5-inch guns. The shelling lasted for only about twenty minutes and was directed mostly against the ridge where Vandegrift had installed his new command post. It was a sleepless night for the two visiting admirals. At midnight the Japanese ships opened up again for forty-five minutes. Some shorts sprayed the Marine SBD squadron's encampment with shrapnel, killing three pilots—including Baldinus, who had hit the *Jintsu*—and wounding two others.

The ridge, to which the Japanese Navy devoted such careful attention, ran northwest to southeast, starting about a mile south of Henderson Field and paralleling the Lunga River until it vanished in a tangle of jungle. On it were dug in two rifle companies of Colonel Merritt Edson's Marine Raider Battalion and the parachutists, a force perhaps four hundred strong in all. Edson suspected, following the capture of Japanese maps and plans in his raid on Taivu, that a large enemy force was going to try to capture the field, and that the ridge, pointed like a knife right at the strip, was the obvious avenue of approach. So the canny one-time aviator turned infantryman was not altogether unprepared when the Japanese started to probe his thinly held lines as soon as the first bombardment ended. The probes grew into a full-scale attack during the night of the 12th–13th, which was held only a short mile from the pilots' dugouts and the airstrip that was the key to Guadalcanal. The night was tumultuous with the roar and flash of artillery, the ceaseless drone of Louie the Louse, and the red glow of flares. September 13 was to be a day of desperate trial for all of the sleepless Americans on the island.

While his pilots were preparing to fight that morning, Roy Geiger was visited at the Pagoda by Archer Vandegrift. The two, Marines together for thirty-three years, took a quiet walk and Vandergrift told his air commander of the message that Turner had shown him the previous night. He ended by telling Geiger that if the time came when the perimeter had to be abandoned, he wanted the planes flown out to fight again. The white-thatched airman turned his gray eyes earnestly on his old friend: "If we can't use the planes back in the hills, we'll fly them out. But whatever happens, I'm staying here with you."

At 0645, the plane carrying Turner and McCain took off for Espiritu Santo. The little air admiral had spent his time on the island talking to the pilots of the Cactus Air Force. He reported by dispatch to ComSoPac: "When I left today material situation OK except for gas shortage and no Marston mat. Personnel very tired—no rest at night due to bombardment or by day because of air alerts." Between 0745 and 0805 that morning, eighteen new F4Fs were ferried into Henderson Field by fighter pilots from the carrier *Hornet*. They had scarcely arrived when the field was caught up in the flurry of another Red alert.,

The Japanese air activities on September 13 were disjointed and indecisive because the Navy, which operated the only aircraft in the theater, had no idea how the Army's attack was progressing or, indeed, if it even had been delivered. The Eleventh Air Fleet's operation order specified an early-morning scouting mission over Henderson Field to determine if it was in Japanese hands. If so, twenty Zeke fighters were to fly from Rabaul and land at the field, there placing themselves under the orders of the victorious Army. Two reconnaissance planes left Rabaul at 0530, escorted by the fighters, to find out what was going on.

The question of who was occupying Henderson Field was answered quite easily for the Japanese scouting planes. They were met by seventeen F4Fs, a sharp combat ensued, and the Cactus fighter pilots claimed three Zekes. Fighting

Five took some lumps, though: one pilot was shot down and killed and another wounded; Ensign Don Innis' F4F was badly shot up, and he bailed out of the flaming plane at 25,000 feet, badly burned. The rest of his division covered him as his chute drifted down into Sealark Channel, between Guadalcanal and Tulagi. He was picked out of the water by a landing boat and returned to the field for evacuation.

This encounter convinced Admiral Tsukahara that the battle was not over, and he sent most of his available bombers down. They attacked "artillery positions on Taivu Point"—which were actually bivouacs for their own service and signal troops. The Bettys were in their bombing run when intercepted over Sealark Channel by Galer with George Hollowell of VMF-224 and Bob Read of 223. The three, flying at 25,000, sighted the Japanese formation 3,000 feet below. Galer led the other two around in a wide climbing right turn, which put them into an excellent position for an overhead run, and then they dove. The Japanese dropped their bombs, partly onto their own troop positions, partly into the water, and turned north just as the three Grummans hit the right rear of their formation. Each pilot got one Betty down in flames. The returning enemy were caught again by seven aircraft of Fighting Five, led by Simpler on his second mission of the morning. Two of his pilots each claimed a bomber. The Navy squadron suffered no loss in combat, but one of their F4Fs crashed during the scramble and was a complete loss.

While Galer and Simpler were handling the bombers, John Smith was having a disastrous tussle with the twelve Zekes. These, sharing the prevailing confusion of the Japanese airmen that day, were efficiently strafing their own troops and installations at Tasimboko when VMF-223's eight Grummans jumped them. From jungle foxholes, the Marine infantrymen watched and listened to the kind of wild fighter dogfight that was rarely seen over Guadalcanal. The Marine and Japanese planes darted in and out of towering cumulus clouds and the whole area resounded with the rattling of machine guns so loud that the effect was that of thunder. One F4F came out of a cloud, diving as only the heavy Grummans could, with two Zekes trying vainly to catch him. He pulled out just over the water, leaving the two frustrated Japanese to pull back up. Correspondent Richard Tregaskis watched two far-distant planes, one chasing the other, pop suddenly out of a wall of cloud, enter a steeply banked turn, and disappear back into it. A few moments later, they reappeared, like two figures on a miniature merry-go-round. Spectacular as it may have been to watch, the fight went badly for the Marines. Smith and Phillips got one Zeke each, but the squadron suffered the usual fate of F4F pilots who tried to dogfight the nimble Japanese. Haring was killed and Scotty McLennan and Chamberlain, a visitor from VMF-212, did not return from the mission. Two others brought badly damaged airplanes back to Henderson Field.

The day's combats accounted for four of the eighteen F4Fs flown in that morning before they could be assigned to squadrons—indeed, before anyone even recorded their Bureau numbers. The remaining fourteen were divided equally between the two Marine fighter squadrons.

At 1730 two float Zekes flew directly across Henderson Field at 500-feet, turned, and came back again before the dazed antiaircraft gunners thought to do anything about it. Pursued by shellbursts far behind them, the planes dived on a Marine SBD which was returning from a search mission and shot it down right on the field. All the men of the Cactus Air Force saw it crash, burn, and explode, killing its pilot and gunner. The Japanese escaped unharmed.

The antiaircraft gunners, not to be caught flatfooted again, opened up furiously on a large formation of aircraft which appeared in another ten minutes. Unfortunately, these turned out to be Navy SBDs. The remaining squadrons of the *Saratoga* air group were arriving from Espiritu Santo for duty at Henderson Field. Twelve SBDs of Scouting Three flew in, led by Lieutenant Commander Louis J. Kirn—christened "Bullet Lou" during his football playing days—luckily unharmed by the trigger-happy gunners. After them came six TBFs of Torpedo Eight, bringing the first torpedoes to add to Cactus' arsenal. At last the air striking force that Vandegrift and McCain wanted so badly was on the island.

As darkness fell on that bloody Sunday, the sounds of battle rose again from the ridge. Red Mike Edson was manning the line with only 300 Marine raiders and parachutists—all that stood between the Japanese and control of Henderson Field. Their struggle started almost as soon as it became dark, but did not become intense until 2100. Louie the Louse then reappeared and dropped a green flare directly over the center of the field. The *Tenryu* and her accompany-

Float Zero

ing destroyers, back again in Savo Sound, began a bombardment that lasted for an hour. During that hour the understrength Raider battalion was assaulted by 2,000 Japanese soldiers. The outnumbered Marines gave ground slowly and reluctantly, and by 2300 the enemy withdrew to regroup. Shortly after midnight, the noise of the Marine artillery picked up again until it became almost a continuous roar, and machine gun and rifle fire up on the ridge swelled to a crescendo. Then came the sound of naval gunfire again: four Japanese destroyers had joined the battle, while another seven landed 1,700 more troops of an Army detachment on the island. At 0200 an enemy mortar barrage hit the ridge, and the Japanese came forward again. After half an hour of desperate struggle, Kawaguchi's men began to melt back into the jungle. Edson and his men fell back to the final part of the ridge, less than 1,000 yards from Henderson Field. But here they stayed. The Japanese were broken. The field and its men and planes had been saved because Edson's Raiders held. And because the field had been saved, Guadalcanal had been saved—until the next time the Japanese wanted to try for it.

At dawn on the 14th, Captain J. A. Thompson of the 67th Pursuit Squadron led two of his pilots off in the only three P-400s that could be flown. The shark-toothed Bells strafed the ridge, coming in just a few feet over the heads of Edson's Marines, and flashing over the bodies of 500 of Kawaguchi's men. Ground fire from the scattered growth around the bottom crippled two of the Army fighters, both of which made dead-stick landings back on the field. But after this attack the Japanese general ordered his shattered brigade to begin a retreat back to the headwaters of the Matanikau River. Only a few sporadic Japanese scouting missions and ineffectual attacks by seaplanes took place during the remainder of the day. Tsukahara's pilots were exhausted too. The men of Guadalcanal had weathered their second major crisis.

The September battles ended with a stroke of luck for the Cactus Air Force. Marion Carl, missing for five days, walked back in. Or rather, he rode in. Shot down over Koli Point, he had bailed out and had been pulled out of the water by one of Martin Clemens' native constabulary. Corporal Eroni took good care of his charge and brought him back proudly in his boat.

Carl was sent for by Geiger as soon as he heard the good news. The general gleefully alluded to the fact that Smith, his squadron commander and rival as a high-scoring fighter pilot, had just shot down his sixteenth plane, while he, Carl, had only twelve. "What are we going to do about that?" inquired Geiger. Carl thought for a minute, then answered: "Goddammit, General, ground him for five days!"

9

IF AT FIRST ...
September 15–October 4

The Japanese drive of mid-September ended in clear failure. But it was not in the nature of this nation to admit failure or accept defeat. As the tempo of the Army's combat operations on Guadalcanal slowed, that of the planning staffs abruptly became feverish. Literally overnight the Navy Section of Imperial General Headquarters produced a new strategic concept and the outlines of a plan for carrying it out. The main import of their directive was to decree a holding strategy in New Guinea, which had hitherto been their major objective, and assign first priority to the recapture of Guadalcanal. The directive also recognized the importance of adequate ground reinforcements for the island. The entire Japanese 2nd Division of 10,000 men, plus the regimental-sized Aoba Detachment, were to be landed by the Navy, along with their heavy artillery, the lack of which the Japanese already on the island had felt keenly. And at last the full significance of the Cactus Air Force was recognized by the enemy. "We ... decided to gain control of the air at any cost ..." records the historian of Japanese naval operations in the South Pacific. From his headquarters in Truk, Admiral Yamamoto issued an order the next day implementing the new plan. Broadly, it stated that the Combined Fleet's objectives were (1) the transportation of Army troops and heavy artillery to Guadalcanal; and (2) to destroy American air power, an important aspect of which was the completion of an adequate airfield at Buin.

In the latter objective, the Japanese acknowledged the ruinous tactical disadvantages of having to fly their fighter aircraft 540 miles to reach their enemy. The Buin airstrip would cut this distance almost in half and give the Zekes enough time over Henderson Field to shoot down the elusive Grummans.

Going from the general to the specific, Yamamoto's order went on to outline the operations to be conducted. The big seaplane tender *Nisshin* was to land desperately needed tanks and heavy artillery on Guadalcanal on the night of September 20. The Eleventh Air Fleet was to destroy American air power on the island in attacks on the 19th and 20th. In support of these efforts, the Second and Third Fleets would move south again and "annihilate" American naval forces.

Yamamoto's order was, in effect, a hasty resetting of the earlier stage, a plan to use his considerable preponderance of air and naval power while the Army built up its forces for yet another try. Unlike the two previous thrusts against Guadalcanal, though, this plan explicitly acknowledged that Geiger's beleaguered little air force had an importance out of all proportion to its size. Its destruction was a prerequisite to the recapture of the island.

Troop reinforcements started to come in to both sides. For the Americans the 7th Marine Regiment was brought in by Kelly Turner on the morning of the 18th. These 3,500 men gave the weary First Division its first addition of strength in six weeks. The cost of doing so was a carrier, *Wasp,* covering Turner's convoy, sunk by an enemy submarine on the 15th. The Japanese came to the island in smaller groups, a few hundred at a time from almost nightly "Rat" landings.,

While each side built up its ground forces, the air war entered a lull. The period from September 15 to 27 was relatively quiet as far as the Marines and the Henderson Field flyers were concerned. Almost two weeks of bad weather prevented any large-scale Japanese air attacks on the field. Many missions were flown by the SBDs against enemy ships, all of which were without result. The nibbling daily attrition of pilots and aircraft continued through disease, mishap, or enemy action. Life remained disagreeble and dangerous.

For some of the South Pacific's aircraft there never was a vacation, not even during periods of relative peace. This was true in particular of the patrol flying boats. The PBYs

never were part of the Cactus Air Force, but they were an
essential if unglamorous element of the air campaign of
Guadalcanal. Without them the Navy would not have been
able to keep track of the Japanese Combined Fleet as it
prowled restlessly north of the Solomons, and the Henderson
field pilots would not have received warning of many a
Cactus Express.

The PBYs started to gravitate to the South Pacific after
Midway. There were two Patrol Wings in the Pacific Fleet,
each controlling four or five patrol (VP) squadrons. Patwing
Two sent a squadron down from Pearl Harbor in June, and
by the first of August Patwing One had one based in the
South Pacific islands too. To aid the attack on Guadalcanal,
Rear Admiral McCain, Commander Air Forces, South Pacific, had these two squadrons and part of a third. Their
assignment was to search the sea areas north and east of
Guadalcanal. Their searches were based on Segond Channel,
Espiritu Santo, where the seaplane tender *Curtiss* operated
nine BPYs from VP-11 and VP-23; Maramasike Estuary, on
the east coast of Santa Isabel, where nine more "P-boats" of
VP-23 were serviced by the *Mackinac;* and Graciosa Bay on
the island of Ndeni in the Santa Cruz group, which was
occupied on August 7 by the old four-stack destroyer *McFarland,* now turned seaplane tender. *McFarland* had with her
two PBYs from VP-11 and three of VP-14. A few boats also
were located at Nouméa and Suva.

This slender force was far too small for the job it had to
do, the pilots and crews shortly were overworked, and the
primitive facilities and uncharted harbors from which they
operated began to exact a slow toll of the PBYs. Two of them
grounded in Efate Harbor on August 1 and had to be
scrapped; one failed to return from search on the 6th; one
went down at sea that same day and another two days later;
and on the 8th one struck a reef in Maramasike Estuary and
sank. In a week, McCain had lost almost one-fifth of his
patrol planes.

The Battle of Savo Island and resulting loss of control of
the sea in the southern Solomons made the forward position
of *Mackinac* and VP-23 in Maramasike Estuary too exposed
and they returned to Espiritu Santo on August 9. The few
PBYs still in New Caledonia and the Fijis were concentrated
at Santo, with an advanced base at Ndeni. Replacements
trickled down from Pearl Harbor by twos and threes, and two

additional half-squadrons were sent down too. By the first of September parts of VP-51 and VP-72 were supplementing 11, 14, and 23 in the South Pacific.

The PBY were scarcely overarmed, mounting a 50-caliber machine gun in each of two big glass blisters on the port and starboard sides amidships, a 30-caliber in the tiny bow-turret, and another firing through a tunnel in the bottom of the fuselage. Nevertheless the P-boats seemed to get more than their fair share of combat, and did not always come out as badly as their low speed, general ungainliness, and weak armament suggested they ought to. On August 26, plane No. 5 of VP-14 (14-P-5 in the concise notation of the Navy) sighted one of Admiral Nagumo's carriers heading back to Truk after the Battle of the Eastern Solomons. The PBY too was sighted and intercepted by a combat air patrol of eight Zekes. Her left-side rudder and elevator cables were shot away in the first attack, but she remained controllable. The fight lasted for twenty-five minutes, the big flying boat dodging from cloud to cloud while the Zekes riddled her with cannon and machine-gun fire. Her oil tanks and lines punctured, 14-P-5 evaded the Japanese fighters, flew for another forty minutes while her oil slowly drained, and then ditched on the lonely atoll of Ontong Java northeast of the Solomons chain. Her crew stayed there for a week until they were picked up by another PBY.

On September 5, Lieutenant (j.g.) F. C. Riley of VP-23 on patrol from Ndeni sighted a Japanese four-engined Kawanishi flying boat (the Allied code name for the type was Mavis). The P-boat, flying at 300 feet, pulled up to 3,000, which put her above the scattered clouds, added full power to bring her speed up to a magnificent 135 knots, and began slowly overtaking the unsuspecting Japanese. In fifteen minutes she had come up on the Mavis' starboard beam, a thousand feet above. Riley then sprang on his prey like a maddened elephant, diving down to a position 350 feet above, his gunners spraying her from the bow turret and the port blister. The bow gunner was told to fire at the enemy's engines while the waist gunner concentrated first on the Japanese gun positions and then moved forward to the engines too. The PBY then crossed over the surprised Mavis, giving first the tunnel gunner and then the starboard waist gunner shots, too. About fifteen seconds after the start of the

Kawanishi H6K5 "Mavis"

fight, the Japanese flying boat's inboard starboard engine
burst into flames and the enemy pilot dropped her onto the
water. Immediately afterward, the other starboard engine
caught fire too, and the Mavis' whole starboard wing dropped
off. Seven men of the Japanese crew jumped into the water.
Riley flew 23-P-11 back, its crew basking in the rare glow of
a victory in air combat.

Only the next day, two PBYs of Patrol Squadron Eleven
fell in with another enemy seaplane better able to defend
itself. The two boats poured machine-gun fire into the Mavis
with no evident result, but the big Japanese plane, impassive
as a Sumo wrestler, gave more than it got. One of the PBYs
landed on the water sixty-five miles west of Ndeni out of gas,
full of bullet holes, and her plane captain dead. She sank, but
not before her surviving crew was rescued.

Having his patrol pilots forsake their real business for
the unaccustomed thrills of air fighting was something that
Admiral McCain obviously would not tolerate—particularly
if there was a chance that they would come out second-best.
He issued an order forthwith reminding them with some

asperity that their primary mission was to obtain information and directing them henceforth not to seek combat with enemy aircraft.

The P-boats' increased activity north of the Solomons was noted by the Japanese with some concern. Yamamoto's plans for support of the Army's mid-September offensive on Guadalcanal included as one of its elements the destruction of the American seaplane base at Graciosa Bay. Apparently the Japanese were unaware that the "base" never consisted of anything but a seaplane tender which could up-anchor and clear out in a matter of hours. If not, they found out shortly. A Japanese submarine sent to reconnoiter the Santa Cruz Islands found *Mackinac* in Graciosa Bay on the 11th and shelled her, but ineffectively.

The PBYs closely monitored the intricate movement of the Japanese Second, Third, and Eighth Fleets as they maneuvered north of Guadalcanal during the September crisis. As always, close contact maintained meant losses sustained. On the 11th, one was shot down by a combat air patrol from Nagumo's carriers. But the careful reconnaissance of the Japanese fleets helped to preserve the flying boats themselves. On the 11th, the two destroyers that Yamamoto sent down to Graciosa Bay were sighted, their objective was realized, and the two tenders there, *Mackinac* and *Ballard*, withdrew immediately. The destroyers shelled the place on the night of the 12th, but there was nothing left to hit.

Chased out of Ndeni, the BPYs never returned. Instead, they used another of the Santa Cruz Islands, the melodiously named Vanikoro, located ninety miles farther southeast, for their advanced base. Despite its lovely name and appearance, Vanikoro seethed with deadly strains of malaria that made it impossible to consider for any permanent base and dangerous to keep a seaplane tender there much longer than a week. The patrol planes developed a kind of shuttle that would take one of them out 800 miles from Espiritu Santo on a search and then into Vanikoro. There the plane would lay over for a day while it was fueled and repaired and the crew rested on the tender. Then it would go out on another search, from which it would return to Santo. McCain's daily air-search plan generally involved sending out a dozen aircraft each morning; in the search sectors where air opposition was expected, the Army's B-17s were sent out rather than the slow and underarmed PBYs.

For the ultimate combination of tedium and danger, probably nothing in the first year of the Pacific War matched the experiences of the PBYs during the Guadalcanal campaign. At least the men of the Cactus Air Force had combat missions and aircraft suited for them. Not the P-boats. Theirs was the humdrum function of looking—just looking. Most of the time they didn't see anything. But the men knew that when they did find the enemy, they were in for a difficult few minutes at best, and at worst slow death from thirst and exposure in a life raft. But it was rough duty, and would get no easier in the months to come. They kept it up, day after day. During the first two months of the fighting for Guadalcanal, they slowly developed proficiency as the eyes of the Navy in the South Pacific.

On the 21st of September the Cactus Air Force lost one of its best friends when Rear Admiral McCain was relieved as Commander Air Force South Pacific by Rear Admiral Aubrey W. Fitch. It was McCain before any senior American commander who realized that Guadalcanal would become the bottomless pit into which Japan would hurl her naval and air strength, and that Henderson Field was the key to the island's striking power as well as its survival. "The planes must find these ships that run in and hit you at night and must strike them before dark," he wrote in a farewell letter to Vandegrift. Admiral McCain carried back with him to Washington a lasting respect for Marine aviation. Before he left Nouméa, the Marines on their part had learned admiration for the chain-smoking little Mississipian whose nose and chin almost met. His strategic vision and the vehemence with which he made the case for giving the Cactus Air Force the dive bombers and torpedo planes it needed probably saved the First Division and the island. John Sidney McCain thought much and saw far. As ComAirSoPac he was in the right job at the right time. Immensely proud of his wings, and thirsting for combat, the flying admiral was immured in Washington for two years before he came out again as Mitscher's alternate in the command of the Pacific Fleet's fast carriers. Worn out, he died the night he came home from the war.

The third week of September was a time of particular weariness and frustration at Henderson Field, devoid of either the incentive of crisis or the exhilaration of success. The rains were worse than usual and the tired pilots began to feel more and more exposed inside the field's perimeter. Their fatigue showed in their inability to hit their targets—not a single hit was obtained on an enemy ship during the whole month—and in a high accident rate. The hard old Marine Geiger was impervious to frustration and had tremendous endurance. But he recognized the signs of trouble among his pilots. In his brusque way he perhaps wanted to show the sympathy he could not admit outright by sharing their dangers in the air. Or perhaps he grew impatient with their complaints about the wretched condition of the field. But, for whatever reason, Major General Roy Geiger, aged fifty-seven, took off in an SBD at 1130 on September 22, flew over to the Japanese encampment at Visale, and dropped a 1,000-pound bomb on it. The Old Man was twelve years past the age when he was officially supposed to fly only with the assistance of a younger copilot. Jiggs Geiger probably looked rather more human to his pilots after his escapade. As far as anyone knows, no other officer of his age and seniority has ever personally flown an aircraft into combat.

The Eleventh Air Fleet now outnumbered the Americans two to one in fighters and three to one in bombers, and only awaited good weather to undertake their long-sought-for destruction. That was what the whole Japanese campaign turned on now: the crushing of the troublesome handful of aircraft on Guadalcanal.

On the 27th the weather finally broke, and the Japanese were able to make their first air attack on Guadalcanal in almost two weeks. At 1230 Kennedy, the New Georgia coastwatcher, reported eighteen enemy bombers escorted by fighters passing overhead. The Cactus Air Force scrambled in a frenzy of activity, but did not intercept the Bettys until they had arrived over the field. Eight Grummans each from 223 and 224 took off, and eighteen from Fighting Five. The Marines worked over the bombers, while the Navy squadron tangled with the thirty-eight Zekes that escorted them down. Their claims totaled five Bettys and five Zekes, Marion Carl getting one bomber and sharing another with 224's Kirk Armistead. However, the attack was effective. An SBD was destroyed on the field by bombs, and four others damaged; three TBFs were so badly damaged that they required major overhaul and two others were temporarily out of commission. Geiger's striking power was substantially reduced: only eigh-

teen SBDs and two TBFs were available at the end of the
day.

The 27th was the last day on Guadalcanal for Flight
300. Turner Caldwell, Chris Fink, Walter Coolbaugh, Barker,
and Brown, the five remaining pilots of the original eleven,
were flown out that afternoon. The eleven gunners were still
walking, and they went out along with their pilots. All the
rest of their lives the airmen from the *Enterprise* would remember their month on that rain-soaked island. They came
to Henderson Field at a particularly critical time for the
fortunes of the Marines. With Mangrum's truncated squadron, they turned back the first of the Cactus Expresses the
day after they arrived on the island. Then for thirty-three
more days they played a valiant part in the frustrated, heroic
history of the Cactus Air Force in late August and September.

The 28th, too, was clear, and the Japanese sent twenty-
seven Bettys off the Kavieng strip shortly after 0800. They
were escorted by almost every fighter that could reach Guadalcanal from Rabaul, forty-two Zekes. However, the coast-
watcher-Cactus team worked perfectly this time. Fifteen
F4Fs from VF-5, nine from VMF-223, and ten from VMF-
224 scrambled in plenty of time and made a perfect interception far out from Henderson Field. The enemy fighters were
completely ineffectual. All thirty-four Grummans fell on the
hapless bomber formation like hawks on chickens and scattered it. Four Bettys were shot down and three others had to
ditch on the way home because of battle damage. One Zeke
was shot down by Lieutenant Colonel Bauer, the visiting C.O.
of Efate-based VMF-212. Not one American plane was lost,
although five F4Fs were damaged.

The Eleventh Air Fleet was staggered by the results of
the day, and its staff met during the evening to consider what
could be done. What was decided was thus expressed by the
Japanese historian: "In today's attack our bombers suffered
heavy damage; therefore it was decided that tomorrow's attack will be carried out by fighters."

The reduction of Geiger's air striking power in the raid
of the 27th brought prompt but discouragingly small reinforcement up from Espiritu Santo. Four TBFs from Torpedo
Eight's rear echelon flew in on the afternoon of the 28th.
With them came three more of Scouting Three's SBDs and

three from a squadron new to Henderson Field, the lost *Wasp*'s Scouting 71. One of the SBD pilots was Lieutenant Commander John Eldridge, the skipper of VS 71. His stay on Guadalcanal would provide the Cactus Air Force with another of its quiet legends. Like Turner Caldwell, Swede Larsen, and Lou Kirn, John Eldridge went far beyond the demands of duty to carry out assignments that were too often a disagreeable combination of the dull and the dangerous.

The attack group that took off from the Rabaul and Kavieng strips on the morning of September 29th was different in composition from all the previous ones. It included twenty-seven Zekes, about the usual size of the fighter escort, but only nine Bettys. The latter were going along only to navigate for the fighter pilots. Coastwatcher Kennedy watched the bombers go over New Georgia and then return within a few minutes. They had taken the Zekes to within sixty miles of Henderson Field before they turned back. Thirty-three F4Fs were scrambled from Fighter One, but only VF-5 made contact with the enemy. Leroy Simpler, leading fourteen aircraft of his squadron into combat, had a brief skirmish with the Zekes near the field. One of his pilots was shot down and killed; one of the Japanese fighters also was shot down. Rather typically, the Japanese records state that they engaged "thirty enemy fighters" and shot down eight of them. Equally typically, the Americans claimed to have downed four Zekes.

The morning of the 30th brought in a distinguished visitor when a B-17 carrying Admiral Nimitz landed on the muddy field in a pelting rain. In the low visibility his pilot almost missed Guadalcanal altogether, and only chance prevented the Commander in Chief of the Pacific Fleet from having to ditch in the lonely expanses of the Coral Sea. Vandegrift, secretly delighted that the admiral had arrived on such a particularly bad day, showed him around the perimeter and had him talk to Geiger and Woods at the Pagoda. He wanted to impress upon Nimitz what he regarded as his main mission—holding the airfield.

Early the next morning a small group of officers and men, hastily selected and notified the night before, met in front of the general's command post to receive decorations from Nimitz. Among them were a dozen or so pilots of the Cactus Air Force. John Smith, Bob Galer, and Marion Carl were given the Navy Cross. Dick Mangrum and McAfferty of

VMSB-232 represented the bombing squadrons, receiving Distinguished Flying Crosses. Red Kendrick and Bill Lees of VMF-223 also were awarded DFCs, as were Hollowell and Kunz of VMF-224; Fighting Five's Clarke, Stover, Register, Halford, and Wesolowski and First Lieutenant J. T. Jarman of the 67th completed the group. The little ceremony over, Vandegrift drove his visitor to Henderson Field in a blinding rain. After one aborted take-off from the swampy airstrip, the admiral's plane had to wait until the rain ended and the sun dried the field. The impartial mischief of the Intertropical Convergence Zone's weather probably made as much of an impression on Nimitz as the arguments of the Marine generals. But then, CincPac was a most perceptive officer, and probably required neither to convince him that the field and its planes and pilots just then were both sword and shield for the Americans in the Pacific.

The weather cleared again on the 2nd and the Eleventh Air Fleet resumed its fighter sweeps against Guadalcanal. This day's raid caught the Cactus Air Force almost completely flatfooted. None of the coastwatchers sighted the thirty-six Zekes that came down, with nine bombers leading them. The Bettys, escorted by nine fighters, turned back when almost in sight of the island, and the remaining twenty-seven Zekes headed in at high speed. Cactus' radar picked them up half an hour out, which was just not enough time to scramble the sluggish F4Fs and get them to altitude.

The Zekes came down on the American formations out of the sun. They were slightly outnumbered by the thirty-three fighters that Cactus launched, but that did not matter. This time they had the altitude advantage, and they used it well. VMF-223 was hit first and hit hard. Red Kendrick, the gifted Harvard Law graduate, and Bill Lees, both of them decorated only the day before by Admiral Nimitz, were shot down on the Zekes' first pass. John Smith came out of a cloud and found three Zekes right ahead of him. One ballooned into a ball of flame with the first hits. The other two quickly turned onto Smith's tail and filled his plane with 20-millimeter shells and machine-gun bullets. One of these hit his vulnerable oil cooler and the Grumman's engine began to run roughly. Smitty let down slowly over Guadalcanal, keeping an eye on landmarks, and elected to land dead stick and wheels up in a clearing six miles outside the Marine perimeter, southeast of Fighter One. Marion Carl circled protectively overhead as Smith climbed out of his plane, but no enemy appeared. Smitty started back toward the perimeter. "It was just like a hike," he said later. "There were a few rivers to ford, of course. The whole trip took me just two and a half hours." Part way back, on a hillside, he found the wreckage of an F4F. There was nothing identifiable except the three-bladed Curtiss propeller. Smitty wasn't sure, but he thought this probably was what was left of McLennan's plane, shot down in September. He stopped for a minute or two and thought of Scotty McLennan. Then he went on his way.

The skipper of 224, Bob Galer, was shot down for the second time, but parachuted into the sound off Tulagi and was picked up. George Treptow, flying with 224 on tempo-rary duty from VMF-121, was shot down within the perime-ter and killed. In Roy Simpler's squadron, Lieutenant (j.g.) George Morgan did not come back from the fight. Four Japanese fighters were claimed, Smith's, two by Galer, and one by Simpler. The Japanese records do not allude to any losses (although they claimed fourteen American aircraft), but it is quite certain that they suffered some.

John Smith got back to the fighter strip in midafternoon. The first thing he did was to take a bath in the Lunga River. Then he took a party out to find Red Kendrick's plane, which he thought had crashed very close to Henderson Field. They found it in a small field where Kendrick had tried unsuccess-fully to ditch it, lying on its back. Red was in the cockpit, his finger still tightly grasping the trigger that fired his guns. They wrapped him in the rubber life raft that was part of his seat cushion and buried him beside his plane.

There was not much talk in 223's tents that night. Only nine of the original eighteen pilots were left.

Several other F4Fs were damaged on the 2nd in addition to the six lost. At the end of the day, Geiger was left with only twenty-six operational fighters. This was almost exactly one-third as many as the Japanese now had at Rabaul. Nor were aircraft the only commodities of war that were in short supply. All the squadrons were badly below complement. Geiger was having to make do by rotating pilots from the Marine fighter squadrons based on islands farther south through a two- or three-week tour with 223 or 224. Bombs, too, were running short. Marine Air Wing 1 wrote ComAir-SoPac on October 2 requesting 1,800 of them, pointing out that 120 bombs had been used in one recent day's operation.

Continued fair weather on October 3 allowed the Japanese to keep their campaign against the Cactus Air Force moving. A group of Bettys led twenty-seven Zekes down the slot an hour earlier than usual. This time they were picked up by one of the coastwatchers, and the fighters scrambled well in advance. The Marine radar saw the Japanese bombers turn back eighty-five miles out. As was their custom, the F4Fs awaited the enemy close to the field. Smitty was afraid that if they went out even under radar control to look for the Japanese and missed them, the Grummans were not fast enough to catch them in a tail chase.

The two Marine fighter squadrons—what was left of them—were the ones that made contact with the Zekes. The wily Marines, experienced ambushers of Japanese formations, avenged the previous day's defeat by catching the enemy unprepared. Marion Carl, leading the single four-plane division that VMF-223 was able to send up, shot down one Zeke, as did two of his pilots. Ken Frazier got two before he was shot down in turn, but he bailed out unhurt.

The star of the day, though, was the visiting Colonel Bauer, flying with 224. He got four Zekes, which, even considering the relative disadvantage of the belly-tank-laden Japanese, was a remarkable performance. But Bauer was a most remarkable man. Tall and dark, with a slightly Indian cast of feature that gave him his nickname of "Indian Joe," he was a famous fighter pilot in the Marine Corps even before the war. A marvelous leader as well as a great pilot, he was worshiped by the younger men, who referred to him as "the Chief" or "the Coach."

While the fight was going on, three more Zekes streaked across the field and strafed it, but two of them were hit by antiaircraft fire and downed.

This was a very bad day for the Eleventh Air Fleet. The Cactus Air Force's combat claims closely match the recorded Japanese losses—the enemy admitted losing nine fighters, with another "badly damaged." Aside from Frazier's plane, the only other American loss was suffered by Fighting Five, one of whose aircraft burned out an engine and crashed in a dead-stick landing at Henderson Field. Not a single Marine or Navy pilot was injured. And Admiral Tsukahara had lost almost 20 per cent of his long-range fighters in one day. The loss was due to more than just the quality of the fighter pilots. The Japanese fighter sweep tactics had been recognized and understood by the Air Wing staff after the raid on the 2nd, and great care was taken to prepare for the enemy on the 3rd. A carefully laid ambush and the icy efficiency of the much-reduced Marine squadrons did the rest. The enemy would not be ready for another air raid for five days and would not attack Guadalcanal again for more than a week.

Around this time, Vice-Admiral Tsukahara was relieved as the commander of the Eleventh Air Fleet by Vice-Admiral Jinichi Kusaka, hitherto commander of the 26th Air Flotilla. It is not clear whether or not this was considered relief for cause. Even in histories, the Japanese were reluctant to go into such matters. But the continued failure of his superior force to "annihilate" the ragtag air force on Guadalcanal cannot have done over much for Tsukahara's reputation.

The short spell of good weather had given the Marines and Seabees the opportunity to fill some of the worst holes in the field, and General Vandegrift reported to Ghormley that it was serviceable for all types of aircraft. Reinforcements came in from Espiritu Santo during the day: five B-17s for temporary duty, six more SBDs from Scouting 71, and an additional three TBFs of Torpedo Eight. Six more pilots for the 67th Pursuit Squadron were flown in by transport. Vandegrift a few days earlier had stated his revised opinion that the P-400s were useful for ground-attack work and asked that the Army squadron be kept at full strength.

The remainder of the air action of October 3 revolved around American efforts to attack an incoming Cactus Express. The *Nisshin*'s critical reinforcement mission was under way. SBD afternoon searches did not get off until 1430, when it was clear that the day's air raid was over. About an hour out, the "B" Sector search sighted the big seaplane tender 190 miles northwest of Cactus, covered by ten Buka-based enemy fighters. The two SBDs were jumped by the Zekes and only escaped by violent maneuvering. Half an hour later, at 1600, the "A" Sector search, the sector to the west, sighted three destroyers running in toward the island. It was clear that something more than the usual Express was coming.

When the "B" sector aircraft's radio message was received at the field, an attack group was hastily organized and took off at 1615. One dive bomber returned with engine trouble, but seven SBDs and three TBFs, led by Scouting Three's Lieutenant F. L. Frank, attacked the *Nisshin* and her six escorting destroyers at 1725. The Japanese ships maneu-

vered radically in tight circles, putting up heavy antiaircraft
fire, and all the bombs missed. The enemy came on at high
speed, and was off Cape Esperance before midnight. A
scratch lot of five SBDs from four different squadrons were
launched at 2220 to attack the dimly visible ships. The leader
of this group was Scouting 71's C.O., John Eldridge: because
his aircraft's radio frequency had not yet been changed to the
one used by Henderson Field, another VS-71 SBD was taxied
up alongside the operations tent and used as a message relay
between him and the Air Wing staff.

Such improvisations were in vain. Only Eldridge and a
plane from Scouting Three contacted the Japanese ships, and
their bombs, dropped in almost complete darkness, missed.
Another flight of dive bombers loaded with flares was sent up
around midnight. It was an eerie night, with the blue exhaust
flames from the aircraft the only illumination of the field.
Overhead, two enemy seaplanes from Rekata Bay clattered
malevolently back and forth through the blackness, occasionally shattering it with a randomly dropped bomb. Out over
the sound, silent bursts of brilliant white appeared and slowly
shrank again into night as flares were dropped and drifted

150 mm. Japanese Howitzer

down under their parachutes. The feeling of formless menace that comes from an enemy not quite seen permeated the field.

Working like ants in the darkness, the Japanese efficiently unloaded the *Nisshin*'s cargo, including a number of dangerous 150-millimeter howitzers. On her way back, the big ship was sighted and attacked twice without any damage, though two TBF pilots claimed hits that proved illusory.

On October 4, Yamamoto issued the order for the operation that had been taking shape in his mind since the Army's failure in mid-September. On a day to be designated later, a high-speed convoy would land the remaining troops of the Army's 2nd Division—called the Sendai because it was raised in that Japanese city—on Guadalcanal. The task assigned this division was the capture of Henderson Field. The landing was to be supported by air attacks by the Eleventh Air Fleet and a bombardment of the Marine beachhead by two battleships. It was to be covered by Kondo's Second Fleet, which would operate north of the Solomons, and by Nagumo's Third Fleet, which would wait for the Americans east of the island chain. The enemy carrier strength had been reinforced by the arrival from Japan of two large converted carriers—*Hiyo* and *Junyo*—whose air groups had just completed their training. It was to be the largest Japanese fleet operation since Midway, one that would pit their large land-based strength and the air groups of five carriers against the tiny Cactus Air Force and the two American carriers operational in the South Pacific. Around the evolution of this plan would revolve the events of the entire desperate month of October on Guadalcanal.

10

CRISIS IN OCTOBER
October 5–13

October 5 was a day of frustrated effort by all the South Pacific air forces. ComSoPac laid on an attack on shipping in the Shortlands anchorage by the *Hornet,* and this was to have been coordinated with a strike on the Buka airfields by B-17s of the 11th Bomb Group and one by the Cactus Air Force on the Japanese seaplane base at Rekata Bay. The whole operation was turned into a fiasco by weather. The Hornet's pilots could scarcely find the Shortlands, let alone hit any ships; only one of the thirteen B-17s located its target, and the Cactus aircraft attacked in small scattered groups.

The afternoon SBD search located another Cactus Express of six destroyers 170 miles west of the island, and two attack groups were organized to go after them. The first, nine SBDs led by Bullet Lou Kirn, found the enemy ships at 1545. Kirn and one of his pilots had very near misses on either bow of the *Minegumo* and damaged her severely; they thought she sank, but the crippled destroyer managed to limp back to the Shortlands at fourteen knots. Another three SBDs dove on the *Murasame* and all scored damaging near misses, putting many holes in her port bow. She too survived a slow return to the Shortlands. The long scoreless weeks endured by the Cactus dive-bomber pilots seemed to be over at last.

The other four destroyers came resolutely on in, despite the crippling of *Minegumo* and *Murasame,* and although ineffectively attacked by another group of SBDs, unloaded west of Lunga Point around midnight. A mixed group of flare-carrying SBDs and TBFs with bombs took off about 2200 to hit some of the dumps where the incoming supplies were initially stored. It was a very black night, and alternating periods of bright illumination and utter darkness can readily induce vertigo and disorientation in a pilot. Red Doggett, one of Torpedo Eight's flying Chiefs, flew right into the water on one of his runs and was killed along with his two crewmen. John Taurman, so recently recovered from his ordeal after the August 24 battle, became lost and finally ditched, out of gas, off San Cristobal. His last words over the radio to Bruce Harwood, who went out looking for him in the darkness, were: "I think I've used up all my luck." He had. He, his radioman Bradley, and his gunner Robak drifted for two days on their damaged life raft before Bradley decided to swim for distant San Cristobal. He made it in a day, and was washed up on the beach nearly dead of exhaustion. John Taurman and Robak were never seen again.

Somehow it all seemed so unfair. But in those islands many Japanese and Americans escaped violent death in battle again and again, only to die purposelessly floating on a beautiful blue sea or stranded on a poisonous island. The loneliness of death suffered in the immensity of a fair, brilliantly sunlit world of water was a unique and dreadful characteristic of the Pacific War.

October 7 was a big day in the career of Louis Woods; he was promoted to brigadier general twenty-five years after he was first commissioned in the Marine Corps. General Geiger had sent his chief of staff to Espiritu Santo on October 1 to expedite the supplies and reinforcements that the Cactus Air Force needed but never seemed to get in time. On Guadalcanal, Woods, as he said later, "spent 90 per cent of my time worrying about supplies, 5 per cent holding what we had, and 5 per cent fighting the Japs." Down south he could devote all of his time to getting men and material onto the island. On the day he made general, he wrote to Geiger that he was trying to get personnel of VMF-121 and VMSB-141 to Guadalcanal as fast as possible. In the case of the former squadron, action already was under way. The escort carrier *Copahee* left Espiritu Santo at daybreak with VMF-121 embarked and headed northwest toward Guadalcanal.

In view of all his activity over supplies, it is worth recording how Louis Woods obtained his first set of general's stars to wear on his uniform. A member of the Air Wing staff persuaded an Army sergeant to solder two pairs of dimes together, file them into five-pointed stars, and polish them. Like so many other improvisations in those days, they worked about as well as the real thing.

The *Nisshin* headed toward Guadalcanal from the Shortlands for the second time on October 8, shepherded by six destroyers. Once again the big seaplane tender carried part of the Sendai division, heavy equipment, and supplies. Once again the Japanese made a maximum effort to provide air protection for the landing.

At 1530 the incoming Cactus Express was sighted, and the pair of SBD search planes that found it ran into a real fight. Although both pilots and a gunner were wounded, they broadcast continuous sighting reports back to the field. Upon receipt of these, a big attack was scrambled. However, their best efforts were to no avail: the dive bombers all missed, and although Torpedo Eight claimed a hit on the *Nisshin* (the second one in a week on the same ship), she was unscathed. Once again, her task was successfully accomplished.

On the plus side, the little escort carrier *Copahee*, with her screening destroyers, arrived at a point fifty miles south of Indispensable Reef on the afternoon of the 9th, and there launched twenty F4Fs of Marine Fighting 121. This squadron had sailed from San Diego early in September and arrived at Espiritu Santo three weeks later. It had previously sent up five pilots to Guadalcanal; now it was coming in as a unit to take over the burden of the island's fighter defense from the three spent squadrons that had been carrying it for weeks. The squadron C.O. was Major Lenoard Davis, called "Duke," an Annapolis man, small, amusing, and easygoing. His exec was a captain named Joseph Jacob Foss, at twenty-seven referred to by the squadron of twenty-two- and twenty-three-year-olds as "old Foos." Joe Foss had been commissioned in the Marine Corps only eighteen months before, stayed on as an instructor at Pensacola, and had a hard time getting into a fighter squadron at his allegedly advanced age. This squadron, young men and "old," was going to produce more fighter aces than any other to see service on Guadalcanal. They didn't get off to a perfect start, though. Upon landing, they were met by the sarcastic John Smith, who informed them that they had landed on the wrong field. They had naturally chosen the mat runway at Henderson Field and completely missed the "cow pasture." Feeling rather foolish, VMF-121 took off again and flew its twenty F4Fs over to the Fighter Strip, three-quarters of a mile away.

By the 11th, the tempo of the Japanese reinforcement operations began to proceed toward a crescendo. The large-scale attack that they had been planning since late September depended for its success on the arrival of a fast convoy which was to land the remaining troops of the 2nd Division and part of the 38th, plus their supplies, artillery, and tank support. Yamamoto dared not send this convoy south of the Short-lands until he was able to provide it with continuous day air cover against the attacks of the Cactus Air Force. And he could not provide such cover until the new airfield at Buin was ready to handle fighter planes. Completion of this strip was delayed repeatedly by lack of construction equipment and almost continual rain. Finally, on the 8th, the field was declared usable, and on the 10th thirty Hamps and Zekes flew down. Yamamoto immediately scheduled his convoy for October 15. The fighters' first assignment was to cover another critical supply mission scheduled for the next day.

Meanwhile, ubiquitous *Nisshin,* with her sister ship *Chitose* and a screen of six destroyers, was to make the last of her runs to Guadalcanal on October 11, carrying another regiment of Japanese heavy artillery. The mission, command-ed by Rear Admiral Jojima, was considered so important that an air attack on Henderson Field with the entire strength of the Eleventh Air Fleet was planned for the day and a night bombardment by three heavy cruisers during the actual land-ing.

The incoming raid was not detected by the coast-watchers. Cactus' radar picked it up at 1220, 138 miles away, which allowed enough time to scramble the fields and even get some of the F4Fs to altitude before the Japanese arrived. Fourteen Grummans of VMF-224 and three from 223, led by Bob Galer and his lean, nervous flight leader, Kirk Armi-stead, made the interception. Fighting Five missed the enemy altogether, the 67th's P-39s—newly arrived to replace the old P-400s—couldn't get high enough, and VMF-21 rendez-voused too late to catch more than a corner of the fight. The Japanese came in two groups: the first was the now conven-tional fighter sweep of seventeen Zekes, the second the main attack force of twenty-seven Bettys and thirty Zekes. The first group had only a brief brush with the Americans. The second was scattered by bad weather en route. Eighteen of the bombers went down below the clouds and were jumped by the two veteran Marine squadrons. Their bombs fell far short of the field, and the F4Fs claimed six of them, a seventh cripple being downed by the 67th's Captain Sharpstein. Two Zekes were shot down and the rest, scattered by weather and battle, landed at Buin, Buka, and Rabaul. VMF-121's Art Nehf, out of gas, ditched in Savo Sound and was pulled out of the water by a Higgins boat. Lieutenant Stern of the 67th Pursuit went missing. The enemy attack was a clear failure.

In the middle of this busy day two of the legendary Guadalcanal fighter pilots left after six weeks on the terrible island with which their names would always be associated. John Smith and Marion Carl were evacuated, leaving only four pilots of VMF-223 remaining. Smith cannot be called an unsung hero—he got the Medal of Honor for his nineteen victories. But the true measure of John Smith's value to the Cactus Air Force is found, not in heroism—of which he had much—but in tactical skill and leadership as a fighter squadron commander. By some he was considered arrogant and supercilious. Perhaps. But he was a true professional, and that was what it took to make fighter pilots out of a dozen boys in fifty days. His friend and rival, Marion Carl, totally different in temperament but no less skilled as a pilot and leader, helped him to make 223 the pre-eminent squadron of the early days on Guadalcanal. With their departure the days of the classical air battles over the island would soon draw to a close.

Geiger was well aware through CINCPAC intelligence that another express was on its way down on the 11th and that it would be preceded by a bombardment group. The Nisshin and Chitose were sighted 200 miles away just before 3 o'clock that afternoon. No attack group was organized. Geiger did not want one coming back after dark to land on a field that might well be full of shell holes. However, sections of SBDs or individual aircraft continued to track Admiral Jojima's ships until after 2200. Then, starting just before midnight, large flashes and explosions were seen and heard to the northwest of the field. It was a naval battle.

The Navy, forewarned as usual and, for once being able

to do something about it, was expecting the Japanese. Rear Admiral Norman Scott, commanding an odd lot of two heavy and two light cruisers organized to provide close support for a reinforcement convoy, was sent forward to await the enemy. At 2346 he found himself fortuitously crossing the "T" of the unsuspecting Japanese 6th Cruiser Division. Confused, with obsolete radar on his flagship, and unable to visualize the situation, Scott conducted the battle without particular distinction, losing an opportunity to sink all three enemy heavy cruisers by prematurely ordering a cease fire. However, the Japanese heavy cruiser *Furutaka* and destroyer *Fubuki* were sunk, the flagship *Aoba* damaged, and the division commander, Rear Admiral Goto, killed. The battle was greatly admired at the time, and American victory claims were extravagant. It did prevent the bombardment of the field, and Scott lost only a destroyer, although the light cruiser *Boise* was badly damaged. However, while the shooting was going on, Admiral Jojima's ships were quietly offloading their supplies off Tassafaronga, unmolested.

At 0515 the next morning the first attack group took off to look for cripples from the previous night's fight. John Eldridge and Al Cooley had sixteen SBDs between them, with a heavy escort of F4Fs and P-39s. In the early light just after take-off, they flew over the aftermath of the battle, huge oil slicks with American and Japanese small boats moving slowly through them. The destroyer *Duncan,* abandoned, drifted slowly through the sound, her sister ship *McCalla* alongside picking up survivors. North of the Russells they found the survivor of *Goto*'s two destroyers, as well as two other destroyers, *Shirayuki* and *Murakumo,* that had rescued many of the Japanese survivors during the early morning hours. Eldridge's five SBDs missed in their attack on the first target; one of Cooley's pilots near-missed *Murakumo* and left it trailing oil. A second group located the same two destroyers at 0800 and made an expertly coordinated attack on them. John Dobbin with fourteen F4Fs from VMF-224 and 121 strafed both ships and kept the antiaircraft fire down to a minimum. Bullet Lou Kirn with six SBDs from his own squadron, VS-71, and 141 got three near misses on the *Murakumo.* While the fighters and dive bombers were keeping the ship occupied, Swede Larsen led his six TBFs in a torpedo attack. The big "torpeckers" came in in an inverted V formation that put three of them on each bow of the destroyer: no matter which way she turned, she would present a beam target to a torpedo. Larsen's section coming in first forced the *Murakumo* to commit herself to a starboard turn. Then either Hanson or Abe Katz, coming in from the port side, scored a direct hit. The destroyer, crowded with survivors from *Furutaka* and *Fubuki*, came to a halt in a cloud of steam and smoke, sinking. She was abandoned and scuttled that afternoon.

By early afternoon the *Shirayuki* was joined by the destroyer *Natsugumo* and this pair was attacked at 1645 by another group of Cactus aircraft. John Eldridge, the great dive-bomber skipper, had ten SBDs from three squadrons. Eldridge dove first on *Natsugumo* and hit her just aft of amidships. Two others scored near misses. There was a huge explosion, and the rakish gray destroyer rolled slowly over, doomed. Swede Larsen, dedicated but ever-frustrated, missed getting a torpedo hit on her when he became too wrapped up in trying to coordinate his lone attack with the strafing runs of eight P-39s, and released his fish prematurely.

As the pilots of squadrons newer to Guadalcanal carried out the unremitting, dangerous flights into daily battle, the last link between the island and the two original squadrons of the Cactus Air Force was broken. Dick Mangrum was flown out, the only pilot of 232 still able to walk when he left Guadalcanal. The others were all dead or had gone out weeks before as stretcher cases. With him went the remaining four pilots of John Smith's 223. It says much for the endurance of human beings that they lasted as long as they did. Six weeks of constant combat while living as men had to live on that island were more than enough for one lifetime.

Despite the defeat of Goto's bombardment force, on the night of the 11th–12th, Admiral Yamamoto's plans for massive reinforcement of the Japanese Army on Guadalcanal were unfolding without any serious setback. To ensure the success of the fast convoy scheduled for October 15, a bombardment of Henderson Field by the battleships *Kongo* and *Haruna* was to be carried out on the night of October 13–14. On each of the two succeeding nights, cruisers were to shell the field. The Second and Third Fleets sortied from Truk on October 11 to take up supporting dispositions north and east of the Solomons. And, as usual, it was specified with particular care that the Eleventh Air Fleet was to destroy all American aircraft on Guadalcanal.

While the first moves of Yamamoto's complex operation were being made, the Americans were carrying out one of their own, also with the landing of reinforcements on Guadalcanal as its objective. Admiral Turner sailed from Nouméa on October 8 with the Army's 164th Infantry embarked on his transports. Distant support for the transports was provided by Task Force 17, built around the carrier *Hornet*, and Task Force 64, with the new battleship *Washington*. Scott's four cruisers were in direct support until they were sent ahead to intercept Goto. The trip from New Caledonia was without incident and Turner's ships arrived off Lunga Point a little after sunrise on October 13.

Although the 13th started out well for the Americans, it was not allowed to end that way. Vice-Admiral Kusaka had picked it as the day that he would attack Henderson Field with the entire strength of the Eleventh Air Fleet. Neither the coastwatchers nor the radar picked up the Japanese raid until it was too late. Kusaka sent down twenty-seven Bettys with an escort of eighteen Zekes. Cactus' forty-two available F4Fs were still climbing for altitude when they saw the bombers, glinting silvery at their altitude of almost 30,000 feet, drifting slowly across a cloud-dotted blue sky, antiaircraft shells bursting far below them. The Japanese bombed Henderson and the Fighter Strip with considerable accuracy, putting thirteen holes in the runway and setting fire to 5,000 gallons of gasoline. VMF-121 had a brief brush with them as they were on their way out: Tom Mann claimed a Zeke, and Big Bill Freeman dove on the leader of the Betty group and shot him down. In doing so, the inexperienced young pilot gave every other bomber in the formation a shot at him, and he ditched his riddled plane in the water just east of the field.

Two hours later another group of eighteen Bettys and eighteen Zekes came over while most of the Grummans were still on the ground being refueled. Joe Foss led twelve F4Fs from VMF-121 after them, but was jumped by some Zekes that he failed to see. Just as he was wondering why everyone in his formation had suddenly dived out of it, a stream of tracers went by his head. The Zero that tried for him overshot, though, and pulled up directly in front of him. Foss gave him a single light burst and the Zeke blew up in a thousand pieces. The excited captain then was thoroughly shot up by three more Japanese fighters, one of which hit his oil cooler. In seconds his engine, drained of oil, froze, and he dove for the field still chased by the Zekes. Unable to slow up until his pursuers left him, Foss, "coming in like a rocket ship," sideslipped desperately at the last minute to lose speed, then bumped the length of the strip still going like a streak, madly pursued by an ambulance. Somehow he got away with it, and returned in a few minutes riding on the ambulance's running board, much chastened.

The Bettys, unhindered, bombed the fields again, but caused relatively minor damage. All in all, the two raids constituted, as Torpedo Eight's war diary said, "the worst bombing the island has experienced." However, the damage was not nearly as severe as the Japanese thought.

Just after dark a Betty flew across the island, with the waving white fingers of the Marines' big searchlights groping for it. The big Japanese 150-millimeter howitzers fired sporadically. Now and then white flares ballooned briefly around the perimeter. The day's bombings, the sense of ineffectiveness occasioned by the failure of the fighters to intercept the enemy planes, the artillery fire, the unfamiliar noises and lights in the muggy darkness, combined to create a sense of brooding menace over the whole island. At 0138 the popcorn-machine noise of one of the Japanese float biplanes was heard overhead, and colored flares began to float down from the blackness: a red flare over the west end of Henderson Field, a white one over the middle of the strip, and finally a green one over the east end. Then, with a roar, sixteen fourteen-inch guns on two Japanese battleships fired together out of the night.

The airmen, sleepless since nightfall, ran stumbling through the darkness to the foxholes and slit trenches that they used for air-raid shelters. For over an hour they lived through a nightmare of rumbling shells, concussions that shook the ground, deadly steel splinters that ricocheted from the coconut palms, fires, and, above all, hideous noise. Many artillery bombardments of both world wars were more prolonged, but few provided such a concentration of huge guns on so small a target. Fourteen-inch guns are of practically unheard-of-size for land artillery. Whether or not it was a record did not matter to the men of Henderson Field. To those who were there, it was always "the bombardment," as if there had never been another. Some—a very few—were better able to take such horror in stride. VMF-121's Danny Doyle shared a foxhole with three squadron mates. Toward the end of an hour, a nearby gasoline dump was spouting roaring flames hundreds of feet high, parked planes were blazing all over Henderson Field, an ammunition depot was cooking off with spectacular display, and flares drifted down periodically from Japanese aircraft flying overhead. When a temporary lull in the noise came, Doyle leaned over and inquired of one of his neighbors: "Say, do you think it would reveal our position if I lit a cigarette?"

From the bridge of the *Kongo*, Vice-Admiral Takeo Kurita, Commander Battleship Division Three, watched with quiet professional satisfaction as Henderson Field turned into a sea of flames. His ships fired 918 fourteen-inch shells into the perimeter, and most of them landed on the field and in the coconut grove between the field and the sea where the pilots and aircrewmen lived. Fortunately for the airmen, and for Guadalcanal, only 293 of those shells were high explosive; the remainder were armor-piercing, very thick-walled with a correspondingly reduced explosive charge. These simply blew big craters in the ground. But the high-explosive shells, designed especially for shore bombardment, had an enormous blast effect and spread wicked steel splinters hundreds of yards. It was these that did much of the damage.

PT Boat

The two battleships were illuminated from the beach by the big searchlights the Marines used for antiaircraft work and taken under fire by the five-inch battery. Four PT boats, newly arrived at Tulagi, went out after the big ships and gave Admiral Turita something to think about. But the battleships were not hit and retired according to plan about 0230. Bettys continued to fly over and drop bombs sporadically through the darkness. There was to be no sleep on the island that night.

Behind them the battleships left utter chaos. The radio station was completely demolished, and Cactus could not even get the bare fact of the bombardment to Admiral Ghormley for almost three hours after it had ended. Incredibly, only forty-one officers and men were killed. But these included the commanding officer, executive officer, a flight leader, and two other pilots of Marine Scouting 141, all killed when a shell landed in the middle of the dive-bomber pilots' camp. The Pagoda was damaged so badly that Geiger took advantage of the opportunity to get rid of what he had long suspected to be a prime aiming point for the Japanese, and ordered it bulldozed out of existence.

The island's offensive power was wiped out. Virtually all of Geiger's aviation gasoline went up in flames. Of the thirty-nine SBDs that had been operational on October 13, only seven were in flyable condition the next morning. There were only two P-39s and four P-400s that could be flown. All the TBFs were destroyed or out of commission. With a major Japanese offensive imminent, the Cactus Air Force was left with seven dive bombers with which to oppose it.

11

"MIRACLES
ARE STILL WITH US"
October 14–16

The big guns of the Japanese battleships had ripped and chewed the Cactus Air Force, but had not destroyed it. Through some fantastic luck the Fighter Strip was almost untouched, and twenty-nine of the island's forty-two fighter planes remained operational. Geiger was to need them all on the 14th. The Eleventh Air Fleet, sensing that its adversary finally was ready for the kill, continued its maximum effort against Henderson Field.

The Cactus fighters, jumpily alert and knowing how much depended on them, were scrambled at 0930 on the strength of a coastwatcher's report. Whatever he saw wasn't the bombers, though. The frustrated F4F pilots landed after an hour and still were on the ground refueling when the day's first raid came in at noon. Twenty-six Bettys bombed the field unopposed, but since almost all the operational American planes were on the Fighter Strip, no appreciable damage was done. An hour later another eighteen bombers came over, but this time they were met by every fighter that would fly and taken completely by surprise. They had been convinced that the night's battleship bombardment had destroyed the island's aircraft, and the failure to intercept the first raid probably reinforced this belief. Fighting Five claimed five bombers, and the Marines four more and three Zekes as well. The Japanese records are most reticent about what happened to this raid, saying only that the bombers suffered "some damages" and admitting "the bombing raid was not very successful." Quite likely the American claims were nearly correct. To inflict these losses, though, cost them one of 121's pilots.

The shape of the menace to Guadalcanal became clear when the morning search planes found two groups of Japanese ships heading toward the island. The most ominous of these was a force of six transports and eight destroyers. This was the fast convoy, the safe passage of which was the whole object of Yamamoto's huge operation. It had sailed from the Shortlands on the morning of the 13th, taking a roundabout route north of Santa Isabel. The second force was Admiral Mikawa's Eighth Fleet, the cruisers *Chokai* and *Kinugasa* with two destroyers. Together they gave dreadful promise of more night bombardment and massive reinforcement of enemy ground forces.

Early in the afternoon Colonel Toby Munn, Geiger's aide, drove over to the 67th's area from headquarters. Three of the Army pilots and a mechanic were standing around, and he called them over: "I want you to pass the word along," he said, "that the situation is desperate. We don't know whether we'll be able to hold the field or not. There's a Japanese task force of destroyers, cruisers, and troop transports headed this way. We have enough gasoline left for one mission against them. Load your airplanes with bombs and go out with the dive bombers and hit them. After the gas is gone we'll have to let the ground troops take over. Then your officers and men will attach themselves to some infantry outfit. Good luck and good bye." While the Colonel was saying his few words, the little group had to hit the dirt twice when Japanese artillery shells exploded nearby.

The Marine ground crews worked feverishly throughout the morning and early afternoon, interrupted by air raids, to repair some of the damaged dive bombers. By 1445 four were ready and went out with four P-39s and three of the old P-400s to attack the transport convoy. They were met by heavy antiaircraft, and had no luck. An hour later, nine of VS-3's planes were patched up sufficiently to allow a second attack on the transports before it got too dark. Two wrecked B-17s had been drained of gas and this was enough to fuel the planes. Kirn led his eight pilots accompanied by the flyable P-39s and P-40s and some of 121's Grummans, and they too attacked in vain through severe antiaircraft fire that shot down one of the 67th's Bells. When they landed in the darkness on the cratered field, another of the Army planes ran off the runway and crashed into a stack of Marston mat. Geiger forbade further flying that night.

When the Cactus Air Force took stock at dusk on October 14, its situation seemed utterly hopeless. The flying that it had had to do to keep the Japanese bombers away from the field and try to strike the oncoming convoy had used up almost all the aviation gas on the island and Geiger had to look forward to helplessly watching the enemy ships approach while his aircraft sat on the ground. Even had he the gasoline, there now were only five flyable SBDs on Guadalcanal. For the first time since aircraft came to the island, the Marines seemed clearly doomed.

Admiral Fitch at Espiritu Santo, spurred by Vandegrift's situation report on the evening of the 14th, moved fast to give the Cactus Air Force all the help he could. The only SBDs in the South Pacific not already at Guadalcanal at the time of the bombardment were the eight planes of Lieutenant Commander Ray Davis' Bombing Six, from the *Enterprise*'s old air group, and nine spare aircraft at Espiritu Santo with no pilots to fly them. Fitch already had sent Davis up to Cactus that morning. He then ordered Colonel Bauer's VMF-212 to furnish the pilots to ferry the nine spares to Guadalcanal. Once these pilots had been flown back by transport plane, Bauer was to bring the twenty F4Fs of his squadron up from Efate to Santo and wait there. Finally, Fitch considered the possibility of having Task Force 17 fly ten of the *Hornet*'s SBDs up to the island, but deferred action on that.

Next was the aviation gas problem. Some help already was on the way. Two big special-purpose barges (called PAB barges) carrying thousands of gallons of aviation gas, oil, and Marston mat had left Santo on the 10th, each towed by a tug. Two cargo ships and a pair of destroyers accompanied the barges on their slow crawl to Guadalcanal. However, the PABs had been intended to supplement Geiger's normal supply of gas and were well on their way before the present crisis arose. So Fitch made two other decisions. First, the old *McFarland*, which was about to relieve *Ballard* as the resident seaplane tender at Vanikoro, was ordered to go by way of Guadalcanal and deliver 750 drums of gasoline and twelve torpedoes. An airlift was organized to ferry drums of fuel up from Espiritu Santo, and ComSoPac was asked to order all available Army and Marine transport aircraft in the area to this duty.

Two stark dispatches to Ghormley composed by Vandegrift late on the night of October 14 clearly stated the extremity of his situation: "Urgently necessary this force receive maximum support of air and surface units." "Absolutely essential aviation gas be flown here continuously."

As night closed in on the island again, so did a pervading sense of doom. Almost no planes. Almost no gasoline, except what could be drained out of the wrecked planes that littered the edge of the field. And the Japanese cruisers were coming inexorably down through the darkness. The hours crawled slowly by, the men waiting sleeplessly in their dugouts and shelters for the dreadful ordeal of another shelling.

It came finally just before 0200. Once again there was the incongruously comic sound of one of the little float biplanes, then the brilliant flares that swayed slowly down, showing everything in pitiless flickering light. *Chokai* and *Kinugasa* had sixteen eight-inch guns between them, and they fired 752 shells onto both airstrips in half an hour. Sixteen big artillery rounds bursting every forty-five seconds caused more heavy damage, but this bombardment lacked the shattering emotional impact of that of the previous night. Behind its cover, however, the Japanese troop convoy anchored off Tassafaronga and began unloading its 4,000 men.

When dawn finally came, the Marines had the sickening humiliation of seeing the enemy transports lying only ten miles westward, lighters and small boats unloading them while Zekes and float biplanes confidently flew cover overhead. The Japanese were certain that the American aircraft finally had been eliminated.

They almost had been, but not quite. The night's bombardment left only three SBDs that could be flown. Using gas drained from wrecked planes, two of them taxied to the head of the runway at Fighter One, where all the surviving aircraft were now operating. One of them fell into a crater in the taxi strip in the predawn darkness. The other, piloted by Lieutenant Robert Patterson of 141, carefully felt its way to a spot designated by Joe Renner, the field's operations officer, who had carefully reconnoitered the "cow pasture" after the shelling. A small group of men watched tensely as Patterson put on full throttle and slowly started rolling down the strip.

Japanese Float Bi-plane

Then suddenly one wheel went over the edge of a giant
shellhole, and the SBD ground-looped into total wreckage.
Patterson and his gunner somehow escaped injury, and he
begged for permission to take the remaining plane. Just at
dawn he finally got off and flew over alone to attack the
transports. After take-off, he found that a hydraulic leak kept
him from retracting his wheels or using his dive flaps. The
indomitable Patterson dove on one of the enemy ships regard-
less, wheels down and without flaps, got a hit with his bomb,
and survived.

While mechanics drained gasoline from wrecked F4Fs to
keep Cactus' planes flying, someone on Geiger's staff recalled
that Louis Woods had cached quite a bit of gas in drums

hidden around the field. "By God, find some!" ordered Geiger. A colonel from the division staff set out to look for the almost-forgotten dumps, most of which were covered with earth. He took a supply major with him on his feverish hunt, so that if one were killed the other still would know where the dumps were located. The engineers found two hundred drums in their part of the perimeter, and another hundred were discovered on the beach south of Kukum. The colonel found one cache of a hundred, one of forty, and another of twenty-five drums. From almost nothing, the Cactus Air Force had found a two-day supply of gas. Now the planes, such as were left, could go on flying. Ironically, much of the worry about gas could have been avoided. Woods had written to Geiger early in October, reminding him of the hidden dumps. When he returned to Guadalcanal in November, his letter was discovered in Geiger's shirt pocket—unopened.

At 0600 Duke Davis led five F4Fs off to strafe the transports. One of the fighters was flown by Smokey Stover of Fighting Five and he ran into air opposition in a very literal sense. Stover had made two runs on the enemy ships when he sighted one of the ubiquitous Japanese float planes and attacked it head on. He pulled up just a little too late and his right wing struck the biplane's top wing. Stover watched his disabled opponent crash on Guadalcanal and returned to the field with a square yard of black fabric wrapped around his wingtip. On it was the blood-red circle that was the standard Japanese aircraft marking.

Lieutenant William Woodruff was in charge of all the SBD maintenance on Guadalcanal. His mechanics had labored throughout the previous day and all night, interrupted only by the air raids and bombardments, to patch up the damaged dive bombers, the overworked men delivering them one at a time during the morning. As fast as they did, Al Cooley, the C.O. of MAG-14, whom Geiger had made bomber commander, would send each plane out to bomb the Japanese ships. A couple of hits were made in such dangerous single-plane missions, but this sort of thing was far too costly for the results obtained. A better alternative was presented during the morning by Major Jack Cram, Geiger's junior aide and the pilot of his personal aircraft, a PBY-5A amphibian. When Geiger first came to Guadalcanal and observed the situation, he had told his aide, "Until we get out of this one, you'd better just fly supplies in." Since then Cram had been using the PBY to fly "everything from toilet paper to beans" up to the island.

Cram flew into the Fighter Strip late in the afternoon of the 14th with a torpedo slung under each wing of the big amphibian. Swede Larsen had asked for these a couple of days before, but by the time the PBY brought them up from Nouméa, Torpedo Eight was out of business. Cram and Joe Renner spent the night in a foxhole during Mikawa's shelling, and the general's aide was filled in on just how bad things were: "They've got our backs molded into the wall. We've had a permanent Condition Red all day. No sirens now unless at least fifteen Jap planes come in. The F4Fs can't meet all the raids. We haven't enough gas or ammunition to send them up each time. . . . If they ever try to break through what's left today . . . God help us, Jack . . . it'll be bad."

The next morning, Cram walked purposefully back to the operations tent at the Fighter Strip. He had just visited Larsen's squadron and found that most of them were back up in the hills with the 7th Marines, equipped with small arms and fully expecting to do a little land fighting. All their TBFs were still down. If anyone was going to use those torpedoes, it wasn't going to be Torpedo Eight, but the talk had given him an idea. In the tent, Cram found Toby Munn and proposed his idea: "Toby, I've been over to see the boys in the torpedo squadron. I think we could hook up a manual release for these torpedoes on the PBY." Munn and Cram went to see Geiger; the General was badly worried about the situation and readily agreed to let his aide make the torpedo attack that he proposed. "Jack, you and Joe go see how much protection you can get. See the fighter and bomber squadrons," Geiger added.

While Cram's crew rigged manual releases for the two torpedoes that could be operated from the PBY's cockpit, Renner, Cram, and the squadron commanders planned a coordinated attack on the Japanese transports. Geiger stopped the single-plane SBD attacks, and Woodruff's mechanics were able to put together a twelve-plane attack group by 1000. The 67th furnished three P-39s and a P-400. Four F4Fs comprised the remainder of the fighter cover. The dive bombers were to climb out from the strip in a wide circle, rendezvous, and make their dives from the landward side. Cram was to climb out in the reverse direction, and make his torpedo run from the Savo Sound side of the enemy ships. This having been arranged, the major thought he'd better find out how to make a torpedo attack. He had never made one.

Roy Simpler, whose brother was a torpedo pilot but who had had no torpedo experience either, gave him a briefing of sorts: "You won't have to worry about it in this plane, but you should be under 200 knots when you drop, and about 200 feet. It'd be a good idea to come in so that two of the ships are overlapping, so if you miss one you might hit the other." To help appreciate this, it should be remembered that the twin-engine PBY was a *very* slow patrol flying boat with a normal cruising speed of perhaps 90 knots, and possessing the acrobatic ability of an anvil. Which is to say that Cram's mission, despite the humorous aspect introduced by his plane's performance characteristics, would involve his almost certain death. Jack Cram knew this perfectly well, but he was a Marine. Renner drove Cram to his plane in a jeep when everything was all ready. "This will be the most screwed-up show in history, but there's no other choice," said Renner. "If it works, miracles are still with us."

The dark-blue PBY climbed slowly away from the field, inching toward the 6,000 feet of altitude that Cram thought he would need to start the attack. He had his whole crew with him, bow gunner, flight engineer, two waist gunners, and a tunnel gunner. Only the copilot's seat was vacant. No one ever flew in that seat except Geiger.

According to the tactics agreed upon by Cram, Al Cooley, and Duke Davis, the SBDs rendezvoused east of Henderson, then swung around to attack the Japanese transports from the west. When Cram saw the first bomber roll into its dive, he was out over Savo Sound. He shoved the yoke forward and the unwieldy boat nosed over into a long dive. He was so preoccupied with his approach that he forgot all about his airspeed, which was abruptly brought to his attention by the less-than-gentle flapping of the boat's big parasol wing. Cram glanced at his air-speed indicator and was horrified to see it showing 240 knots, far in excess of what a PBY could safely take. Scared half to death, he eased gingerly back on the yoke. Still going like an elderly blue streak, the PBY flashed over the enemy's screening destroyers at 200 feet before they ever saw him. The major took aim at the transport farthest from him, and yanked first one release handle and then the other. The two torpedoes dropped into the water; one boiled straight into the side of one of the ships and exploded; the other porpoised and missed. Cram rolled the PBY into a left turn and headed back to the field, pursued by several Zekes, which shot him up thoroughly. He could see his bow gunner, who had never fired a shot in combat, blazing away at random and found time to call him on the intercom, "Lead them and let them fly into the tracers."

The big amphibian fled back to the field as best it could, with Duke Davis' fighter pilots trying to keep the Zekes off. But when Cram dived past Henderson Field and arrived over the Fighter strip, he still had one persistent enemy on his tail. Fighting 121's Roger Haberman had just entered the landing circle a few seconds before with a badly shot-up Grumman. He was in a left bank, his wheels down, starting to turn onto final landing approach, when he saw Cram's "Blue Goose" appear with the Zeke on his tail. Haberman kept the F4F in its turn, added full power, and kept its wheels down: he had no time to take the necessary twenty-nine turns on his hand crank to get them up. He missed his first attempt to get into a firing position, but turned and came right back. This time he got his plane, squirting oil furiously all the while, within forty feet of the oblivious Japanese before cutting loose with all six guns. The Zeke vanished in a flash and shower of debris that hid Haberman's F4F from sight, and flaming pieces of the enemy plane hit just beyond the edge of the field. Haberman then resumed his interrupted landing approach. Cram landed safely on the short Fighter strip, followed by the exuberant fighter pilot, who had just scored his first victory.

The General's PBY was riddled, the starboard engine hit, the fuel tanks holed, the tail surfaces almost shot off, and the port gunner's blister shattered. Word was relayed rapidly to its owner, who immediately cooked up an elaborate rib. Geiger sent for his aide, who arrived to find the Old Man glowering.

"Understand you got that plane shot up!"

"Yes, sir."

"How bad?"

"One hundred and seventy-five bullet holes, sir."

Then Geiger launched into an intricate tirade, citing destruction of government property, courts-martial, and so on, until the tired and somewhat shaken Cram was ready to get mad too. "You ungrateful old son of a bitch!" he thought—and then saw Toby Munn, a silently shaking witness to this all the while, give him a wink. Only then did he realize. "Jack, that was a damn fine job," the General said, and invited him to lunch. After the meal, Geiger told Cram to "fly it out if you can get it fixed," went back to his headquarters, and wrote out a citation for the Navy Cross for his aide.

The pounding of the Japanese transports went on through the afternoon. A flight of eleven B-17s sent up from the Espiritu Santo-based 11th Bombardment Group got three bomb hits on one of the ships. Two more coordinated attacks were made by SBDs and the 67th, and three of the ships were set on fire. The cost, though, was not negligible. Three of 141's planes were lost with their crews.

Between 1030 and 1330 the *Kyushu Maru, Sasako Maru,* and *Azumasan Maru,* all burning, were beached to keep them from sinking. Just a little before 1600 the Japanese convoy commander, Rear Admiral Takama, decided that his position under continuous air attack was too dangerous to be maintained. He had unloaded all of his troops and perhaps 80 per cent of the supplies aboard the remaining three transports. These three ships and their escorting destroyers, therefore, got under way and headed north to get out of range of the American aircraft, pushed along by a final strike by three SBDs of VB-6. It was Takama's intention to come back that night and complete the unloading of the three transports.

On the 15th the Eleventh Air Fleet sent down twenty-seven Bettys and nine Zekes, which came over the field at 1245, unopposed. What few fighters were left were unable to intercept, except for Dave Richardson of VF-5, who shot down one of the escorting fighters. His wingman was shot down off the mouth of the Tenaru River, but was rescued. One of the Japanese bombs destroyed a Fighting Five F4F on the field. With that loss, the squadron had exactly one plane left in commission.

Flights in and out of the Fighter Strip continued during the tumult of the day. Three R4Ds flew up from Espiritu Santo carrying twelve drums of gasoline each. Each 55-gallon drum was about an hour's supply for an F4F. The transport planes, landing under shellfire, hastily rolled the drums out onto the strip and took off with fifteen pilots of Fighting Five, the 67th, and VMSB-231. Six of the spare SBDs were ferried in by some of Joe Bauer's pilots from VMF-212. While planes landed and took off again, all around both airstrips, exhausted, red-eyed mechanics worked into their forty-eighth hour of continuous repairs on dozens of damaged aircraft. Gassing and arming crews pushed themselves as hard as the pilots who flew the worn-out planes they serviced. In the 67th, pilots were belting their own ammunition.

The things that were done by the men of the Cactus Air Force gave them another of the ambiguous victories so characteristic of the Guadalcanal campaign. Six Zekes were shot down during the day. The cost to the Cactus Air Force was three SBDs, one F4F, and two P-39s. Four pilots and three air gunners were killed.

October 15 was not a successful day for the Japanese. The historians of the Eleventh Air Fleet, writing about it five years later, adopted a distinctly defensive attitude: "Whereas our Zero fighters could not operate satisfactorily due to their radius of action and the enemy had its base quite close and thus had the advantage, the expected results were not obtained during this escort." The postponed unloading of the other three transports, which it was hoped to accomplish during the night never came off. What were called "liaison discrepancies" between the Japanese Army and Navy resulted in the ships returning to the Shortland Islands without having accomplished their mission. Admiral Tanaka, writing years later, avoided the circumlocutions so dear to his countrymen. "This attempt to land a completely equipped army force ended in failure," he said. That it did so was entirely due to the heroic and superhuman efforts of the pilots and ground crews of an air force that was not supposed to exist any more. But what made it like so many such victories in weeks past was that there was no relief for the victors. Things kept going very much as they always had. The ordeal of the Cactus Air Force was not to end so soon.

There was yet more drama and tragedy in the Solomons that October 15. The supply convoy that had sailed from Espiritu Santo a few days before was sighted by a scout plane from the Japanese seaplane tender *Chitose* seventy-five miles off Guadalcanal, and Nagumo's carriers organized an air attack. The supply ships wisely turned back, but the destroyer *Meredith,* towing PAB barge No. 6, and the tug *Vireo* kept on toward Guadalcanal. Just after noon, twenty-seven aircraft from the *Zuikaku* arrived and smothered *Meredith* with bombs and torpedoes. The attack was seen from miles away by a patrolling B-17, and photographed. In Espiritu Santo, the photo showed only a tug, a drifting barge—and an ominous oil slick. This was all that would be known for a while about the end of the *Meredith*.

In Espiritu Santo and Nouméa a feeling of desperate crisis was growing. Admiral Fitch ordered all ships in the harbor at Santo except the seaplane tenders to retire to Efate and New Caledonia, and the tenders to keep steam up and be ready to get under way. Ghormley sent a dispatch to Nimitz expressing the gravest view of the situation: "It appears to be all-out enemy effort against Cactus, possibly other positions also. My forces totally inadequate [to] meet situation. Urgently request all aviation reinforcement possible."

With this message, Robert Ghormley signaled the end of his naval career. On the evening of October 15, Pearl Harbor time, Admiral Nimitz met with his staff, considered the crisis, and decided that "the critical situation requires a more aggressive commander."

During the early morning hours of the 16th of October, big Japanese ships came back for the third successive naval bombardment of Henderson Field. This time it was the heavy cruisers *Myoko* and *Maya*, the former the flagship of Vice-Admiral Kondo, commander of the Second Fleet. They fired 1,500 eight-inch shells, starting twenty-five minutes after midnight, and kept it up for an hour. However, relatively little damage was done to the Fighter Strip or the airmen's living quarters.

Geiger's objective on the 16th was to try to inflict the maximum possible damage on the Japanese troops and supplies that had been landed the previous day. His resources, after three nights and two days of bombing and shelling, plus combat losses, were thin indeed. He had ten SBDs in flyable condition thanks to the almost incredible exertions of Woodruff's mechanics. The Army squadron had four P-39s and three P-400s left. These seventeen aircraft were the remaining offensive capability of the Cactus Air Force. Since it was obvious to the Americans that a major enemy land offensive against the field was imminent, Task Force 17, built around the *Hornet*, was sent north to add the strength of her air group to Geiger's handful. *Hornet* aircraft were over Guadalcanal most of the day, and in addition attacked Rekata Bay. The Cactus pilots flew seven ground-attack missions during the day, using anything from two to sixteen aircraft. As the 67th's history records: "The day ... was a weary succession of taking off, bombing and strafing, landing to refuel and rearm, and taking off again."

The planes that went out, flew up the beach to Kokumbona, and came back again were in poor shape to start with and were just about flying by the end of that long day. Of three P-400s that went out on one mission, one had only a single 30-caliber macine gun still operating, one had no guns working at all, and the third carried no bombs. Fortunately there was no enemy air opposition, but an SBD of Marine Scouting 141 was shot down by antiaircraft fire.

Japanese air efforts during the day were focused on the *Hornet* force, which was sighted late in the morning by one of their patrol planes, but which various attack groups were thereafter unable to relocate. At 1500, nine Val dive bombers flew down from Buin, searched in vain for the carrier, then headed back by way of Guadalcanal. There they found a target, and a valuable one. The old four-pipe destroyer *McFarland*, sent up from Espiritu Santo crammed with 40,000 gallons of aviation gas, a dozen torpedoes, and miscellaneous ammunition, had anchored off Lunga Point early in the afternoon and started to offload her priceless cargo. She was just starting to get under way, with a barge alongside taking off the last 350 drums of gasoline, when the Vals dove on her. One bomb hit the barge, which immediately turned into an exploding inferno. *McFarland*'s little 3-inch antiaircraft guns got one of the dive bombers, but the last one hit her on the fantail, killed twenty-seven men, and destroyed her rudder.

At exactly the moment that the *McFarland* was attacked, Joe Bauer was leading his VMF-212 into Guadalcanal after a long overwater hop from Espiritu Santo. As he circled the Fighter Strip, watching the eighteen other planes of his squadron land, he saw first the smoke and flame of the burning barge against the blue sea, then the Vals diving. His gas tanks almost empty after the trip, Bauer set out alone after the eight surviving dive bombers. He caught them only a few hundred feet up and, in full view of a hundred pilots on the Fighter Strip, shot down four of them in a matter of seconds. It was a stunning accomplishment, even for the Cactus Air Force, and was to win the Chief the Medal of Honor.

McFarland had singlehandedly relieved the gasoline

shortage by landing 20,000 gallons. Steering with her engines, she crawled to Tulagi, carrying 160 evacuated Marine and Navy men, some of them bad combat-fatigue cases, besides her own crew. She took out with her some of the enlisted men of VMF-224, VF-5, and VMSB-231. Four R4Ds that flew in forty-eight drums of aviation gasoline took back out with them Roy Simpler and five other pilots, ending the service of Fighting Five on the island after thirty-six days. John Dobbin went out with eleven pilots of VMF-224, and the last four pilots of 231 left too. With these departures, MAG-23 relinquished its control of the tactical operations of the Cactus Air Force to MAG-14, and only the valiant 67th Fighter Squadron remained of the original outfits on Guadalcanal.

12

BATTLE
FOR THE FIELD
October 17–25

The first phase of Yamamoto's plan had been a partial success. The remainder of the Sendai division had been landed, and at least some of the ammunition and rations. The Second and Third Fleets, not having sighted any American fleet units by 2100 on the 15th, retired north by prearrangement for refueling on the 17th and 18th. About midday on the 16th, enemy patrol planes sighted the *Hornet* task force south of Guadalcanal, but by then the Japanese fleet was 600 miles away and too low on fuel to do anything about it.

Geiger got an urgent dispatch from Fitch at 0325 in the morning of October 17, passing along word from Pearl Harbor that the Japanese were planning two air raids on Guadalcanal during the day, and that the first enemy aircraft would be taking off from Buka at 0500. CINCPAC's radio intelligence operation, always excellent, this time was superb. The first raid arrived at 0720, eighteen Vals and eighteen Zekes from the temporarily land-based air groups of the carriers *Hiyo* and *Junyo*. They were intercepted by eight F4Fs from VMF-121, led by Duke Davis, and slaughtered. Joe Foss, who was sleeping late that morning, awakened to the sounds of engines and machine-gun fire, and stepped out of his tent to watch. One bomber dropped its bombs in the water near Tulagi and fell flaming after them. Another glided into the sound, smoking, its impact marked by flames and a puff of black smoke. Six of the dive bombers were shot down, two by Davis himself, and four Zekes for the loss of one Marine plane. No damage was done to the two American destroyers which were their intended targets. These two ships, *Aaron Ward* and *McCalla*, undismayed by the abrupt beginning of their day, opened fire on the Japanese supply dumps at Kokumbona and poured 1,900 rounds of five-inch into them in the next three and a half hours.

Aided by their spotting from three SBDs, the destroyers started large fires, one of them 300 yards across, and much of the ammunition and supplies landed at so much cost two days before were lost to the Japanese. The 67th's P-39s and P-400s joined in the attacks after the ships had finished, and a flight of six B-17s flew up from Santo and made a devastatingly successful bomb drop. The destruction of these supply dumps later was blamed for the subsequent failure of the Japanese Army's offensive, but it appears more likely that that Army's predilection toward frontal assaults on fortified positions was a more important contributor to defeat.

Although ComSoPac may have felt Guadalcanal was virtually blockaded and may have become overly preoccupied with what the enemy was going to do—as opposed to what the Americans could do—the men of the Cactus Air Force were still full of spirit, Lieutenant (j.g.) C. H. Mester of VS-71, flying the afternoon search of the sector that included Rekata Bay on the 17th, dove on a Japanese float biplane that was just taking off and shot it down. His slow SBD immediately was pounced upon by four more biplanes and a float Zero which chased him down the Santa Isabel coast and finally shot him down. Mester and his badly wounded gunner, Forwood, survived and found their way to one of the Santa Isabel coastwatchers.

Geiger lost some of his oldest hands when Bullet Lou Kirn and the remaining pilots of Scouting Three left Guadalcanal. There were eight of them left.

The night of October 17–18 was chosen by the Japanese for the last sizable run of the Cactus Express before the Army's big attack on Henderson Field. Three cruisers and eight destroyers anchored off Tassafaronga around midnight and another five destroyers off Cape Esperance. Four of the destroyers shelled Henderson Field and the Fighter Strip for ten minutes, but little damage and no casualties resulted. The shelling and the poor condition of both fields effectively kept any American aircraft from interfering with the landing, which went off without a hitch. It was so satisfactory to

Coronado

General Hyakutake that he sent a message to Yamamoto setting October 20 as the date for the seizure of the airfield.

On the morning of October 18, a big four-engined Coronado patrol flying boat landed in the harbor of Nouméa and Vice-Admiral William F. Halsey, Jr., stepped out of it into a waiting launch. In the launch was Admiral Ghormley's aide, who handed him a double envelope containing a very short dispatch: "you will take command of the South Pacific Area and South Pacific forces immediately."

"Jesus Christ and General Jackson!" the admiral commented. "This is the hottest potato they ever handed me." With that, Halsey went aboard Ghormley's flagship, the old destroyer tender *Argonne,* and relieved him.

If it had been any other admiral than Halsey, the men of the Cactus Air Force probably would have had little interest in who happened to be holding down the job of ComSoPac. They had their hourly preoccupations with survival and with such comforts as they might find in the rain, mud, dust, and heat of Henderson Field, and in any case would not expect any vice-admiral ever to get within five hundred miles of the place. But Halsey had become publicly known in the early months of the war as a commander who looked, talked, and acted aggressively, and such a personality was long overdue in the South Pacific. Even if later tales of Marines cheering and dancing among the foxholes of Guadalcanal sound rather unlikely, the men were glad to see Bill Halsey in charge.

Admiral Kusaka's almost continuous offensive against Henderson Field and its planes went into its eighth day on the 18th, when he sent fifteen Bettys and nine Zekes down to

Guadalcanal. Kennedy on New Georgia gave the Cactus Air Force an hour's warning and the two Marine fighter squadrons prepared an ambush that would have done credit to John Smith. Sixteen F4Fs, eight each from 121 and newly arrived 212, were involved. Major F. R. Payne, exec of 212, led his eight off first, followed by Joe Foss's flight. A take-off mishap delayed the take-offs of Foss's last two men and the first five planes circled over the strip waiting for them. Foss looked back during one of the turns just in time to see three Zekes joining up on the unsuspecting latecomers. The other planes dove down on the likewise unsuspecting Japanese and shot them off the tails of their squadron mates before the latter even knew they were in trouble. The other six Zekes then came down on Foss's flight and a melee ensued; four of the total of nine Japanese fighter planes had been shot down when it was over. By the time the bombers arrived, most of their fighter protection was scattered, and planes from both squadrons lit into them. Foss was coming down in an overhead run on one of them when it suddenly blew up without his having fired a shot. Another pilot had got it first. Unperturbed, Joe flew through its wreckage, fired a couple of shots at the bomber next to it, dived through the formation, and then came up under a Betty on the other side of it, standing on his tail. On the verge of a stall, he fired a quick burst that hit the bomber's left engine. The Betty burst into flames, nosed over into a steep glide, then shed a wing and spun into the channel halfway between Guadalcanal and Tulagi. Incredibly, three of the Japanese crew survived without a scratch and were fished out of the water. The raid cost the enemy three bombers and four fighters, and the Marines only one plane in the take-off accident. VMF-121 and 212 each had a pilot missing, but both were later recovered safely.

It was a good day for Geiger as far as combat was concerned, but he still had a great deal more to worry about than Japanese bombers. Operations from Henderson Field were still harassed by sporadic Japanese artillery fire, and the strip could not be used most of the day on the 18th. To give his planes and pilots an alternative to the Fighter Strip, he started another strip under construction to the eastward, out of range of the enemy guns on the other side of the Matanikau River. The aviation gas problem was still a worrisome preoccupation for both Geiger and Fitch. The admiral ordered the minelayers *Southard* and *Hovey,* two more of the gallant ex-four-piper destroyers, to load 175 drums of gasoline each on deck and run up to Guadalcanal. More substantial aid was forthcoming when a search unit of ships found the tug *Vireo* and a drifting PBA barge that had been sighted the day before from the air. The tug *Seminole* took the barge under tow for the island. She was loaded with 2,000 drums of gasoline, almost ten days' supply for the depleted air force.

While the Cactus Air Force fought on among the towering clouds over Guadalcanal, the Sendai division marched invisibly through its dark jungles far below. It was moving from the assembly and supply areas near Kokumbona toward the positions from which it was to assault and overwhelm the American airfield on the night of October 20. Already, though, its march through the damp forest was slowing down, and it was proving impossible to bring along the artillery pieces and ammunition carried to the island at the cost of so much effort and blood.

The Eleventh Air Fleet kept formations of Zekes patrolling over Henderson Field from midmorning to midafternoon on the 19th, but there was only one brief brush between them and the Cactus fighter pilots.

The fighter pilots were up almost all day covering two most important arrivals. The old *Southard* arrived early in the morning with her 175 drums of aviation gas, and at 1300 the *Seminole* towed PAB Barge 4 into Tulagi. With her arrival Geiger could breathe a little more freely. Now he could keep his airplanes flying for a while.

The *raison d'être* for all the Japanese actions and American reactions of the past week, the Sendai Division, still writhed unseen through the wet darkness of the Guadalcanal jungles. The Japanese had to hack their way along, moving with agonizing slowness in a long single file that stretched and undulated through the trackless rain forest like a blind earthworm. General Maruyama was nowhere near where he was supposed to be on the 20th, and sent a message to Yamamoto postponing the attack on Henderson Field until the 22nd. Nagumo's and Kondo's fleets, which had refueled on the 17th and 18th in preparation for the big day, steamed to and fro in frustration, advised of occasional tantalizing glimpses of American ships.

Henderson Field was still closed for flight operations by Japanese artillery fire through October 22. The enemy was using at least one of his big 6-inch howitzers and some

75-millimeter mountain guns. These fired sporadically, and the Marines attributed the fire to a single piece, called either "Pistol Pete" or "Millimeter Mike." Besides closing Henderson completely, the Japanese shells began falling within 500 yards of the Fighter Strip. Things were slowly closing in on the Cactus Air Force.

The fickle weather was good enough on October 23 for Admiral Kusaka to send the largest force of bombers in several weeks, sixteen Bettys with an escort of twenty-eight Zekes. They arrived at 1130. Colonel Bauer, who had taken over as fighter commander when Colonel Wallace left, scrambled everything he had, twenty-four F4Fs and four P-39s. The result was a classic fighter melee. Joe Bauer, an aggressive, inspiring leader, was willing to meet the Zekes on their own terms. "When you see Zeros, dogfight 'em," he ordered.

Duke Davis and Joe Foss each led a flight of F4Fs, as did Major Fred Payne, Bauer's exec. Foss was following Davis' eight planes when they sighted five enemy fighters at their altitude. Both flights turned toward the Japanese, and in his turn Foss looked up to see a whole pack of Zekes diving on them. He quickly led his flight into a turn and dove to pick up speed. The Japanese fighters piled into Davis, and both formations broke up in a dogfight. Foss eased in behind a Zeke that was on the tail of an F4F and let him have a burst from all six guns at a range of only a few feet. As almost always happened, the enemy fighter exploded, its engine whirling off from the cloud of pieces, its burning wings sailing down like fiery maple seeds. He dove onto the tail of another, followed him into an ill-advised loop, and at the top of it, inverted, gave him the burst that blew this Zeke up, too. A couple of minutes later Foss collected a burst in his engine and once again had to make a long dead-stick glide back to the strip, reflecting ruefully that this was the fourth F4F he had crashed or brought back shot up. Overhead, one of the biggest dogfights ever fought over Guadalcanal was coming to an end. Columns of black smoke in the jungle and on the sea marked places where enemy planes had crashed, and a lone Japanese slowly floated down in his parachute behind a spinning fighter.

None of the Marine fighters were lost, although one plane landed in such bad shape that it was promptly rolled over to the boneyard. Seven others were shot up in varying degrees. Joe Bauer's assessment of the situation had been proven right. It would have been suicide for an F4F to dogfight a Zeke a month before, but the attrition of September's and October's hard fighting had cost the Japanese their best fighter pilots, and their replacements lacked experience and skill. As always happened in such confused combats, claims were grossly overstated, totaling twenty Zekes and two Bettys. It is not known what their losses were, since the Japanese narratives glossed over the events of the day even more than they usually did. That they were quite heavy is highly probable.

Spectacular as the dogfighting of the 23rd was, it affect-ed the course of events not at all. General Maruyama, who had further delayed his attack to the 23rd, now postponed it another twenty-four hours to 1700, October 24. However, this decision was not communicated to the western arm of his two-pronged force and it attacked on the previous schedule—a full day early. It was almost completely wiped out by Marine artillery fire.

Far out at sea on the 23rd, hundreds of miles from the island, one of Fitch's PBYs located a Japanese carrier. He held contact until he was relieved by another flying boat, which shadowed the enemy through most of the day. At dusk three more PBYs carrying torpedoes took off to attack the Japanese ships. The Japanese had repeatedly sighted Admiral W. A. Lee's Task Force 64, built around the new battleship *Washington,* most lately on the 22nd. But they had not yet seen the American carriers and it made them most uneasy to be tracked continuously by PBYs while their adversary's main strength remained unlocated. It made them still more uneasy when one of the night-flying boats located and made a torpedo run on a cruiser. With their fuel supply again depleted, Nagumo and Kondo refueled quickly at a rendez-vous 450 miles north of Guadalcanal early on the 24th, and headed south, feeling themselves in a strategically inferior position.

The same day, a thousand miles southwest of the Japa-nese fleets, the American carriers about which they were so concerned were rendezvousing below the New Hebrides. For more than a month the *Hornet* had been the only Ameri-can carrier in the South Pacific. Today she was joined by the veteran *Enterprise,* back from her repairs at Pearl Harbor, with a splendid new battleship, *South Dakota,* for an escort.

The two carrier forces, Task Forces 17 and 16, respectively, were commanded by Rear Admiral Thomas Kinkaid, recently a cruiser division commander, with his flag on *Enterprise*. Had Halsey not been unexpectedly ordered to take over the whole South Pacific, he would have been commanding the carriers. However, from his headquarters in Nouméa he issued specific orders to Kinkaid. *Enterprise* and *Hornet* were to run north along the New Hebrides chain, round the Santa Cruz Islands, then retire southwest to cover Guadalcanal.

It rained most of the night of October 23–24 on Guadalcanal, but Maruyama's sodden, patient infantrymen reached their jump-off positions south of Henderson Field by noon of the 24th. The Fighter Strip was soaked and virtually unusable —the dawn SBD patrols were unable to take off until 0700. Roy Geiger, temporarily commanding on the island while Vandegrift was conferring with Halsey in Nouméa, put in an emergency call to Fitch for more aviation gas and sent Jack Cram down in the PBY for a load of artillery shells. The big air battle of the previous day had used up most of the gasoline on the island, and the Marine artillerymen had almost fired themselves out of ammunition. The PBY and four R4Ds took off from Espiritu Santo with the ammunition and gasoline, but had to return when Geiger reported the strip too wet to take transports.

The rain kept Japanese aircraft away from the island all day, and restricted American flying to routine searches and a few ground-attack missions. It abated somewhat in the afternoon in time to permit the landing of the transport planes carrying their desperately needed cargoes.

General Maruyama's long-expected general attack against Henderson Field finally started at 2200 on the night of the 24th, in the middle of a torrential rain. To the surprise of the Americans, though, it came from the south, along the line of Bloody Ridge, the scene of Edson's epic battle in mid-September. But the Marines rapidly recovered from the initial shock, stabilized their lines, and stood off six successive charges during the night and early morning hours. The battalion commander running the battle, Lieutenant Colonel Lewis Puller, began feeding in an Army battalion piecemeal to reinforce his thin line. A Japanese colonel with a small party pushed through into the rear of the Marine position. His exploit resulted in a report that the airfield had been captured, and this was passed first to General Hyakutake at

17th Army Headquarters, then on to Admiral Yamamoto. This was the message which the Navy had been awaiting for two months. It was the prearranged signal for a number of things to take place. The 26th Air Flotilla of the Eleventh Air Fleet was to fly down to Guadalcanal and land on the field—as it was originally scheduled to do on August 7, the day the Marines seized it. A force of three destroyers was to run through Indispensable Strait and land Japanese troops at Koli Point, east of the field. A cruiser-destroyer force was to move in and furnish gunfire support to the Army on Guadalcanal, and this was to be further assisted by Mikawa's Eighth Fleet and Kondo's Second Fleet. Now the message had been sent and all these things were started in motion.

October 25 was a Sunday, to become famous in the annals of Guadalcanal as "Dugout Sunday," the day that enemy artillery, planes, and ships combined to keep most of the people on the island in their foxholes all day. However, not many men of the Cactus Air Force spent that Sunday in a dugout. It was the most active day yet in the short, chaotic history of that organization. It started very badly, with Henderson Field closed by artillery that fired a round into it every ten minutes, and the Fighter Strip a swamp usable only with extreme danger. Nothing was able to take off at all except for six SBDs flown by brave Marines from VMSB-141. They left at dawn for the regular morning searches. One of them sighted the three destroyers thirty-five miles away rushing in toward Guadalcanal at 20 knots.

The Eleventh Air Fleet sent down a big two-engined reconnaissance plane with an escort of eight Zekes to find out if the field was ready for occupation. They arrived at 0800 and circled overhead while the fighter pilots, unable to get their F4Fs off the strip, watched in helpless anger. Finally, either because its pilot wasn't sure what he was seeing or just out of bravado, the big plane dove and flew the entire length of the Fighter Strip right down on the deck. Every machine gun, rifle, and pistol on the field fired at him and he pulled up into a steep wingover, then dove straight into the trees beyond the field to explode with a shattering roar. It was a most satisfactory outcome as far as the besieged Cactus flyers were concerned. Someone was seen later trying to take a flying boot off a dismembered leg in the wreckage.

Japanese fighters were still circling overhead like vultures as the sun dried the strip sufficiently to operate aircraft. About 0930 Joe Foss took off with four other F4Fs to tangle with the Zekes. They met six of them at 1,500 feet and set up a "scissors"—always turning into the opponents and meeting them head-on—which enabled them to climb safely to 6,000 feet and have enough air room to begin dogfighting the Japanese. The flight claimed five Zekes.

The three destroyers sighted earlier in the morning by one of the SBD search planes were off Lunga Point shortly after 1000. Pursuing two old destroyer-minelayers, they encountered, overwhelmed, and sank the tug *Seminole* and a yard patrol craft carrying gasoline from Tulagi to Guadalcanal. The two fleeing four-pipers, *Trever* and *Zane,* escaped, in part because the Japanese destroyers were attacked and strafed repeatedly by a flight of four F4Fs from VMF-212. The ships reversed course, briefly shelled the beach until one of them picked up three hits from one of the Marines' 5-inch coast-defense guns, and retreated back whence they had come.

The four fighters from 212 had turned back the destroyers were jumped on the way back to the field by some of the forty Zekes that kept up an almost constant patrol over Guadalcanal through the day. One of the four, Jack Conger, used up all his ammunition shooting up the ships and downing an enemy fighter. Just off the beach, he was engaged by another Zeke, and in the course of the fight found himself slightly below his opponent's tail. Determined to get him, guns or no, he pulled back on the stick and chewed the Zeke's tail off with his propeller. Both planes went down out of control. Conger bailed out of his spinning F4F, swung twice, and hit the water. A moment later the Japanese pilot dropped into the sound in his chute. A landing boat picked up Conger and headed over toward the other swimmer. The Japanese tried to kick the boat away, and Conger reached out with a boat hook and snagged his belt. The Japanese pulled out a huge Nambu pistol, pointed it at the Marine, and pulled the trigger. Nothing happened. Then he turned the gun on himself, again with no result. A sailor grabbed the pistol, and the reluctant survivor was hauled aboard to ride back to shore with his late adversary.

Behind the three Japanese destroyers, intending to furnish additional fire support for the abortive Koli Point land-

Nambu Pistol

ing, came the old light cruiser *Yura* and five destroyers, commanded by Rear Admiral Takama, commander Destroyer Squadron Four. This group was picked up 110 miles away by one of the morning SBDs at 0830, but it was not until after noon that the field dried sufficiently for an attack group—five of the twelve flyable SBDs—to take off safely with bombs. The group was led by Eldridge. They found the *Yura* and her consorts thirty miles northeast of Florida Island at 1300. The five dive bombers circled high overhead as the flight leader quickly designated the targets each was to attack. Then John Eldridge throttled back, "split his flaps"—opened the SBD's wing-mounted dive brakes—and rolled over into a near-vertical dive on the Japanese cruiser. He didn't use his bombsight; long experience told him just where he should keep his tight-turning target in relation to his engine cowling. Gentle but increasing pressure on left rudder kept the plane from skidding in its headlong dive; slight aileron turns were all that was necessary to keep the cruiser where she belonged.

At 3,000 feet Eldridge reached forward and pulled a handle on his instrument panel, feeling a slight jolt as his bomb released. Then he pulled out smoothly, he and his gunner briefly subjected to three or four times the normal force of gravity. A few seconds later his 1,000-pound bomb made a direct hit on the thin-skinned old Japanese cruiser, and she slowly shuddered to a halt. The next man near-missed the destroyer *Akizuki*, Admiral Takamas flagship, and another pilot put a 500-pounder in the water next to the *Yura*. Near misses would be almost as dangerous to ships as hits, since the force of the explosion was transmitted through the water to the hull plates.

An hour and twenty minutes later three P-39s attacked the crippled *Yura* and two of them near-missed the cruiser. At 1500, Ray Davis of Bombing Six came out with three other SBDs, including Coit and Doughty, who had been in on the first mission. Davis got a near miss on the *Akizuki* and Coit another one on the *Yura*. The cruiser was flooding fast, and her captain got permission to beach her on Fara Island, but it was too late. Eldridge was back again at 1630 leading a group of four SBDs, four P-39s, and three F4Fs. One of the Army planes got a direct hit on the cruiser with a 500-pounder, which was seen by a coastwatcher on Santa Isabel, and there was another near miss on the *Akizuki*. Half an hour later six B-17s attacked the cruiser and claimed two more hits. The old *Yura* was too heavily damaged now to be saved. She was abandoned by her crew west of Cape Astrolabe, Santa Isabel, and her sinking was hastened by torpedoes from two of her escorts. *Akizuki*, a boiler room and starboard engines disabled, managed to crawl to safety. Using only part of an available striking force of twelve dive bombers and four P-39s, the Cactus Air Force had sunk a 5,000-ton cruiser and driven off the rest of the Japanese bombardment group. Admiral Mikawa hastily reversed his course and, in the inimitable phraseology of the Japanese accounts of those days, "decided to assemble his forces in rear areas until the recapture of the Guadalcanal airfield was definitely reported."

While Geiger's tiny surviving force of SBDs was dealing with the *Yura*, his fighters were in almost continuous combat over Henderson Field. A log for the busiest part of the afternoon gives a laconic account of the most furious air fighting of the entire campaign:

1423 Condition Red. 16 bombers five miles out at 20,000 feet altitude.

1424 Enemy planes split into groups. 16 bombers coming over in a straight line.

1430 Bombs dropped along beach near Kukum.

1434 One bomber shot down.

1435 Another bomber with motor shot out. Bombers going out.

1436 2 Zeros shot down over field. Another bomber coming down.

1442 Another enemy formation coming in.

1450 Dogfights overhead.

1451 One Zero shot down.

1452 Another flight coming in very low, 10 miles out.

1456 Zeros strafed airfield.

1457 3 Zeros coming in, 5 miles out.

1500 9 dive bombers over field; bombed graveyard of wrecked planes. ["Right in my boneyard," Geiger chortled as he watched.]

1501 8 Zeros to the southwest.

1503 2 groups of enemy planes going out. A few Zeros still prowling around.

1507 6 Zeros coming in at 4,000 feet. Strafe field.

1508 3 groups of planes going out.

1516 Condition Green.

The MAG-23 war diary—which by then really was recording the combat activities of all of the First Marine Air Wing—succinctly summarizes the fighter pilots' day: "Enemy fighter planes were over Cactus at irregular intervals throughout the daylight hours. Our Grummans were almost continuously in the air, landing, refueling, reloading, and taking off again time after time."

Duke Davis' flight intercepted the Bettys (there were nine of them, not sixteen), and claimed five. Joe Foss and his men went up again after the bombers had left and tangled with more Zekes, raising the total day's claims to seventeen enemy fighters and five bombers. The Japanese records show that nine Zekes were lost over Guadalcanal on the 25th—just about one out of every four sent down—and do not mention any bomber losses, although there undoubtedly were some.

By evening of October 25 the two-week-long Japanese air effort was spent, and its objective—the destruction of the Cactus Air Force—still unobtained. The valor of the American airmen, stretched to the limits of human endurance, won against superior numbers. On this heroic day the blood brotherhood that adversity had forged from a handful of pilots, air gunners, and mechanics triumphed for the last time against efforts specifically intended to destroy it. The cost of the victory was high. At the end of the day Roy Geiger had twelve out of thirty-five fighters flying, and his only striking power was eleven SBDs and six Army Bells. The pilots had given him everything they had for two hideous weeks, and now they were drained and exhausted. They didn't know it yet, but the Eleventh Air Fleet was finished. Its losses during those two weeks in October were twenty-five twin-engine bombers and close to eighty fighters. Its power was so reduced that it never again was to undertake a major bombing mission against Henderson Field.

13

SANTA CRUZ
October 26

With the intervention of the Japanese and American carrier forces, the scene of the critical battle for the control of the air over Guadalcanal shifted from the skies over Henderson Field to the open-ocean areas west of the Solomons. The great gray ships of both Navies had almost four hundred aircraft between them, strength that dwarfed the shattered Eleventh Air Fleet and the few dozen survivors of the Cactus Air Force. The outcome of the imminent battle between the carriers, their aircraft serving the functions once performed by guns, could decide the extent to which the Japanese would be able to land soldiers on Guadalcanal without American air interference. With a decisive Japanese victory, the Marines inevitably would be overcome. If the Americans triumphed, their supply lines to the beachhead would be safe at last and the island's security against counterattack guaranteed. So, as the air fighting subsided over Guadalcanal, the burden of the battle momentarily was to be assumed by the fleets.

The Japanese had two fleets, Nagumo's Third and Kondo's Second, spread far apart in one of their characteristically complex dispositions. Admiral Nagumo's fleet was built around the two largest and most modern carriers in the Imperial Navy, *Shokaku* and *Zuikaku,* veterans of Pearl Harbor, the Coral Sea, and the Eastern Solomons. They had with them a light carrier, *Zuiho,* converted from a submarine tender. The three carriers had a screen of one cruiser and eight destroyers. Forty miles south of them was a force of two battleships, four cruisers, and seven destroyers. Its functions were to provide surface gunfire support to the carriers, should this be needed and, more important, to furnish an imposing-looking target between the carriers and the Americans that might absorb bombs otherwise destined for vital flight decks. A hundred miles west of Nagumo was Kondo with two battleships, five cruisers, and fourteen destroyers. Kondo's fleet included a single carrier, *Junyo*, flying the flag of the aggressive Rear Admiral Kakuji Kakuda, commander Carrier Division 2.

Kinkaid's forces were tactically concentrated, *Enterprise* and *Hornet* steaming within sight of each other. The "Big E" was screened by four cruisers and six destroyers. In ships the American admiral obviously was heavily outnumbered. However, in carrier battles it is aircraft that matter, not ships; Kinkaid was outnumbered here, too, 212 to 172.

The Japanese air groups had been reinforced since the Eastern Solomons battle, but not sufficiently to make up for the losses of August 24 and the slaughter of their fighters by the Cactus Air Force on August 29. However, the squadrons of *Shokaku* and *Zuikaku* in particular were commanded by highly skilled and experienced aviators who had been in every battle since Pearl Harbor. Some of them were survivors of Midway. These men were the very best in the Imperial Japanese Navy—and, after Midway, they were all that were left.

The Americans had one experienced air group, *Hornet*'s and one brand new one, *Enterprise*'s Air Group Ten. The *Hornet* group, led by Commander Walter Rodee, was one of those conglomerates of squadrons snatched from other carriers or hastily reformed after decimation at Midway. It included VF-72, one of *Wasp*'s two fighter squadrons, commanded by the violently outspoken "Mike" Sanchez; Scouting Eight and Bombing Eight, both of them original *Hornet* squadrons, were led respectively by "Gus" Widhelm, one of naval aviation's more famous characters because of his combativeness and colorful vocabulary, and Lieutenant James Vose. The torpedo squadron, VT-6, was one that had been re-formed when the first one of that number, the *Enterprise*'s, was wiped out at Midway. Its skipper was Lieutenant E. B. Parker, nicknamed "Iceberg" for good and sufficient reason.

Air Group Ten was the first of the newly trained air

groups to get out to the Pacific, and the first to be assigned a number instead of the name of its parent ship. Its commander was Lieutenant Commander Richard Gaines. Lieutenant Commander John Collett, a suave, handsome regular, was the C.O. of Torpedo Ten. Bombing Ten's skipper was John Thomas, and Scouting Ten was commanded by James R. Lee, called "Bucky." The outstanding man in the air group, though, was the fighter squadron commander, Jimmy Flatley. A quick, small, nervous man, he was a superb flyer and fighter, deeply religious and a born leader who had an almost telepathic rapport with his pilots. One of them recalls sitting with him in the carrier's ready room while some of the squadron's planes were landing. Suddenly the crash alarm sounded on deck above. Flatley looked up slowly and said, "That was Bobby, wasn't it?" He was right—it had been the pilot he *knew* it was. This intuitive sensitivity made the pilots of Fighting Ten worship Jimmy Flatley. But this remarkable man was not only a pilot and leader; he was a tactical innovator. Along with another squadron commander, Jimmy Thach of Fighting Three, he developed fighter tactics built around the two-plane section as the basic unit that enabled Marine and Navy pilots to win against the almost impossible odds of 1942 air fighting in the Pacific.

The Japanese had been shadowed all the morning of the 25th by one of Fitch's Vanikoro-based PBYs, but the Americans were not located by the enemy, except for a surface-ship force built around the battleship *Washington*. That force, under Rear Admiral W. A. Lee, was staying near Guadal-canal, waiting to intervene if enemy ships threatened the beachhead again. The Japanese, attributing to the Americans the same complicated tactical subterfuges that they themselves favored, assumed that Lee was a decoy and that the unseen carriers were lurking on one of their flanks, waiting to strike from ambush. Their nervousness was increased by the apparent immunity of the American PBYs, despite strong fighter patrols around their carriers. The Japanese, convinced that a trap was waiting to be sprung on them, reversed course. Kinkaid, on the strength of the PBY's report, sent out a search and attack group late in the afternoon, but the patrol plane, dodging enemy fighters, had missed their turn north. The carrier planes therefore failed to find the Japanese, who had withdrawn out of range. Shortly before midnight, Yamamoto ordered his fleets to expect a battle on the 26th, and they turned south once more.

A PBY night striking force left Espiritu Santo on the afternoon of October 25 and two of the three boats found the Japanese carrier force at around 0200 the next morning. One of them dropped two 500-pound bombs close aboard *Zuikaku,* engulfing her bridge in smoke, flying right over the big carrier at low altitude. Another, flown by Lieutenant Commander J. O. Cobb, skipper of VP-91, made a torpedo run on the destroyer *Isokaze,* the first one ever made under full radar control. Cobb's radar operator picked the ship up at twelve miles and coached him in on the correct compass heading. The PBY gradually let down in the darkness until the highly inaccurate pressure altimeter was indicating only 100 feet. Cobb skittered over the invisible surface of the sea until his target suddenly loomed up ahead of him. He pulled the release lanyard, but they were in too close; the torpedo did not have enough of a run to arm its exploder mechanism and *Isokaze* escaped. But this visitation was too much for the nervous Admiral Nagumo. He convinced himself that he had been led into a trap by the wily Americans, and at 0250 reversed course to the northward at 24 knots. An hour later Kondo's Second Fleet followed suit.

Fitch's PBYs maintained intermittent contact with the Japanese through most of the night. About 0300, one of them accurately reported Nagumo's position, then some 200 miles northwest of Kinkaid. In another of the communications foul-ups that plagued naval aviation throughout the whole Pacific war, the flying boat's contact report was not relayed to Kinkaid for another two hours. Those two hours were to cost the Americans all the tactical advantage of knowing where their enemy was, and a carrier that they could ill afford to lose.

Both fleets sent off air searches before dawn. Nagumo launched sixteen seaplanes from the battleships and cruisers and eight torpedo bombers from the carriers. Sixteen SBDs from VB-10 and VS-10 took off from *Enterprise* starting at 0512, and fanned out in two-plane teams, each team to search a 15-degree sector out to a distance of 200 miles from the ship. The sectors to be searched ranged from 235 degrees— southwest by west—around to due north. Each SBD carried a 500-pound bomb.

With the fleets so close together and the air searches

spreading out like waves from a pebble dropped in a pool, it did not take very long for them to discover each other. The weather was good, scattered fair-weather cumulus clouds at 1,300 feet and occasional tropical rain showers. The first pair to see anything was Bombing Ten's Welch and McGraw, searching the western sector, who passed one of Nagumo's carrier aircraft on a reciprocal course about eighty-five miles from the *Enterprise*. Half an hour later they found the battleship-cruiser force that was bringing up Nagumo's rear. The two SBDs pulled up into the clouds and took a careful count of the Japanese ships before radioing a contact report back to the *Enterprise* at 0630. At exactly the same time, one of the Japanese float planes, having sighted the American carriers, was making his report to Nagumo.

The three Japanese carriers had a total of sixty-seven aircraft waiting for this moment. Further confirmation came a few minutes later when one of *Shokaku*'s Kates sighted the *Hornet*. At 0710 eighteen Zekes were launched by the *Shokaku* and were joined by another nine fighters from the *Zuiho*. *Zuikaku* launched eighteen Kate torpedo bombers. Finally, the fighters were followed off the *Shokaku* by the attack-group commander, Lieutenant Commander Mamoru Seki, leading his squadron of twenty-two Vals.

The American carriers were twenty minutes behind the Japanese in getting their attack groups off, and when they did their tactics virtually preordained failure. *Hornet* had only fifteen SBDs, six TBFs, and eight fighters "spotted"—arranged in takeoff order—on her flight deck. Why her remaining dive bombers and torpedo planes were down on the hangar deck is not clear. Perhaps her deck was still spotted for the night launch for which her air group had been standing by most of the night. At any rate, *Hornet* launched the twenty-nine planes she had on deck at 0730, then frantically started bringing up the rest on both her elevators. The first wave was commanded by Gus Widhelm, who had six other SBDs from his own squadron and eight from Vose's. The dive bombers climbed to 12,000 feet, with the four fighters above and ahead of them, while Parker's six TBFs stayed down at 800 feet. They headed off toward the Japanese fleet at 0750.

Enterprise started launching her air group, such as there was of it, at 0750. Twenty of her SBDs had been committed to the morning search and to antisubmarine patrols, and only

Nakajima 97 "Kate"

three dive bombers were left for the attack group. Jack
Collett had only eight torpedo planes. Dick Gaines, the CAG,
had a ninth TBF, but carried only bombs. This minute force
was escorted by eight F4Fs of Fighting Ten, one division led
by Jimmy Flatley himself, the other by Lieutenant John
Leppla.

Admiral Kinkaid on *Enterprise* was understandably anxious to attack the Japanese carriers as soon as possible.
Midway had shown that the cardinal rule of carrier warfare
was to get in the first blow and cripple the enemy flight decks.
In applying this lesson, though, Kinkaid and his staff forgot
another one, that air attacks should be concentrated and
coordinated. He ordered *Enterprise*'s Air Group Ten to join
the *Hornet* air group if this would cause no delay, otherwise
to proceed independently to the target. However, as the planes
were being launched, this order was modified. Pilots taxiing up
to the take-off spot on the flight deck saw a sailor holding up a

small blackboard on which was chalked the message: "Proceed without *Hornet*."

The smaller *Enterprise* group, taking less time to rendezvous, started out toward the enemy at almost the same time that the *Hornet* aircraft did. The two groups were flying side by side but several miles apart, spread all over the sky. Gus Widhelm's SBDs were almost 8,000 feet higher than Collett's two divisions of TBFs, while Parker, down on the water, soon mistook the *Enterprise* air group for his own and followed them. Gaines climbed rapidly above the rest of his air group and surveyed them in lonely grandeur 3,000 feet above for the remainder of the mission. Although he was the senior aviator present, it apparently did not occur to him to get closer to the *Hornet* group for mutual support en route and for greater impact in the attack.

About 0800, as *Hornet*'s first attack group and the *Enterprise* aircraft started toward the Japanese, *Hornet* began launching her second wave. This consisted of nine SBDs, nine TBF's, and an escort of seven F4Fs. Walter Rodee, *Hornet*'s CAG, commanded these aircraft, flying a tenth TBF. None of the torpedo planes carried torpedoes, but were loaded only with four 500-pound bombs. This was another error of judgment. The torpedo, when skillfully used, was one of the most dangerous weapons that could be employed against a ship. Using TBFs as horizontal bombers, with small bombs at that, was equivalent to sending them out without any weapons at all. By 0810 seventy-five American aircraft, flying in three loose-knit groups ten miles or so apart, were on their way to attack Nagumo.

The Japanese were not without their problems either. At 0650, shortly before their first attack wave was launched, their carriers were sighted by Lieutenant Commander Bucky Lee and Ensign Johnson of VS-6, flying the 298–314-degree search sector from *Enterprise*. The two SBDs climbed to altitude, sending their contact report four times without getting any acknowledgment from the ship. As they closed to within fifteen miles of Nagumo's ships, they were jumped by the enemy combat air patrol. Lee shot down a Zeke with his forward guns, and Johnson claimed two more. Both SBDs made for clouds in the hope of losing their opposition and, in the process of skipping from cumulus to cumulus, lost each other too.

Lee's contact report alerted most of the other search

pairs, and those who received it abandoned their now superfluous missions and headed over toward the enemy carriers. Lieutenant Ward and Ensign Carmody from an adjacent sector arrived first and were maneuvering into a dive position when the Japanese CAP, fresh from driving off Lee and Johnson, jumped them. Their rear gunners, Baumgartner and Liska, each claimed a Zeke in the resulting melee, but the two SBDs were driven off without having made an attack. While the enemy fighters were thus embroiled, though, another pair arrived led by Lieutenant Birney Strong, a veteran of old Scouting Five and the Battle of the Eastern Solomons. Strong and Chuck Irvine, his wingman, climbed to 14,000 feet unobserved and unobstructed by any air opposition. There they picked out a carrier that was visible through the scattered clouds.

At about 0730, his position perfect, Strong throttled back, split his flaps, and rolled into a vertical bank—a lot of bottom rudder, and the SBD turned, simultaneously nosing over into a seventy-degree dive. Irvine followed a few thousand feet behind. Their target was the *Zuiho*. The first she knew that she was under attack was when Strong's dive bomber flashed out of the clouds, then pulled sharply back up into them, closely followed by Irvine. In rapid succession two 500-pound bombs hit aft on the flight deck of the small carrier, blowing a fifty-foot hole in it and starting a brief fire. *Zuiho* was in no danger of sinking, but Captain Obayashi shortly reported her unable either to recover or to launch aircraft. The SBDs were vainly chased for forty-five miles by vengeful Zekes, and each of their gunners claimed one enemy fighter. Strong's and Irvine's two little Douglases had put one of Nagumo's carriers out of the battle and, moreover, escaped without a scratch.

At 0800 the second Japanese attack group took off from the two carriers that remained operational. Its leader was Lieutenant Commander Shigeharu Murata, commanding *Shokaku*'s torpedo squadron, with twelve Kates. He had with him twenty Vals of *Zuikaku*'s dive-bomber squadron, and the same ship furnished the fighter protection, sixteen Zekes. Murata's group headed toward Kinkaid just minutes after Widhelm and Gaines took departure toward the Japanese.

The earlier launch of the first Japanese wave and the higher cruise speed of their aircraft now began to affect the balance of the battle. The two leading American groups were only sixty miles from their own ships when they were sighted by Lieutenant Commander Seki's inbound aircraft. First they saw Widhelm's dive bombers, but by the time the Japanese fighter leader realized they were enemy, the two groups had passed each other. Just a few miles farther on, though, they sighted Air Group Ten, and this time the Japanese made no such error.

About thirty minutes out on their course, the aircraft of Air Group Ten were still gaining altitude. The TBFs were flying in two divisions of four planes each, the first led by Jack Collett, the other flying to his left and a little behind. They were at 6,000 feet, climbing at 120 knots. A thousand feet above them on each bow was a division of Fighting Ten's F4Fs. The four on the port side of the formation were Leppla's division; on the starboard side, Jimmy Flatley's. The last thing for which the group was prepared was a fight. Some of the TBFs hadn't turned on their radio transmitters and many of the fighters hadn't even charged their guns. The two divisions of F4Fs were gently weaving back and forth to maintain position over the slow-climbing SBDs and TBFs. No one was keeping any sort of lookout this close to their own task force. This cost them dearly. "Eternal vigilance or eternal rest," said Flatley later in his candid report of the affair.

Flatley looked out to port, preparatory to starting another weave, to see the sickening sight of Jack Collett's TBF spinning seaward in flames, and Leppla's division diving in behind the TBF formation to dogfight with a group of Zekes. The attacking formation was the escort fighter group from *Zuiho,* nine Zekes led by Lieutenant Hidaka. The Japanese attack was well executed, Hidaka having come in from above the lumbering American formation out of the sun. The three Zekes that hit the TBFs each scored, one shooting Collett's plane down, the other two damaging a pair of the torpedo bombers so badly that both had to return and ditch near the task force. A fourth TBF went down in flames, and no one got out. Three chutes were seen from Jack Collett's aircraft, but he and his crew were never seen again.

Leppla, taken by surprise, committed a tactical error fatal to him and his division. Instead of warning Flatley and turning toward the other four F4Fs—which would have enabled them to shoot the enemy off his tail—he turned into the Japanese fighters. This embroiled him in a dogfight with the far more maneuverable Zekes, left him far astern of the formation he was supposed to protect, and deprived him of Flatley's support. The fight was over quickly. Leppla bailed out of his crippled plane, but plunged over a mile into the ocean, streaming a partially opened chute behind him. Two others in his division were shot down, to be picked out of the water later by a Japanese destroyer.

The shattered *Enterprise* formation regrouped as best it could. Only three SBDs, five TBFs, and Flatley's division of fighters were left. Meanwhile, Widhelm's *Hornet* dive bombers, ahead and to port of the remnants of *Enterprise*'s Air Group Ten, crossed their bow and drifted over to starboard on a more northerly course. About 150 miles from the *Hornet,* at 0920, they sighted the Japanese Vanguard Force of battleships and cruisers. This force had a combat air patrol of nine Zekes, which immediately were engaged by the four-plane division of Fighting 72 accompanying the SBDs. These four fighters, led by the squadron's fiery skipper, Mike Sanchez, dropped back to fight the Zekes, and Widhelm's fifteen SBDs continued on.

Five minutes later the dive bombers sighted two of the carriers of Nagumo's fleet, *Zuiho* still smoking. Two big black bursts of antiaircraft fire appeared in front of them, and in less than a minute the *Hornet* aircraft were under attack by the Third Fleet's CAP. Gus Widhelm had his defense organized to a fare-thee-well. His rear seat gunner, Stokely, acted as fire-control director for the whole formation: over the intercom he told Widhelm what the enemy fighters were doing, and Gus would turn one way or another as much as he could to throw off the fighters' aim without reducing the gunners' field of fire.

The Japanese fighters tried stubbornly and skillfully, but they could not break up Widhelm's compact formation. They could only claw savagely at its extremities, and this began to cost the dive bombers one plane after another. Lieutenant (j.g.) Philip Grant of Bombing Eight was shot down first, both he and his gunner killed. Lieutenant (j.g.) Fisher, his wingman, suffered severe damage to his plane and landed it in the water. He and his gunner were not recovered. Next Lieutenant (j.g.) White turned back, his left aileron shot off, and bullets through a shoulder and one of his hands. Painfully wounded, his plane only partially controllable, he somehow got back to the task force and landed safely aboard the

Enterprise. All the remaining twelve SBDs were riddled by machine-gun and cannon fire and two of the rear gunners wounded. Widhelm's oil line was cut and his plane began to trail smoke. Straight and true on his compass course, he flew on toward the distant carriers. Santa Cruz is an obscure battle, lost now in the great events that took place afterward. But there are few moments in the long history of the United States Navy as heroic as that which saw the indomitable little formation from the *Hornet* crawling slowly through an embattled sky two miles above the Pacific, led by a doomed plane defiantly trailing its long black smoke plume.

Just a few miles short of Nagumo's carriers, Widhelm's engine, finally drained of its oil, jerked stiffly to a frozen stop, and Gus started a long glide toward the sea, calling to the remaining pilots of his division to keep in formation and join the one behind them. Then he dropped his bomb and Stokely fought off the Zeke that harassed them almost all the way down, while Widhelm busied himself with the practical problem of ditching his plane without power.

Jimmy Vose took over the leadership of the *Hornet*'s remaining dive bombers and selected the largest of the two carriers he could see as their target. It was *Shokaku,* Nagumo's flagship, damaged at the Coral Sea, damaged again at the Eastern Solomons two months before. Only fate was to save her today. One after another the SBDs plunged from the sky like tiny black insects attacking some leviathan. Beautiful, luckless *Shokaku* was hit by six 1,000-pound bombs that wrecked her flight deck and hangar deck, and started fires that would have been fatal had she not already flown off all her aircraft.

If *Hornet*'s torpedo planes could have made an attack coordinated with that of her bombing squadrons, Santa Cruz might have come out better for the U.S. Navy. But "Iceberg" Parker's big TBFs, flying far below the SBDs, had become confused and followed the remnants of the *Enterprise* air group instead of staying with their own. When Widhelm called them upon sighting the Japanese carriers, they did not hear him, nor did the oncoming *Hornet* second wave.

Hornet's dive bombers were the only American aircraft to locate and attack a prime enemy target in strength. The rest of the planes, scattered in threes and fours because of Japanese opposition and the helter-skelter way they had been launched, wasted their weapons in futile attacks on targets that were unimportant. The *Enterprise* group's survivors split into two parts after they recovered from the attack by *Zuiho*'s fighters. The five surviving TBFs, only four of which carried torpedoes, and Flatley's division of F4Fs stayed together. When Gus Widhelm announced his sighting of the enemy carriers, the *Enterprise* torpedo bombers heard him and turned to port, since that was the side on which his group *had* been. They hadn't seen the *Hornet* SBDs cross over ahead of them onto their starboard hand. Thus they turned in the wrong direction, away from Nagumo's carriers. Ten minutes later they sighted the battleships and cruisers of the Vanguard Force. The torpeckers circled in frustration for another ten minutes, vainly seeking a carrier. Then Thompson, leading the four TBFs, asked Flatley if his planes had enough gas to continue on search. The fighter commander had to say no. His short-range F4Fs had dropped their wing tanks to fight Hidaka's Zekes, and they had been in the air almost two hours now. Thompson had little choice but to attack one of the Vanguard Force, so his four TBFs made an ineffectual try at the battleship *Kongo*, then headed back. The F4Fs fought off an attack by a trio of Zekes, orbited until Japanese attacks on the *Enterprise* ended, and finally landed aboard with little left in their gas tanks but fumes.

The third and last of the American attack groups was *Hornet*'s second wave. Its efforts were even more disjointed and futile than those of its predecessors. Just as it was passing over the Vanguard Force, Lieutenant Lynch, leading its contingent of nine SBDs, thought he heard a transmission from Widhelm's force to the effect that no carriers were in sight. Since Widhelm was sixty miles ahead of him, Lynch concluded that the carriers must be beyond the effective range of the American aircraft, and decided to go after one of the ships of the Vanguard Force. He called Commander Rodee and told him that he proposed to attack a nearby cruiser unless otherwise directed. He received no reply. Lynch selected the *Chikuma*, a handsome heavy cruiser, and his nine Douglases plunged down on it, one close on the other. Their bombing was good: two hits were made on the bridge, wounding the captain, and three others were scored, one of which disabled the torpedo tubes aft of the bridge and another, exploding in the engineering spaces, put the forward port engine out of commission. The ship suffered severe personnel casualties and some flooding. The ten TBFs with this attack group flew on for another twenty minutes in search of more lucrative targets. Then they returned to the Vanguard Force and made an ineffectual high-altitude bombing attack on the damaged *Chikuma*.

Their attacks over, their power expended, the scattered air groups returned in small formations to the task force, some brushing briefly with Japanese survivors similarly engaged. There they waited, circling in clouds, dodging their own antiaircraft fire, until they could be landed aboard. That was to be determined by the enemy.

14

FLAMES ON THE SEA
October 26

While the Americans, hastily launched, gallantly but inexpertly led, flew on to dissipate their strength, the first Japanese attack group pressed on in toward Kinkaid's two task forces. The brush between *Zuiho*'s fighters and the *Enterprise* attack group took place about 0840, and Commander Gaines, an interested spectator, radioed word back to his carrier. *Enterprise* and *Hornet* had thirty-six fighters in the air, twenty-one from *Enterprise*'s Fighting Ten and the remainder from the *Hornet*'s Fighting Seventy-Two. Because the Japanese attack was expected from the northward and *Enterprise* was the northernmost of the two carriers, she was assigned fighter-direction responsibility for both task forces. This was to turn out to be a most unfortunate decision.

The first thing that went wrong was that, despite the ample warning from the outbound striking groups, the carriers' air-search radars were unable to sort out the incoming Japanese raid from other targets on the scopes until they were only forty-five miles away. Second, *Enterprise*'s inexperienced fighter director officer (the previous one had gone with Halsey to SoPac Headquarters) had positioned his combat air patrol very badly; most of them were kept within ten miles of the carriers at altitudes of 12,000 feet or less—three or four thousand feet below the usual approach altitude of Japanese dive bombers. Third, once the Japanese were picked up, the FDO quickly lost control of the situation. The confused F4Fs were subjected to a barrage of contradictory orders, which rarely included any definite vectors. They were told alternately to look high, then low, then high again for the

165

same raid, and given directions in such terms as "port bow" or "starboard quarter" relative to *Enterprise,* which was not only twisting and turning constantly, but was not even visible to most of the fighter pilots. The result was the same thing that happened at the Battle of the Eastern Solomons, although for different reasons. The Japanese dive bombers reached their pushover points with the slow-climbing Grummans still several thousand feet below them.

Enterprise went into a local rain squall about 0900, just before the Japanese started deploying for their attack. A handful of Vals dove on her, but the sheltering clouds saved her from any damage. The unlucky *Hornet* found no such refuge, and was selected as the prime target for the enemy aircraft. Lieutenant Commander Seki's twenty-two Vals started their dives from 15,000 feet, virtually unopposed except for a huge volume of antiaircraft fire. The first plane got a hit on the carrier's flight deck aft. The next two bombs were near misses. Then the squadron commander pushed over into his dive; his plane was riddled by one or two shell bursts in quick succession. The graceful Val slowly rolled over into an almost-inverted attitude, dove straight onto the *Hornet*'s island, glanced off the big flat stack, and went through the wooden flight deck onto the hangar deck, where two of its bombs exploded. It was an end worthy of "Mamo" Seki, a great dive-bomber leader and a Samurai.

Just as the Vals were starting their dives, the torpedo-carrying Kates came up from astern of the *Hornet.* Two torpedoes hit in the carrier's engineering spaces, and she slowly slid to a halt in clouds of smoke and steam. Three more bombs struck her, and finally a flaming Kate crashed into one of her forward gun galleries. Happy, efficient *Hornet,* less than a year old, launcher of Doolittle's stunning bombing raid on Japan, was left a shattered wreck in five minutes crippled by an attack of almost textbook perfection. It was the last such attack that would ever be made by carrier aircraft of the Imperial Japanese Navy. But that was no consolation to *Hornet*'s men.

Lieutenant Dave Pollock of Fighting Ten was back orbiting *Enterprise* with his wingman after having led his division of F4Fs in futile attacks on the dive bombers that crippled the *Hornet.* Looking down at the formation, he noticed that two destroyers had halted. (They were picking up the crew of a ditched SBD.) Then he saw something else that made him stiffen—the unmistakable thin white trace of a torpedo erratically circling round the two ships. Pollock rolled over into a steep dive and plunged down toward the deadly moving trail of bubbles, firing a long burst from his guns when he was within range, and then pulling up steeply for another run. He was hoping to detonate the torpedo, or at least indicate its position to the ships. To the edgy gunners of the task force this aircraft come out of nowhere apparently to strafe a destroyer was not a rescuer but a target. *Enterprise* and the two destroyers opened up on Pollock without troubling further about fine points of aircraft recognition. He was undamaged, but his attempt was in vain. The crazily circling torpedo (fired by a Japanese submarine) hit the destroyer *Porter* with a huge explosion and the ship eventually had to be abandoned.

While the *Hornet*'s engineers and damage-control men were working frantically to save their ship, it became the *Enterprise*'s turn to be a target. Starting at 1009, the second Japanese attack group hit her. The dive bombers from the *Zuikaku* apparently never rendezvoused with Murata's torpedo planes from *Shokaku,* and they arrived half an hour ahead of the Kates. Instead of making the kind of closely coordinated attack that had worked so successfully against the *Hornet,* the Vals attacked independently. Once again the combat air patrol, badly misdirected by *Enterprise,* was too low and too late, and the Japanese were opposed largely by a torrent of antiaircraft fire from the "Big E" herself and her major escorts, the battleship *South Dakota* and the light cruiser *San Juan.*

The enemy attackers did not do very well, considering that they had no air opposition, but they were encountering modern navy antiaircraft fire for the first time. Forty-eight 5-inch guns on the four big ships of Task Force 16, plus scores of the new 40-millimeter Bofors guns on the *South Dakota* and *Enterprise,* shot the squadron to pieces. The battleship alone was credited with twenty-six aircraft, which was pretty good, especially since there were only twenty in the attack group. Multiple counting of falling enemy aircraft was even a worse problem for ships than for fighter pilots. But the enthusiastic claims were almost justified in this case. Only two of *Zuikaku*'s Vals scored hits on the well-handled *Enterprise.* One bomb went through the forward part of the flight deck, the forecastle deck below it, and out through the ship's side before it exploded, blowing a parked plane over the side. The second hit just abaft the forward elevator and exploded three decks down, killing forty-three and wounding seventy-five of the carrier's crew and putting the forward elevator out of commission. Only a handful of the Vals survived the attack: the plane of Lieutenant Takahashi, the *Zuikaku*'s dive-bomber leader, was riddled by an F4F; his rudder jammed hard over, he flew in circles for hours before he finally ditched. He was the only one of the Japanese bomber squadron commanders to survive the Battle of Santa Cruz.

The torpedo planes of the second enemy attack group were the *Shokaku*'s, a dozen strong, led by Lieutenant Commander Shigeharu Murata, the Japanese Navy's greatest expert on aerial torpedo tactics. Because of his skill, he had been chosen to plan and execute the torpedo-plane portion of the Pearl Harbor attack. Murata had dropped the first aircraft torpedo of the Pacific war on December 7, 1941. Now, as his squadron headed in toward the *Enterprise* at 1040, he had only a few more minutes to live.

The man who was to kill him was a lieutenant from Fighting Ten named Stanley Vejtasa. He was so blond they called him "Swede," and he was a crack fighter pilot. Vejtasa's division, after having shot down three of the Vals that had earlier attacked the *Hornet,* was orbiting ten miles away from the *Enterprise* when his wingman called out "Tallyho, nine o'clock down." There, 10,000 feet below them, standing out clearly against the blue sea, were Murata's shiny dark green Kates. Swede and his wingman, Lieutenant Dave Harris, dove at 350 knots, preceded by the two pilots of his second section, who had gone off after some Zeros a minute or two before. The Japanese were flying in a stepped-up column of three three-plane sections and a two-plane section; evidently one of the original twelve planes had turned back or had some trouble on the way. Vejtasa and Harris made a high-side run on one of the three-plane sections and each set a Kate on fire. As Swede broke away, he saw a fifth F4F join in the fight: Dave Pollock, separated from his division, had come down to help. The Japanese formation then broke up and flew into a cloud, Vejtasa following closely behind. In the gray murk he came up astern of the man on the left side of another of the three-plane Vs, got him squarely in the center of the glowing cross and circles of his gunsight, and squeezed the trigger on his stick grip. After two short bursts the Kate blew up. Vejtasa then skidded over to the right, behind the section leader, and shot his rudder off before the plane caught on fire. The third Kate started a shallow turn and Swede, still in heavy cloud, slid in astern of it and set it on fire with a single long burst.

Pulling up, Vejtasa saw another Kate above him and tried to make a low side run, but missed. Following it out of the clouds, Vejtasa hastily broke away as the task force's antiaircraft guns opened up. The Japanese plane headed straight in on the destroyer *Smith,* crashed on its forecastle, and blew up with a tremendous roar. Circling around the task force, Vejtasa saw two of the Kates that survived his onslaught and the volcano of antiaircraft fire retiring close to the water. Seeing another F4F preparing to attack, he dove on one of the two Japanese planes and set it on fire. Flaming, it went on for another five miles before it flew into the sea. The other Kate was "attacked" by Ensign Donald Gordon of Fighting Ten, who was out of ammunition but made a head-on run, hoping that his guns would somehow fire. They didn't, but the Japanese pilot, flying only a few feet above the water, dug his wingtip in trying to evade Gordon and cartwheeled to his destruction in a huge shower of spray.

Probably only five of *Zuikaku*'s Kates even got close enough to the *Enterprise* to drop their torpedoes (although the ship thought she sighted nine tracks). None scored hits. In all probability only two survived the attack.

Just after 0900, *Junyo,* Rear Admiral Kakuda's one-ship carrier division (her sister ship *Hiyo* had retired to Truk after an engine room fire on the 22nd) launched its first attack group, eighteen Vals and twelve Zekes. Its leader, Lieutenant Masao Yamaguchi, commander of the *Junyo*'s dive-bomber squadron, sighted the burning *Hornet* around eleven, but he had been sent to get *Enterprise.* His group was over Task Force 16 a few minutes later, but the Big E was hidden by low clouds. Yamaguchi radioed back his intention to hit the *South Dakota,* but Admiral Kakuda quickly ordered him to find and strike the carrier. In a few minutes they had found *Enterprise* and at 1121 about half of *Junyo*'s dive bombers started their attacks. The ship had just started to take her aircraft aboard, but had only landed a few when the Vals came out of the clouds. Those clouds took the sting out of the Japanese effort. They were numerous and low-lying, effectively preventing the steep seventy-degree dives that were so deadly and hard to counter. Yamaguchi's pilots were forced into long shallow glides of forty-five degrees that made them highly vulnerable to antiaircraft fire. *Enterprise*'s gunners claimed eight, which probably was not far wrong. The enemy pilots scored one near miss which caused the big carrier to whiplash badly, flooded a couple of minor compartments, and jammed the forward elevator in the up position. A hundred feet above the water, in the midst of this bedlam, *Enterprise's* radar officer was calmly working on the ship's air-search radar antenna, which had jammed a few minutes before. He got it fixed in time for the radar to pick up the rest of Yamaguchi's attack group seventeen miles away. With all the American fighters low on gas and out of ammunition, it was up to the gunners to fight them off. One dive bomber got a hit on *South Dakota*'s forward turret that wounded her captain and fifty men. Steering control was shifted from the bridge to the after conning tower and, while this transfer was taking place, the big battleship turned, out of control, and headed directly for the *Enterprise* at 28 knots. Luckily the carrier got out of the way. A few minutes later, another of *Junyo*'s Vals put a bomb into the antiaircraft cruiser *San Juan*. It went all the way through the unarmored decks of the light cruiser, out through the bottom, and exploded under her keel. The shock made *San Juan* lose *her* steering control, and for several minutes she too dashed wildly through the formation completely undirected, her bristling battery of 5-inch antiaircraft guns still firing.

At 1145 the attack of *Junyo*'s dive bombers was over. Only six of the eighteen Vals survived, and Yamaguchi and his second in command were both shot down. In terms of actual damage they accomplished nothing to compensate for such losses. But this attack, with its several unnerving episodes, coming after a morning of confusion, may have been the final straw as far as Task Force 16 was concerned. *Enterprise* spent the next hour and a half bringing aboard sixty of her own aircraft and forty-eight of the *Hornet*'s. With the forward elevator disabled and the other two elevators located on the landing area of the flight deck, this went pretty slowly. When the flight deck became dangerously crowded with parked aircraft, landings had to stop while these elevators were used to get planes down to the hangar deck. The TBFs were landed last because they had longer endurance, but the delays necessitated by the damaged elevator and handling almost fifty extra aircraft were too much for the big torpedo planes, some of which had been nearly six hours in the air. Several of them ran out of gas while waiting and had to ditch wherever their engines quit. It was an iron test of mental and physical endurance for Robin Lindsey, the *Enterprise*'s landing signal officer, who had to bring aboard over a hundred aircraft, some with battle damage, all low on gas and flown by exhausted pilots. It was an ordeal of another kind for the ship's plane pushers, who had to manhandle scores of planes back to the two operating elevators and strike them below on the hangar deck, while the aircraft still waiting to get aboard circled impatiently overhead. By 1325, though, all aircraft that had not ditched had been landed. Kinkaid then set a southeasterly course and began a high-speed retirement.

News of defeat and danger came in to Halsey at Nouméa in fragmentary messages, starkly conveying a sense of arriving doom. First came an urgent dispatch from Rear Admiral Good, commanding the cruisers of Task Force 17: *"Hornet* attacked by Jap carrier planes ... several bomb hits, one or more torpedo hits, now dead in water and burning ... preparing take her in tow. Have lost touch with Kinkaid." Then a terse, strained message from Kinkaid: *"Hornet* deep in water, burning ... *Porter* torpedoed. All now."

Hornet had her fires under control by 1000, and her engineers set about the job of connecting her three workable boilers with the one engine room that was still undamaged. At the same time the cruiser *Northampton* came alongside and passed a towline to the carrier. After an interruption caused by the attack of a lone Val that had strayed from the *Junyo*'s first striking group, the ship was under way in tow at 1123. Then the towline broke and everything came to a standstill again while the *Hornet*'s deck force broke out a bigger tow cable and passed it to the *Northampton*. The two ships got moving again at 1330, and Captain Mason then evacuated all of his wounded and unessential crewmen. For almost two hours, the chances looked very good that *Hornet* was going to be saved. But the persistence of Kakuji Kakuda tragically changed things for the Americans.

At 1315 the *Junyo* launched a second attack group,

consisting of her torpedo squadron, nine Kates under Lieutenant Yoshiaki Irikiin, and an escort of five Zekes. This was followed shortly by six Vals and nine more fighters. The torpedo planes were sent out to follow up the earlier attack of *Junyo*'s dive bombers on the *Enterprise*. Irikiin had been informed that his target would be a crippled carrier, the Japanese having, as usual, overestimated the damage they had done. He sighted one shortly after 1500. He did not know that he had found, not *Enterprise*, but the *Hornet*. The Kates came in through heavy antiaircraft fire that cost them seven out of the nine attacking aircraft, and only one hit was scored on the virtually stationary *Hornet*. However, this hit cut off all remaining power on the ship, and left the big carrier completely helpless.

The Vals attacked twenty-five minutes later and neither inflicted any damage nor suffered any losses. Ten minutes after this attack, at 1550, a hit was scored on *Hornet* by a flight of horizontal bombers. There is a minor mystery about these aircraft. The *Hornet*'s action report describes them as nine twin-engine aircraft, bombing from an altitude of 8,000 feet. That is pretty low for aviation people to make a fundamental mistake in identification. Yet Admiral Morison's history says the attack was made by six Kates. If this was so, they were not *Junyo*'s aircraft, since she had none left to fly such a mission, and *Zuikaku* was out of range. It seems more probable that the aircraft were Bettys of the Eleventh Air Fleet, although the Japanese records list no such attack. The final air strike of the day was made at 1702 by *Junyo*'s remaining flyable aircraft, four Vals and six Zekes. One bomb exploded on the hangar deck and reverberated through the empty ship. By then *Hornet* had no one left aboard but her dead. Admiral Murray considered that there was no further hope of saving her, and reluctantly ordered her abandoned. Two destroyers were designated to sink her, and the surviving ships of Task Force 17 headed south in retreat.

An emergency call went out from the *Hornet* to Task Force 16 at the start of the *Junyo*'s 1500 torpedo-plane attack, requesting air cover. Kinkaid had been withdrawing for the last hour, and it soon became clear that *Hornet*'s appeal was not going to change his mind. Prior to setting his retirement course, he sent a dispatch to Admiral Good: "If Murray safe, direct him to take charge salvage operations.

Have been under continuous air attack. . . ." Shortly thereafter, he notified Halsey: "Am retiring southward. Unable to give *Hornet* fighter coverage."

In his action report to Halsey, written in November, Admiral Kinkaid neither alluded to *Hornet*'s request for air cover nor defended his refusal to provide it. His rationale, however, was thus stated in the Task Force 61 war diary: "The planes aboard *Enterprise* had not been gassed, the fires below decks were not completely extinguished. Fighters, bombers, and torpedo planes were all mixed together on flight and hangar decks in whatever order they landed. With the number of planes aboard and Number One elevator out of commission it was not possible to respot the fighters until the excess planes were flown off the ship. Under the circumstances the *Hornet*'s request for fighter coverage could not be complied with."

The records of the air operations actually conducted by Task Force 16 after it started to retire do not indicate, however, that *Enterprise* was as completely immobilized as the war diary entry suggests. The ship launched twenty-five fighters at 1310, landed one back aboard in fifteen minutes, and sent off five more fighters and four TBFs at 1444. At 1510 thirteen of the *Hornet*'s SBDs were flown off to Espiritu Santo to relieve some of the congestion on the hangar deck. At 1520, eighteen of the airborne F4Fs were recovered. At 1635 another thirteen fighters were launched, and nine of those airborne were landed aboard ten minutes later. The remaining sixteen F4Fs were kept in the air as a combat air patrol until dusk.

A more pertinent explanation for Task Force 16's abandonment of the *Hornet* also is contained in Commander Task Force 61's war diary. This entry sets forth the reasons why Kinkaid elected to retire: "With the *Hornet* out of action, the extent of damage to the *Enterprise* not fully determined, and the probability that there were one or two undamaged enemy carriers in the battle area which had not been sighted by our forces, the decision of Commander Task Force 61 to retire at high speed to the southeast was made without hesitation."

It is fairly obvious that this decision was indeed made without hesitation. The question is whether or not some hesitation should have been displayed. Although it is difficult to fault Admiral Kinkaid, who, after all was the man on the spot, his decision might better have been justified by the fact that *Enterprise* was the last operational American carrier fleet in the Pacific and should not have been risked further under conditions of such uncertainty. Oddly, no such reason was put forth. A naval aviator would have understood its importance, but might also have been more disposed to provide fighter cover for *Hornet*. Admiral Kinkaid was not an aviator. He had been a cruiser division commander, and had been given his command because he was appropriately senior and available when Halsey was sent to Nouméa. Let none believe that Thomas Cassin Kinkaid was not an able flag officer. But it should be noted that Santa Cruz was the last battle of the Pacific war in which American aircraft carriers were directly commanded by an admiral who was not himself an experienced flyer.

In reluctant response to the fact of defeat, Halsey sent a brief message at the end of the day to all his task forces: "Retire to southward." The Battle of Santa Cruz was over.

In the hours of darkness early the next day—Navy Day, 1942—the United States Navy, for the first time in its history, abandoned a still-floating warship and left it to an advancing enemy. *Hornet*, flaming throughout her 800-foot length, still was not sunk by the shellfire and ineffective torpedoes of two destroyers, and both of them fled before their job was done. So after midnight the red glow of the burning carrier was sighted from the flag bridge of Kakuda's flagship *Junyo*. Two destroyers of Kondo's Vanguard Group closed the ship and finished her with four huge "Long Lances"—24-inch torpedoes, the best in the world. *Hornet,* seventh holder of a name that had been in the Navy for 130 years, sank wrapped in flames. Somehow it seemed obscene, sickening, like leaving helpless wounded on a battlefield to the mercy of a cruel enemy. To many aviators there that day the story of lost *Hornet* still rouses deep emotion after twenty-five years. To some it was a disgrace as black as any the Navy had ever known.

What happened? The carriers that had fought a numerically superior enemy to retreat in the Coral Sea and the Eastern Solomons, and had crushed him at Midway, failed at Santa Cruz, and failed badly. True, Kinkaid was outnumbered, vastly outnumbered in ships. But the main batteries of the only ships that really mattered were aircraft, and here

things were a lot closer to being equal. Nagumo began the
battle with a nominal 212 planes on his four carriers; Kinkaid
had about 170 on two.

Two tactical errors seem to have cost the Americans
dearly at Santa Cruz. The first was the decision to send the
carrier attack groups against the enemy piecemeal. This decision was Kinkaid's. He made it because he considered it more
important to get in a first blow, however weak, rather than
accept the delay inherent in rendezvousing two air groups,
one of which was itself launched in two separate formations.
Had the two air groups never contacted one another, the
tactic might have been more justifiable. But they were in
visual contact for much of their flight toward the Japanese
fleet, and it would have taken little time to join them up. No
one in the air assumed the initiative to do so. The situation
was compounded by failure of squadrons in the same air
group to fly together and mount coordinated attacks. The
Enterprise's CAG, evidently considering his major function to
be that of scorekeeper, not air leader, flew a kind of surveil-
lance over his tiny force, and *Hornet*'s torpedo squadron, by
hugging the water while the dive bombers went high, ensured
the further fragmentation of that scattered air group.

The second error was the assignment of fighter direction
for both task forces to *Enterprise*. Although this was what the
then prevailing tactical doctrine called for, because the Big E
was closest to the expected direction of attack, it was nevertheless wrong because her fighter director officer was inexperienced. In the battle, according to his captain, "some errors
of judgment on the part of the FDO were undoubtedly made,"
and the result was *Hornet* crippled and *Enterprise* damaged
without any effective air interception whatsoever prior to the
start of the Japanese dive-bombing attacks. *Hornet* pilots who
later looked at the *Enterprise* Combat Information Center
considered it grossly inferior in equipment, layout, and procedure to that of their own ship. The event suggests they were
right.

Aircraft communications were very poor, both with each
other and with the task forces. The high-frequency sets of the
day called for very fine tuning and were inordinately sensitive
to the normal wear and tear on operational aircraft. Until
very-high-frequency radios came into general use in mid-
1944, communications troubles plagued naval aviation con-

tinually. At Santa Cruz, as in the Eastern Solomons, the battle was marked by reports of sightings and attacks that were never received by the people who would have been able to use the information. Although Widhelm's sighting of the Japanese carriers was broadcast and rebroadcast by him, neither Parker, commanding the torpedo squadron, Rodee, leading *Hornet*'s second wave, nor Gaines, the *Enterprise* air-group commander, heard him. If any of them had, the American air strikes might have been more effective than they were.

Frustration and anger were the post-battle reactions of the American pilots at Santa Cruz. They did not feel that they had done very well, individually or collectively. They thought the air strikes were badly conceived, and that the deficiencies of their radios made them badly executed as well. They considered the fighter direction abysmally poor. And, innocent of the pressures and responsibilities of command, they viewed the abandonment of *Hornet* by Task Force 16 as rank cowardice. The squadron commanders made most of these sentiments known in their action reports, and in no uncertain terms. Jimmy Flatley and Mike Sanchez, the two fighter skippers, were so outspoken that both of them secured correspondingly indignant and acrimonious endorsements on their reports by their superiors.

The ships' antiaircraft gunners, however, felt little of this frustration. They thought they had done very well, as indeed they had. Sixty-nine Japanese aircraft were shot down during the battle, and a further twenty-three ditched due to battle damage. Many of the enemy were downed by F4Fs after they had delivered their attacks. But it is likely that at least half were shot down by the antiaircraft guns of the two task forces. Santa Cruz may be considered the advent of modern antiaircraft practice in the United States Navy. It also marked the end of dispersed defense by aircraft carriers maneuvering independently. When the new carriers began to operate in the Pacific a year later, they were grouped together in threes and fours, surrounded by powerful screens of battleships, cruisers, and destroyers.

On October 28, two days after the battle, a PBY on special search near the Santa Cruz Islands sighted a tiny yellow rubber raft on the sea, landed, and taxied up to it. In it were two men in Navy flight suits. The pilot of the P-boat suddenly recognized one of the two men as his flight instructor at Pensacola. He went quickly to the rear of the airplane, where the two were being hauled in through one of the blisters. "What the hell are you doing here?" he demanded of the former instructor. "None of your damn business," retorted Gus Widhelm, "get me a cup of coffee."

15

DEATH OFF SAVO
October 27–November 13

The Marines on Guadalcanal knew nothing of the Battle of Santa Cruz, fought five hundred miles to the eastward between ships and aircraft they never saw. But that battle was as vital to them as if it had been fought over Henderson Field or the waters of Ironbottom Sound. With the Eleventh Air Fleet worn down to impotence by the stubborn resistance of the Cactus fighter pilots, the Japanese could control the air over Guadalcanal only with their carrier-based air power. Now that too was gone. The battle had virtually wiped out Nagumo's air groups. Of the 242 aircraft that he had operational, only 84 were ready for combat the day after the battle. Most of his experienced squadron commanders were dead. Two carriers, one of them his own flagship, were damaged extensively. If the Japanese were yet to recapture Guadalcanal, they would have to try in the face of Geiger's little air force. One hope remained—to overwhelm the few American aircraft with a huge naval surface force.

The failure of the mass night attacks against the Marine perimeter in September and October at last convinced the obstinate Japanese Army high command that different tactics would have to be adopted. What they decided upon after Santa Cruz was a massive reinforcement of their forces on Guadalcanal. The shattered Sendai division was to be joined by the rest of the 38th Division in November and another division plus an independent brigade in December; these units, backed up with heavy artillery, would be employed in daylight frontal attacks against the Americans. In order to succeed, the Japanese calculated that they would have to transport to the bloody island 30,000 more troops, 300 artillery pieces, and 30,000 tons of supplies. To do this would require 150 transport trips or 800 destroyer trips.

Yamamoto, although recognizing the importance of holding Guadalcanal, could scarcely muster the naval forces required to carry out the ambitious plans of the Army. *Shokaku, Zuikaku,* and *Zuiho* had gone home to Japan to have their damage repaired and their depleted air groups replaced. Only the converted carriers *Hiyo,* just returned after engine repairs, and *Junyo,* with a handful of aircraft, remained in the South Pacific. Yamamoto had the Second Fleet, which was built around the two carriers, four battleships, and five heavy cruisers, plus Mikawa's Eighth Fleet of four heavy and two light cruisers. His plan to use these forces to support the Army build-up on the island began to take shape in early November. It was directed toward landing the major combat strength of the 38th Division from transports around November 15. Once again a midmonth crisis threatened Guadalcanal.

While the detailed planning for this climax continued, so did the almost nightly runs of the Express. On the night of November 2 a large force of destroyers landed troop reinforcements and supplies on the island. This landing cost the life of one of the great men of the Cactus Air Force, John Eldridge. He, together with two Marine lieutenants of VMSB-132, Melvin R. Nawman and Wayne Gentry, went out at dusk into a low solid overcast to attack an estimated twenty-one destroyers. All three became lost and crashed in violent thunderstorms that raged that night across the entire Solomons chain. The planes and bodies of Eldridge and Nawman and their crewmen were found afterward on Santa Isabel, but Gentry vanished completely. Eldridge, who had been grounded by Geiger "because he had already done so much," led fourteen attacks on Japanese ships in his thirty-five days on Guadalcanal. He had come through all of these unscathed, only to meet death through the random, insensate power of a tropical thunderstorm. In these beautiful, dreadful islands, nature killed as skillfully as man.

Admiral Yamamoto's plans were essentially complete by the 6th of November. Like most Japanese operations, particularly his own, they involved intricately scheduled coordination between several widely scattered but interdependent forces, each one of only moderate strength. The over-all objective was the landing of the main bodies of the 38th Division and the 8th Special Naval Landing Force with their heavy weapons and supplies on Guadalcanal on the morning of November 13. Yamamoto long since had recognized that Henderson Field was the key to the success of any such operation. His plan, therefore, provided for a bombardment of the field on the night of the 12th by two battleships of Kondo's fleet, and by both Kondo's and Mikawa's heavy cruisers on the 13th. The Second Fleet was divided into two forces, one built around *Hiyo* and *Junyo*, escorted by two battleships, and another which included two more battleships, *Hiei* and *Kirishima*, and a heavy-cruiser division. The latter force was to bombard the field. Mikawa's Eighth Fleet, operating independently of Kondo, was to escort Tanaka's transport convoy and protect it while it lay off Guadalcanal unloading. Yamamoto's total available strength for the operation was two aircraft carriers, four battleships, seven heavy cruisers, four light cruisers, and thirty destroyers—all intended to ensure the safe arrival of eleven transports carrying 14,500 infantrymen and their precious equipment to Guadalcanal.

The Cactus Air Force had been slowly rebuilding its strength around the fragments left after its mid-October crisis. A new Marine Air Group, MAG-11, began to arrive on November 1. Its first squadron on the island was Marine Bombing 132, commanded by Major Joseph Sailer. Joe Sailer was blond and compact, a product of Philadephia private schools and Princeton. In the five weeks of life that remained to him he was to earn a legendary reputation among flying Marines. Another of MAG-11's squadrons, Major Paul Fontana's Marine Fighting 112, started operations from the Fighter Strip on November 2.

By early November, it was clear to all that Roy Geiger, the rock-hard old airman, was suffering from a bad case of combat fatigue. Two months and four days of seeing his always outnumbered young men killed or evacuated, unable to fight any more, had finally broken down even his constitution. Louis Woods was sent up to relieve him as Commander Air, Guadalcanal, on November 7. Geiger was furious and charged his old friend with disloyalty. Woods vainly did his best to reason with his distraught superior, who returned, unmollified, to Espiritu Santo at Halsey's order. In a way it was a tragedy for Jiggs Geiger to be sent back to run his air wing from a desk six hundred miles from the fighting. He knew that he was about to miss the final battle for the island. But for the Cactus Air Force, it was the best thing that could have happened. Fresh, relatively rested, ten years younger than Geiger, changed by his promotion, as he said, "from a kindly old colonel to a blood-thirsty brigadier general," Louis Woods stepped into the direct command of Guadalcanal's air power at the most crucial hour of its short, tumultuous history.

The build-up of Japanese naval shipping and its accompanying radio traffic escaped neither the patrolling B-17s nor Nimitz' communications intelligence organization. Halsey's chief of staff, Miles Browning, had prepared for him on the 9th an accurate assessment of the strength, intentions, and schedule of Yamamoto's forces. Nimitz sent a message to Halsey on November 10, saying: "Excellent indications that major operation assisted by carrier striking force slated to support movement Army transports to Guadalcanal.... While this looks like a big push, I am confident that you with your forces will take their measure."

Halsey's forces were nowhere near as strong as those of the Japanese—he had one carrier, two battleships, four heavy cruisers, four light cruisers, and twenty-two destroyers—and the spearhead of his strength, *Enterprise*, had been crippled badly at Santa Cruz. As late as November 8, Halsey's estimate to King was that the carrier would not be available for 25 knots or even reduced air operations before the 21st. Furthermore, one of his two battleships, *South Dakota*, had a 16-inch turret out of commission because of the bomb hit it had received in the battle.

The Marines felt a deepening sense of uneasiness during the first days of November. The tempo of Express runs had increased perceptibly, and it was proving almost impossible to stop them. A big one came on the 7th, eleven destroyers carrying 1,300 troops. They were sighted 125 miles north of Guadalcanal and the Cactus aircraft swarmed out late in the afternoon to meet them. Seven SBDs of VMSB-132, led by Joe Sailer, dive-bombed the destroyers while three planes of Torpedo Eight made a torpedo run at 200 feet out of the setting sun. As the bombers and torpedo planes attacked, they and their cover of twelve P-39s from the 67th Pursuit Squadron were met by a valiant handful of ten float Zeros and biplane reconnaissance seaplanes which were protecting the destroyers. The combination of highly maneuverable targets and harassment by the little float planes was not enough to keep the Japanese from suffering major damage to the destroyers *Naganami* and *Takanami* in this attack, which was closely followed by another by twenty-two F4Fs.

The Japanese seaplanes put up a very good fight, as they always did. Six float Zeros were vainly trying to catch Major Fontana's VMF-112 when they were jumped by Joe Foss with seven F4Fs. Five were shot down in the first dive, and one of the F4Fs came back for a second pass that accounted for the survivor. Foss recalled with wonderment that all six of the Japanese pilots bailed out successfully, but then, one after another, unbuckled themselves from their parachutes and plunged into the sea. VMF-121's Danny Doyle was seen diving into the sea near one of the destroyers with one wing shot off. Two more F4Fs ditched at sea out of gas, but their pilots were picked up. Joe Foss made the mistake of trying to dogfight with one of the enemy's slow but maneuverable single-float biplanes. Not only did the Japanese pilot escape but his tail gunner put several bullets into the F4F. Foss then shot down another of the biplanes in flames. Then, looking around him, he found the sky suddenly empty. He had become separated from the rest of the squadron in the excitement of the melee. He headed back toward Guadalcanal, or in the direction where he thought it was. But the customary landmarks were covered by squall clouds, and by the time he thought to look at his compass he was thoroughly lost. Foss eventually ditched off Malaita, out of gas, and was picked out of the water that night by a coastwatcher. He spent the night at a mission entertained by hymn-singing Malaitans, and the news was radioed over to Henderson Field. Geiger sent Jack Cram over the next day in his own PBY to pick Foss up. Cram flew him back, the relieved and excited Joe standing behind him, dressed in a pair of sailor's white trousers, smoking a cigar, and talking a mile a minute.

The Express was back again the next night, sighted too late to permit an air attack. It was briefly engaged by Tulagi-based PT boats, but landed its consignment without loss. The Marines, listening to the gunfire off Savo, were glum. It appeared that there was no way to stop the Japanese destroyers from coming in almost any night they wished. This was shown again on the 10th, when Major Sailer and twelve SBDs were unable to score a single hit on five destroyers which went on to land their supplies and men unscathed.

The sixteen-day lull in air operations over Guadalcanal, interrupted only by a minor and unsuccessful raid on November 5, was finally broken on the 10th. Fifteen Zekes appeared, without bombers, and were attacked by a two-plane section of F4Fs, which dove through them, the only aircraft of the thirty-one scrambled even to sight the enemy. The next day, Armistice Day, the Japanese attempted the major air attacks on Henderson Field and on American shipping that Yamamoto's plan called for. At 0930, nine Val dive bombers from the carrier *Hiyo*, escorted by eighteen Zekes, attacked Rear Admiral Turner's force of four transports just arrived off Lunga Point to offload another regiment of Army infantry, the second to reinforce the exhausted Marines. The attack cargo ship *Zeilin*, equipped with combat unloading features, had a couple of plates sprung by a near miss, but the F4Fs shot down four Zekes and five Vals. The ratio of American losses to Japanese was unusually high, however; six of the F4Fs were shot down and four pilots lost, all from VMF-121. An hour later twenty-five Bettys and twenty-six Zekes tried to attack Henderson, and were intercepted by seventeen Marine fighters. Four bombers went down at the cost of one more F4F. It had been a hard day for Duke Davis' pilots. Four of them died, Major Davis himself was wounded, and seven of the precious Grummans were lost.

Early the next day, the 12th, a message was received from Paul Mason in his aerie high in the mountains of southern Bougainville that more Bettys were on their way. Seven F4Fs led by Foss scrambled, climbing to 29,000 feet to orbit over the cloud-covered bay and wait. At 1335 the island's radar picked up the Japanese 109 miles away at an altitude of 20,000 feet and tracked them until they were only thirty miles away, over the east tip of Florida. At that point, radar suddenly lost them.

Admiral Turner's transports had been formed up into air-defense formation off Lunga Point, and were the first to sight the Japanese bombers. They were Bettys, nineteen of them in a great disorderly gaggle. The usually impeccable Japanese formation had come apart as the big planes dove down from 25,000 feet and swung around Florida Island to head toward Turner's reinforcement group. Their rapid let down had given them great speed, and as they turned onto their attack course the Bettys were doing over 300 knots.

Foss saw them too as they emerged from under the clouds that covered Florida and flashed across Ironbottom Sound toward the transports. The seven F4Fs dove at full throttle to head them off. As their air-speed indicator needles drifted past the painted-on red lines at 300 knots, Foss's cockpit canopy suddenly ruptured from unbalanced internal and external pressures and the two walkway strips on his wings blew off. All of the canopies frosted over as the fighters plunged straight down from the cold heights into the warm, muggy dampness near the surface. The Marines, thanks to the tremendous speed of their dive from 29,000, caught the Bettys just as they were starting their torpedo runs. The sky was black with the antiaircraft fire of twenty-seven warships, and white wakes crisscrossed the bay as Turner's transport group swung this way and that to avoid the torpedoes. Just about the time that the seven Grummans from VMF-121 reached the Bettys, they were joined by Major Fontana, with eight more from VMF-112 and by eight P-39s of the 67th.

Now quick bursts of flame and long plumes of smoke began to add to the chaotic pattern of the battle as the American fighters darted in and out of the Japanese formation. Foss pulled up to within a hundred yards of one of the onrushing Bettys, set its right engine on fire with a short burst, and watched it cartwheel into the water. In less time than it takes to read about it, the now-fleeing Japanese were past the ships, running for their lives from the Army and Marine fighters. One of the flaming Bettys sideswiped the cruiser *San Francisco* as it flew by, killing or wounding fifty men. As Foss passed over the ships, a Zeke made a run on him; he pulled up, found the Japanese fighter in his sights, gave him a short lethal squirt, and went back to the bomber that he had been chasing. That too went flaming into the water.

The whole thing was over in less than eight minutes. All but two of the Japanese bombers were shot down by the fighters and ships' antiaircraft—Foss counted twelve of them floating on the water at the same time after the fight—at the cost of three Marine F4Fs and one of the P-39s. None of the transports was hit and they resumed unloading the Army troops. The destroyer *Buchanan* had been struck by a "friend-ly" antiaircraft shell and was damaged badly enough to be ordered south; the *San Francisco,* although she lost thirty men, was only superficially damaged.

By nightfall on the 12th, the stage was being set for what was obviously going to be the biggest battle yet. Admiral Turner's ships, their job done, headed back to Espiritu Santo. The cruisers and destroyers which had protected them remained to intercept the Japanese surface forces closing in on the island. Aircraft reports had come in all day to Vandegrift, Turner, and Halsey as they sighted and tracked the scattered forces deployed by Yamamoto. They found the bombardment force of two battleships 300 miles to the north, heading inexorably toward Guadalcanal. They also thought they had sighted two carriers far to the westward; although this was mistaken ship recognition, it added further to the growing dread felt by the American commanders.

Admiral Fitch, recognizing supreme crisis, had been collecting aircraft reinforcements from all over the South Pacific and sending them into Guadalcanal as fast as they could be found. Twelve more P-39s for the 67th Pursuit Squadron and six SBDs of VMSB-132 flew in on the 7th. An Army B-26 squadron at Suva was ordered to load with torpedoes and hold itself in readiness to fly to Espiritu Santo on an hour's notice. Planes left Santo for Henderson Field throughout the day on November 12. At 0545 three F4Fs went up, escorting six TBFs of VMSB-131, the first Marine torpedo squadron, coming at last to relieve exhausted Torpedo Eight. Later in the morning ten SBDs of Marine Scouting 142 headed north, Major Robert H. Richard commanding, the second dive-bomber squadron of MAG-11. Shortly after noon, a veteran of the early days of the campaign took off again for Guadalcanal: Dale Brannon, now a major, led eight P-38s of his newly formed 339th Pursuit Sqaudron back to the field where, less than three months ago, he had landed with his handful of P-400s. General McArthur, responding to ComSoPac's desperate pleas, sent another eight P-38s from Milne Bay, New Guinea. These big twin-engine aircraft were almost the entire force of modern American fighters in the whole Pacific. If Guadalcanal was finally to go under, it would take much of the South Pacific's air strength with it.

On the field, maintenance crews worked all out on damaged planes. But the best the overworked squadrons could promise General Woods for the next day's battles was

B-26

forty-five aircraft: fourteen F4Fs, seven P-39s, sixteen SBDs,
and eight TBFs. Except for the noises of the jungle, and of an
aircraft engine being run up every now and then, a heavy
stillness fell over the island as night began to fall. In their
tents the pilots rolled and tossed wakefully. They knew that
they were sleeping right on the bull's-eye of the target.

The air-raid siren at the field ended the waiting at 0130
on the 13th. Its warning was taken up by horns in the tank
park, another siren on the bank of the Lunga, and the
captured Japanese ship's bell in the headquarters building.
Over this cacophony, the popping drone of a Japanese catapult observation plane from a battleship slowly grew louder.
Its pilot flew over the field for a few minutes and then started
to drop flares. Green flares. The Marines and the airmen who

had been there on the night of October 13–14 knew what that meant: the naval bombardment was about to begin.

A distant rumble of naval gunfire started at 0150 and rapidly grew to a continuous muted roar. But no shells fell on Henderson. The mutter of the guns was coming from out near Savo, and the northern horizon was bright with continuous flashes which reminded Joe Foss of auroral displays on a winter's night in South Dakota. The men of Guadalcanal watched and listened to the distant naval battle in silence, knowing that it was no ordinary scuffle with the Cactus Express, wondering if their Navy was winner or loser. Most of the firing died away by 0215 and the flashes of big guns were replaced by a few smaller masses of slowly drifting flame that marked dying ships. The pilots watched the flickering lights for a while, and then went back to their tents for the hour or two of sleep that remained to them.

The first search planes of the morning of the 13th went off before dawn. The weather was very poor, with low clouds and intermittent rain. The SBD assigned to the Santa Isabel search saw a Japanese battleship north of Savo when on his way out and attacked it, but missed. Another mission of three more SBDs went out to scout near-Cactus waters for enemy ships. Joe Foss was sent out alone at dawn—0550—to determine damage to our own ships in the night's battle. As the sun slowly lighted the sound between Guadalcanal and Savo, Foss and the SBDs saw the wreckage of what Admiral King later called "one of the most furious naval battles ever fought."

The Japanese had planned a bombardment of Henderson Field during the early morning of the 13th, the two old battleships *Hiei* and *Kirishima* providing the fire power, screened by a light cruiser and eleven destroyers. This force, commanded by Vice-Admiral Hiroaki Abe, had been intercepted just a few minutes before the bombardment had been scheduled to start by a hastily flung-together American force of five cruisers and eight destroyers under Rear Admiral Callaghan, Ghormley's ex-chief of staff. The two forces stumbled onto one another with only the barest of preparation for a naval battle, and engaged in an action at point-blank range which quickly degenerated into a savage melee. One Japanese and two American destroyers were sunk outright. At dawn the Henderson aircraft found the shattered light cruiser *Atlanta* five miles off Lunga Point; a few miles north of her was the veteran heavy cruiser *Portland*, her torpedo-damaged stern twisted into a shape that forced her to steam in circles; the destroyers *Cushing* and *Monssen*, burning and abandoned, lay halfway between Lunga Point and Savo, and three miles northwest of them the Japanese destroyer *Yudachi* in equally parlous state. As the pilots watched, the crippled *Portland* opened fire on *Yudachi* and sank her with six salvos.

Foss and the SBD flight also located the big game first found by the Santa Isabel search plane: *Hiei,* injured by scores of shell hits, screened by three destroyers. For the first time since their long ordeal began, almost three months before, the Cactus flyers had a Japanese battleship in their grasp. The opportunity provided one of the busiest days in Henderson Field's active history. Planes were launched as quickly as they could be gassed and armed, in small groups and, as usual, without regard to formal squadron organization.

The first strike off the field left at 0600, five SBDs of VMSB-142, arrived only the day before, led by their C.O., Major Bob Richard. The dive bombers attacked at 0615 scoring one direct hit amidships with a 1,000-pounder and a near miss. An hour later four TBFs approached the battered monster to deliver the first torpedo attack ever made by Marine aviators. They were led by Captain George Dooley of VMSB-31, newly arrived to relieve tired Torpedo Eight. The twenty-four-year-old Dooley was a determined man—he had almost died in a flaming midair collision as a cadet in the Training Command, and had spent a year undergoing repeated operations before grimly going on to get his wings. Shortly after 0715 his flight scored a torpedo hit on the *Hiei* for a thoroughly satisfying first mission. In another hour Joe Sailer led six of his pilots off for a dive-bombing attack, but failed to score. At 1010 Dooley led his four back for a second torpedo attack, closely followed in by Joe Foss with six F4Fs. Foss's fighters strafed one of the destroyers and then roared in on *Hiei* right down on the water. When they were within a few hundred yards of the ship, Dooley's torpedo hit amidships in a multicolored geyser of water, steam, flame, and debris. The fighter pilots, following their division leader pell-mell, watched Foss make a steep pylon turn within a few feet of the battleship's pagodalike bridge. One later swore that he saw him thumb his nose at the Japanese as he went by.

Another flight of ten SBDs and eight F4Fs went out to look for a reported Japanese carrier force, which turned out to be nonexistent. The fighters, however, had a brush with some Zekes covering the *Hiei* and shot down seven of them.

While the Marine aircraft were beginning their shuttle missions out to Savo and back, badly needed help was on the way from the south. Kinkaid's Task Force 16 had gotten under way from Nouméa on the 11th, the earliest day that the damaged *Enterprise* was able to sail. The Big E had been badly hurt at Santa Cruz: the bomb hit in officers' country had seriously affected her watertight integrity, besides destroying the living quarters of seventy officers. Although fifty-nine men from the repair ship *Vestal* and a Seabee battalion sailed with her and were working night and day to complete repairs, one of her fuel tanks still leaked. More important, it was not known whether her forward elevator was working. No one dared to find out, since it was in the up position; if it were to be tested and jam anywhere below the flight-deck level, the last American aircraft carrier in the South Pacific would be out of commission. With only the after elevator usable, flight operations and respotting aircraft for launch proceeded at half speed.

All through the night of the 11th and daylight of the 12th, *Enterprise* ran north toward the Solomons, her below decks a crackling uproar of rivet guns and welding torches. With her were *Washington* and *South Dakota,* the latter with her forward turret still jammed, two cruisers, and eight destroyers. At 1925 Radio Guadalcanal broadcast the erroneous report of the sighting of two Japanese carriers 150 miles west of the island. The position given was 525 miles northwest of Kinkaid. Task Force 16 closed the reported contact at high speed through the night of the 12th and at dawn launched a search out to 200 miles. So that *Enterprise* might get rid of a few aircraft and thus speed up her flight operations during the expected battle, it was decided to launch Torpedo Ten's nine TBFs for Guadalcanal. The big torpedo planes were loaded with ordinance so that they could attack any targets encountered during the flight to Henderson. Eight of them were given torpedoes and the ninth four

500-pound bombs. Once having landed, they were directed to report to General Woods for orders.

At 0722, after the SBDs reached the ends of their search sectors and reported back no enemy ships, the torpedo planes were flown off 280 miles south of Guadalcanal. The TBFs were preceded by six of VF-10's F4Fs, Lieutenant John Sutherland leading. Torpedo Ten was led by Lieutenant Albert ("Scoffer") Coffin, skipper since John Collett's death at Santa Cruz.

Coffin's TBFs flew at 500 feet, Sutherlands three sections of F4Fs dodging in and out of the towering cumulus a few thousand feet above. In two hours the mountains of Guadalcanal were in sight ahead, and the planes banked left so that they could approach Henderson Field from its threatened western side. At 10 oclock, still at 500 feet, the *Enterprise* flight sighted Savo Island, and behind it the *Hiei*. The nine heavily loaded torpedo planes turned away and added full climbing power to gain altitude. Altitude meant speed, and speed meant survival to the cumbersome "torpeckers." Sutherlands fighters orbited between a few Zekes that were covering the battleship and the depolying torpedomen. The Japanese showed no particular inclination to engage.

Torpedo Ten split into two four-plane divisions and dived from 5,000 feet, heading in on either bow of the *Hiei*. Two or three miles out they broke clear of the clouds, each division in line-abreast formation. At 150-feet altitude, they slowed to dropping speed and opened bomb-bay doors. Coffin's division to port, the other four planes to starboard. *Hiei* desperately fired a 14-inch salvo from her two forward turrets at Coffin's division coming in on her port bow. The ball-turret gunners saw the shells splash into the sea miles behind them. Her antiaircraft fire was weak, most of the gunners probably having been killed in the night battle. A thousand yards from the battleship, the short, fat Mark 13 torpedoes began to drop into the water. The eight blue TBFs, at full throttle, thundered down both of *Hiei's* sides below main-deck level, their crews fleetingly observing her damaged superstructure and guns. Then they were past, zigzagging and skidding frantically to avoid the Japanese gunners. A minute later the geysers of three torpedo hits erupted alongside the ship, one on the port side, one starboard, and one near the stern which wrecked her rudder. *Hiei* painfully swung to starboard, toward the north. Coffin's exultant squadron, unscathed, landed on Henderson Field a few minutes later.

General Saunders, when told of the Japanese convergence on Guadalcanal, promised Admiral Fitch that he would take everything that his 11th Bomb Group could muster north from Espiritu Santo early on the 13th. True to his promise, eight of his B-17s took off at 0300 that morning in a torrential thunderstorm and fanned out toward the Solomons on long 800-mile searches. Two hours later, another seventeen Fortresses left Santo in ones and twos and assembled over San Cristobal a couple of hours later. Fourteen of them, led by Major Donald Ridings, C.O. of the 72nd Bomb Squadron, found *Hiei* at 1110 where Coffin's torpedo planes had left her less than an hour before. The formation wheeled majestically into a bombing run at 14,000 feet and dropped fifty-six 500-pound bombs aimed at the hapless battleship. One of the bombs was a hit, and one a near miss. The B-17s turned back for the 600-mile return to Espiritu Santo.

Ten minutes later, Joe Sailer arrived overhead, leading a flight of six SBDs from VMSB-132. The dive bombers scored three hits with 1,000-pounders. The Marines scarcely had pulled out of their dives when six TBFs swept in on *Hiei's* port bow. Swede Larsen was leading, with Evarts, Divine, and Engel of Torpedo Eight and two pilots of newly arrived VMSB-131. The big Grummans, hell-bent at 200 knots at 200 feet altitude, bored in to 800 yard's range before making their drops. Larsen fittingly capped his long service on Guadalcanal by scoring a direct hit amidships on the battleship. Evarts' torpedo hit on the ship's port bow. Two of the fish missed and two others failed to drop. This was the final mission of the war for the squadron. It might have comforted the crews who died at Midway if they had seen their squadron mates help put under the first battleship ever to be sunk by the United States Navy.

A two-hour respite for the old ship was broken abruptly when Scoffer Coffin led in a flight of six of Torpedo Ten's seasoned pilots at 2:35. Three of the *Enterprise* torpedo planes scored hits.

In a final strike just before sunset, the indefatigable Joe Sailer led a flight of three other SBDs from his own Marine Scouting 132 and four from 141. The weather was steadily

192   THE CACTUS AIR FORCE

deteriorating, and the formation became fragmented; only Sailer located the targets, but was able to make only a near miss by one of the *Hiei*'s screening destroyers. Two planes lost in the rain and clouds failed to return from the flight, the only losses suffered all day by the Cactus Air Force.

The *Hiei*, launched at Yokosuka thirty years before, never fired her main battery of eight 14-inch guns in anger until the early morning of November 13, 1942. Her career in the kind of battle for which she had been designed lasted twenty-two minutes. By sunset of that day she lay sinking off Savo, having absorbed eighty-five shell hits from Callaghan's cruisers and destroyers, and five bombs and ten torpedoes from the besieged island's air striking forces. Captain Suzuki lay dead on his bridge, and 450 of his crew had been killed. The tired, battered ship was scuttled and abandoned by her survivors that night to make one of the most notable additions to the population of Ironbottom Bay. Although the terrible sacrifices of the cruiser and destroyer sailors had given them the opportunity, it should be recorded that the first battleship to be sunk by Americans in the Second World War was sunk because of the attacks of a handful of Marine and Navy aircraft.

Sinking a battleship was fine, but it was not by any means the most important thing that the Cactus Air Force had to worry about that Friday the 13th. There were recurrent reports by several search planes that Japanese carriers had been sighted. Actually none had—target identification from the air is difficult enough for experts, and most of the pilots tended to be a little hazy on ship types. Two strike groups were sent out to attack the nonexistent carriers during the day. But one of the 11th Bomb Group's B-17s really *had* made a critically important sighting: at 0925 he had seen a force of twelve transports, escorted by four "cruisers" and six destroyers, north of Vella Lavella, making for the Shortlands. This was ominous confirmation of the forthcoming major landing attempt on Guadalcanal by the Japanese.

The force which had been seen by the scouting B-17 was indeed the reinforcement convoy commanded by Admiral Tanaka. When first sighted, it was again approaching the Shortlands, having turned back after the defeat of Admiral Abe's bombardment force in the night battle. Admiral Tanaka sailed again for Guadalcanal in the late afternoon of the

13th, preceeded by the four heavy cruisers, two light cruisers, and six destroyers of Mikawa's Eighth Fleet. This force was sighted also on the morning of the 14th. It was apparent that the Henderson Field pilots were going to have another big day.

They were going to be in for a night without the protection of their naval forces too. It had been Halsey's intention to have Admiral Kinkaid detach Lee's two battle-ships during daylight hours on the 13th in time for them to arrive off Savo after dark. He so ordered Kinkaid at 1830. However, the day's flight operations, which required several reversals of course into the southerly wind, as well as numerous "submarine contacts" had delayed Task Force 16, and it was not nearly so close to Guadalcanal as had been planned. Halsey was shocked to receive Kinkaid's answer, which stated: "From Lee's present position impossible for him to reach Savo before 0800 tomorrow." Cactus was once again at the mercy of the Japanese Navy by night.

16

THE LONG JOURNEY
TO DOMA COVE
November 14–15

The night of November 13–14 permitted no rest for the overworked pilots and ground crews of the Guadalcanal strips. At 0130 Louie the Louse reappeared, complete with green flares. A heavy bombardment started, which lasted for thirty-five minutes. Part of the force providing an advance screen for the Japanese convoy, the night visitors were the heavy cruisers *Suzuya*, flagship of Rear Admiral Nishimura, and *Maya*. They fired some 1,000 rounds of 8-inch bombardment ammunition, but scored no hits on Henderson. However, Fighter One was hit, two F4Fs burned, and fifteen others hit by shrapnel. The two big cruisers were finally encouraged to cease their efforts by two PT boats which sortied from Tulagi and made three unsupported attacks on the Japanese.

At dawn on the fourteenth, despite the previous day's hard work, the bad weather, and the cruiser bombardment, the Cactus Air Force went out again. It started the day with forty-nine planes available for combat: fourteen F4Fs, seven P-38s, three P-39s, sixteen SBDs and nine TBFs. None of the ever-ailing P-400s were up. The search planes had started early from the bases to the south, 11th Bomb Group B17s having taken off from Espiritu Santo at 0300 and three PBYs from the lagoon at Vanikoro at 0430.

The regular morning search by SBDs at 0630 reported an enemy force of four cruisers and three destroyers 140 miles west of Guadalcanal heading west toward the Short-lands. The first strike of the morning left at 0715, five SBDs led by the untiring Joe Sailer, and six TBFs, three each from

VMSB-131 and Torpedo Ten. They arrived over their targets at 0800. The ships were the Japanese Eighth Fleet of Vice-Admiral Gunichi Mikawa, the victor of Savo Island and the author of so many of the Americans' troubles since the day of the first landing. Mikawa had with him *Chokai* and *Kinugasa*, heavy cruisers which had been at Savo; Nishimura's two heavy cruisers, *Suzuya* and *Maya*, which had conducted the previous night's bombardment; the light cruisers, *Isuzu* and *Tenryu*; and six destroyers. Sailer's five SBDs attacked *Maya* and started fires with near hits on the port side. The six torpedo planes attacked the *Kinugasa*. All three of the Navy pilots' torpedoes hit and one of the Marines'. As the attack group left, the torpedoed *Kinugasa* was burning fiercely, and it appeared that *Maya* was badly damaged too; however, her fires were soon out and she shortly was able to make 30 knots.

At about the time the Henderson Field searches sighted Mikawa's cruiser force, *Enterprise*, which had held its north-west course at high speed through the night, was 200 miles south-southwest of Guadalcanal. The situation on the island was obscure to Kinkaid. No further contact reports on Japanese carriers had been received since the erroneous ones of the previous day, or, indeed, on any other Japanese forces which might be in range. No word had been passed to him about Vandegrift's status, and it was not even known if Henderson Field was still held by the Marines. The admiral decided to launch a minimum number of search planes so that the largest possible attack group could be held ready on *Enterprise*'s flight deck. At 0620, therefore, ten SBDs were flown off, armed with a 500-pound bomb each, briefed to report enemy ships when they were sighted and then attack them. At 0708 Bill Martin, exec of Scouting Ten, one of the search pilots, reported ten unidentified planes 140 miles north of Task Force 16 and heading toward it. *Enterprise* scrambled additional fighters to reinforce the CAP, and Kinkaid ordered the immediate launch of the attack group. Thirty-seven minutes later Jimmy Flatley and ten F4Fs were being sent down the flight deck, followed by seventeen SBDs of VB-10 and VS 10. Since no contact had been made on enemy ships, their orders were simply to fly north toward Guadalcanal and attack whatever Japanese forces were located. The group, led by Scouting Ten's skipper, "Bucky" Lee, rendezvoused and took departure from the Task Force at 0800. Kinkaid, his striking power committed without any definite target, and unsure of the situation on Guadalcanal, had taken a desperate gamble. Actually the aircraft sighted by Martin were not Japanese—only enemy flying boats operating singly were patrolling the Solomons that day. What he probably saw was either *Enterprise*'s own CAP or the product of keyed-up imagination. The attack group had been launched for nothing. Luckily, Task Force 16 was close enough to Guadalcanal for Lee's aircraft to have a chance of locating something.

Contact was made by *Enterprise*'s search aircraft far to the north just as Lee's attack group was being launched. Lieutenant (j.g.) R. D. Gibson and Ensign R. M. Buchanan of VB-10, who had the 330–345-degree search sector, sighted Mikawa's fleet at 0750, ten miles south of Rendova. From 0815 to 0914, the two SBDs orbited the Japanese cruiser-destroyer force at 17,000 feet, sending amplifying reports back to the ship every fifteen minutes or so. Mikawa was frequently hidden by scattered low clouds and his cruisers put up heavy and accurate antiaircraft fire. Gibson was inaccurate in his ship identification, since he believed the force to include a couple of battleships and a small carrier. After holding contact with the enemy force until they had only enough gas left to make one attack and then head for Guadalcanal, Gibson and Buchanan dove down-sun at the crippled *Kinugasa*, which was leaving a noticeable oil slick behind it. Both bombs hit, and the cruiser began to burn again. The two dive bombers then headed for the barn, landing at Henderson at 1120 to end a five-hour mission.

Ten minutes after Gibson and Buchanan broke off contact with Mikawa, it was regained by Ensigns Hoogerwerf and Halloran of Bombing Ten, turning onto the final leg of the 315–330-degree search sector from *Enterprise*. The two ensigns were too green and too excited to think of anything like making a contact report. They climbed to 17,500 feet and each dove on an undamaged cruiser. Hoogerwerf missed, but thought that Halloran had hit his target; however, he never saw his wingman again after their attack, and he continued alone back to the ship.

Lee intercepted one of Gibson's contact reports at about 0820, but had failed to understand the position. This was given to him again at 0844 by the *Enterprise*, along with orders to attack the enemy ships. Reasoning that the Japanese were probably steering eastward toward Guadalcanal, Lee plotted a course to intercept them southeast of New Georgia. As the SBDs, flying at 15,000 feet, turned left to their new course, Flatley's F4Fs high above sighted the green backbone of Guadalcanal fifty miles to the north, and shortly thereafter, far below, the *Washington* and *South Dakota* crawling across the brilliant blue sea toward the island. At 0930 Lee's formation arrived where his navigation said the Japanese ships should have been if they had been going eastward. No enemy was in sight. Instantly grasping that they must have been heading for the Shortlands instead of Guadalcanal, Lee turned west to fly up along Mikawa's course. Unfortunately the F4Fs' radios were tuned to the *Enterprise* CAP frequency, not the SBDs' attack frequency, and eight of Fighting Tens escorting aircraft missed Lee's turn. The attack group continued parallel to New Georgia, "covered" only by the lonely Stan Ruehlow and his wingman, but able easily to brush off an attack by two float Zeros. Flatley's division flew northwest on the old course until Rekata Bay was in sight, then turned around and returned to the *Enterprise*. Shortly after 1000, the SBDs sighted the burning *Kinugasa*, with two destroyers standing by, both of which opened the same accurate antiaircraft fire that Gibson and Buchanan had noted earler. A few minutes later, at 1015, the remainder of Mikawa's ships came into view.

Lee ordered the five SBDs of Bombing Ten to attack the heavy cruisers in the formation and the second division of Scouting Ten to attack the light cruisers. Then he took his own division down below the clouds to look for the carrier that Gibson had reported. When it became apparent that none was present, Lee's division dove on a light cruiser too. The attack of these sixteen SBDs resulted in heavy damage to the light cruiser *Isuzu*, one of whose boiler rooms flooded, and a near miss on Mikawa's flagship, *Chokai*. After they left, the *Kinugasa*, badly damaged by the torpedoes of the Henderson Field TBFs and by Gibson's and Buchanan's 500-pounders, sank. Lee's attack group landed at Cactus at 1315 after one of the longest attack missions ever flown by American carrier aircraft. Ruehlow's two F4Fs had preceded them.

The heart of this greatest of the Japanese attacks on Guadalcanal was the eleven Army transports and cargo ships carrying most of the troops and all of the heavy equipment of the 38th Division. The troops convoy left the Shortlands for the second time about 1300 on the 13th and steamed down the Slot at 11 knots, screened by twelve destroyers of the veteran Destroyer Squadron 2. Rear Admiral Tanaka, whose flag flew in the *Hayashio*, concerned over the delay which had resulted in his countermarch of the night before, had a premonition of disaster to come. He had been involved in earlier attempts to land troops on Guadalcanal in the face of air attack.

Tanaka's force was sighted shortly after dawn by one of the early-morning search planes from Cactus, but was incorrectly reported as consisting of a battleship, cruisers, destroyers, and another of the "possible carriers" that seemed to be in every contact report. An Australia-based B-17 of the Fifth Air Force sighted and reported the transports again at 0730. An hour later, two SBDs flying the 345–000-degree sector of *Enterprise*'s dawn search radioed back to the ship that they too had sighted the convoy. After making a report, these two planes attacked one of Tanaka's transports. Both missed, and one was shot down by escorting Zekes.

Tanaka had sighted Bucky Lee's attack group at its closest point of approach to him a little before 1000, and started his destroyers making smoke and his convoy zigzagging. His turn was to come shortly. After General Woods and Colonel Cooley had evaluated the conflicting contact reports variously describing the transport convoy, it became clear that this was the prime target for which the Cactus Air Force had been searching for a day and a half. Around 1020 Joe Sailer and Bob Richard were airborne for the second time that day with nineteen dive bombers between them, accompanied by Coffin and seven TBFs. This strike was escorted by six F4Fs. At 1100 the dive bombers were over Tanaka's four squirming columns of transports, watching the destroyers vainly trying to hide them with smoke. Sailer led his squadron down on two ships of one column, while Richard's planes dove on the third transport of the same column and a nearby destroyer. The pilots of VMSB-132 hit one of their targets with two 1,000-pounders, and a second ship with four. Bob Richard's VMSB-141 racked up six hits on their transport, but missed the destroyer. As the two dive-bomber squadrons rolled into their dives in succession from the starboard side of the Japanese formation, Scoffer Coffin's seven torpedo bombers expertly attacked the same column of transports from the port side. Coffin's own division got two hits on their target, and the other one hit on a second ship. This well-executed strike was the most destructive of the whole day's efforts: Coffin's TBFs sank the *Canberra Maru* and *Niagara Maru*, both damaged by the SBD attacks, and the *Sado Maru*, carrying the senior Army commanders, was so crippled by bombs that she turned back for the Shortlands, escorted by two of Tanaka's destroyers. Nine of the aircraft were lost.

For the second day in a row the mechanics and ordinance men at Henderson Field gassed and armed aircraft as fast as their small numbers and primitive facilities permitted, and the MAG-14 staff sent them off as soon as a decent-sized strike group was ready. Torpedoes were in short supply because of the numbers that had been expended in the attacks on *Hiei* and *Kinugasa*, and Coffin's attack on the transports used up all of the remainder. As part of the desperate effort to keep the field operating, six of VMSB-131's TBFs, escorted by an R4D, left Espiritu Santo at midmorning for Henderson, carrying torpedoes.

The next strike took off from Cactus in two flights about 1334. One included Bucky Lee and Glenn Estes of Scouting Ten, only half an hour after they had come back from one of the longest carrier missions ever flown, and seven SBDs of VMSB-141. The second flight included Lieutenant Richey of Scouting Ten and three more Marines of 141. Their attacks were completed by 1445; they had hit three of the ships with 1,000-pounders and sunk one of them, *Brisbane Maru*. All thirteen of the dive bombers were back within two hours. Ten minutes after Lee and Richey were airborne, Bill Martin took off with eight more of Scouting Ten's SBDs. After looking around northwest of the Russells for the phantom Japanese carriers, they too attacked the transports and scored four hits. Chuck Irvine of VS-10, having missed going with one of the earlier strikes, took off alone at 1355. Although attacked by Zekes, he dove, scored a direct hit on his target, and returned safely to Henderson.

Fifteen of "Blondie" Saunders' B-17s, some of which had been on alert since 0345 took off from Espiritu Santo just after ten loaded with four 500-pound bombs apiece. One flight attacked the transports at 1500 and the second at 1515; they thought that they scored a bit on one ship and shot down six of the Zekes which were furnishing fighter cover for Admiral Tanaka. Although Tanaka's memories of that terrible day were confused and chaotic, one thing which stood out in his mind when he wrote about it fourteen years later was the wobbling fall of the bombs from the high-flying Forts.

At 1305, *Enterprise* launched her eight remaining SBDs and an escort of twelve F4Fs with orders to attack the transports and then proceed to Guadalcanal to join the rest of Air Group Ten. After this group was flown off, the Big E retired southward to Nouméa with only eighteen fighters left on board to protect her. Her part in the battle was over. Now it was up to her pilots and planes, flying from the mud and Marston mat of Henderson Field instead of her teak flight deck.

Enterprise's attack group included three planes from Scouting Ten and five from Bombing Ten. It was led by Jimmy Flatley, on his second trip north that day. Tanaka's depleted transport force was sighted five miles northwest of the Russells at 1530, and beyond it the smoke columns from the damaged ships. The SBDs came down from 15,500 feet in difficult crosswind dives. Each of the three scout pilots attacked a different ship and each made a direct hit. The first two bomber pilots missed; the next two got a near miss and a hit respectively on two different transports. The last man went after the ship missed by the first two and put his 1,000-pounder dead amidships. It slowed to a stop, burning. Behind the SBDs, eight of Fighting Ten's F4Fs followed to make two strafing runs on the troop-packed ships. One of the fighters lagged a little behind the rest and was immediately jumped by four Zekes, two from ahead and two astern. He quickly looped and shot down one of those behind him in flames. Japanese fighter opposition did not amount to much. Not one of *Enterprise*'s aircraft was even hit in this highly successful attack, in which the transports *Shinanogawa Maru* and *Arizona Maru* were sunk. Flatley's group landed on Guadalcanal about 1600. He had spent almost seven hours in the air since 0900, and some of the dive-bomber pilots more than eight.

The men of Air Group Ten, used to the comfort and relative security of a carrier, were not exactly prepared for life on Guadalcanal. Fighting Ten's Cliff Witte, parking his plane at Fighter One, spotted Art Nehf of VMF-121, with whom he had gone through flight training. He hopped out and walked over to ask Nehf what the odd-looking puffs of dust were that erupted from the ground every now and then.

Witte had barely greeted his friend when another dust cloud appeared at the end of the strip, and he was astonished to see Nehf suddenly hit the dirt face down. He was quickly informed that these phenomena were the bursts of Pistol Pete's shells and advised to emulate his battle-wise companion immediately.

The weary ground crews watched the last attacks of the day leave the field between 1530 and 1545: Joe Sailer leading five planes of his squadron, Scoffer Coffin again with four TBFs, Glen Estes of Scouting Ten and three Marines from 142. Seven fighters from 121 went out too, one of them flown by Joe Bauer, anxious to see a little action himself after two days of sending his pilots into it. Finally, John Thomas took off leading seven SBDs of Bombing Ten.

Major Sailer's pilots got two hits with 1,000-pound bombs and Coffin's flight another two with 500-pounders. Estes and the three Marine dive-bomber pilots with him sank the *Nako Maru*, sixth of Tanaka's original eleven ships to go down. The F4Fs provided cover for these three groups, but Thomas' squadron never made contact with the fighters that were supposed to protect them. They went on the mission anyway, without fighter cover, approaching Tanaka's shattered formation of destroyers and transports from the southwest at 12,000 feet. Four of the transports were still on course for Guadalcanal, two or three destroyers were heading back to the Shortlands, and black columns of smoke from three of the Army transports were visible along the track of the convoy. Before Thomas' pilots had a chance to select their targets, the Zekes were on them. The first section was attacked by what one of their gunners estimated to be ten of the enemy fighters. One made a beam run on Thomas, two or three others attacked from astern, another head on. A Zeke which had just passed under the second section, to the starboard of the skipper's, crossed Thomas' tail and showed his belly as he pulled away. Thomas' rear-seat gunner opened up with his twin thirties, and the Japanese burst into flames, flipped over onto his back, and dived into the sea. Despite this distraction, Thomas managed to go into a seventy-degree dive over one of the transports and scored a hit. One plane was badly shot up and spun out of the combat, but managed to make it back to Henderson Field with twenty-eight holes in it.

The second section was attacked at the same time as

Thomas. A Zeke made a head-on run on Wakeham and Robinson while another came in from astern. A 20-millimeter shell hit Robinson's engine, which started a fire and made it quit. He sideslipped as he dropped out of the formation, which put out the fire, then dove steeply, which started his engine again. With the Zeke glued to his tail he went down almost vertically, rolling alternately to left and right to throw off the aim of the Japanese pilot. He pulled out at 2,500 feet, having kept his 1,000-pound bomb to increase his speed. Although his air-speed indicator was showing 320 knots, the persistent Zeke stayed with him; he split-S'ed down to 200 feet and tried to scrape his enemy off on the hills and coconut palms of one of the Russell Islands. After hedgehopping all the way across the island, Robinson nosed over to pick up speed, then pulled up sharply toward the clouds. The Japanese decided to pursue the matter no further, acknowledged the standoff with a good-natured rocking of his wings, and headed back for the transports. Robinson's battered "Ten Baker Eleven" landed at Henderson at 1630 with sixty-eight holes in it. Welch and Wakeham never returned. Tiny Jeff Carroum, the fourth man in Welch's section, had the kind of adventure that many airmen had to undergo in the South Pacific—only perhaps a little more so. After Carroum put his bomb on one of the transports, a Zeke shot up his engine and he ditched twenty-five miles off the Russell Islands. He and his radioman, Hynson, were unable to get the life rafts out of the SBD before it sank, and they had to rely on their Mae Wests to keep them afloat while they swam toward the distant islands. Hynson died of exhaustion after a day, but Carroum lived through three days of drifting across the sunlit sea without food or water. Eventually washed ashore he was fed and housed by friendly Melanesians and picked up by a PBY two weeks after he was shot down.

The disastrous result of Thomas' attack was the first setback in a day of almost uninterrupted American success. Unhappily, though, it was not to be the last. Colonel Bauer, the worshiped Guadalcanal fighter commander, was shot down at the very end of the day. He, with Foss and Furlow of VMF-121, had provided high cover for the final attacks of Joe Sailer, Coffin, and the mixed VS-10–VMSB-142 flight. As the SBDs and TBFs left, the three F4Fs went down to make a strafing run on some of the surviving transports. Then they ran for home, right down on the water. They should not have

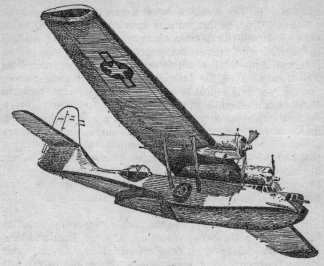

PBY

been down low. One of Woods's biggest worries during the battle was over the nonappearance of the Japanese fighters, and he told his own fighters to stay at high altitude. But the Coach, pugnacious as ever, wanted to get a shot at the enemy, and yielding to temptation was to cost him his life. Two Zekes attacked them from astern, and Bauer turned into them. One blew up, and Foss and Furlow went after the other. He led them over a Japanese destroyer, which broke up the fight with its antiaircraft fire. When the pair returned, they found the Coach just swimming out of an oil slick left by his downed aircraft. Foss tried unsuccessfully to drop him his life raft, but it would not release. Bauer pointed toward Guadalcanal and waved to him; unable to raise Cactus on radio, the two F4Fs rushed back at full throttle.

Joe Renner and Foss were taxiing to the end of the strip in the field's rescue amphibian only minutes after the two fighters landed. They waited, agonized and frustrated, while a squadron of Army B-26s just arriving from Nouméa landed, one after the other. Aircraft landing always had precedence over aircraft taking off, and the bombers were low on gas after their long trip. It was after dark when the "duck" finally was airborne. The scene below as they approached the Russell Islands from the blackness was weird. The light from five burning ships flickered from the bottom of low-lying nocturnal clouds, with an occasional bright flare as more of the Japanese Army's ammunition exploded. Renner and Foss circled helplessly in the darkness, unable to see a thing down on the water. Eventually despairing, they went back to Henderson. Sometime that night, Indian Joe Bauer died a lonely death swimming through a black sea lit fitfully by the fires and the flickering shadows on the clouds. Perhaps it was a wound, perhaps exhaustion, perhaps a shark. The legend that had grown around him in a few brief weeks had helped his hard-driven pilots to surpass themselves when it was vital that they do so. Now, like others before him, he was taken away just as his supreme usefulness had passed.

A few miles away across the dark water, on the dimly lit bridge of the destroyer *Hayashio,* a tired Rear Admiral Tanaka was taking stock of a disastrous day. Seven of his eleven transports were gone, and as many destroyers had returned to the Shortlands, laden with 5,000 survivors. Seven of the covering Zekes had been shot down. The crews of his four remaining destroyers, which had been zigzagging at top speed under attack and firing almost continuously for ten hours, were near exhaustion. A Japanese patrol plane caught a distant glimpse during the day of Rear Admiral Lee's *Washington* and *South Dakota* with their escorting destroyers heading north, and they had been reported to Tanaka as four cruisers and four destroyers. It was clear to the Japanese admiral that the American ships would be waiting for his surviving transports off Cape Esperance. Mikawa's Eighth Fleet, which was supposed to have provided cover for the troop convoy, had been forced back to the Shortlands by the attacks of the Guadalcanal-based Marines and Air Group Ten. Furthermore, Tanaka did not know whether or not Vice-Admiral Kondo's Second Fleet planned to leave its covering position near Ontong Java to intercept the American force. His alternatives were to go on, unescorted, to probable destruction off Guadalcanal, or to turn his stricken remnant around and await developments out of range of American aircraft. His dilemma was resolved for him by a dispatch late in the afternoon from Yamamoto ordering him to continue on to Guadalcanal. Somewhat later, radio communication was established with the Second Fleet and Tanaka learned that the battleship *Kirishima* and the heavy cruisers *Atago* and *Takao* were being sent in to provide support for the troop landings. Shortly before midnight, the three big ships were sighted directly ahead of *Hayashio*.

The light cruisers and destroyers of Kondo's force first made contact with the two American battleships shortly after 2300. The customary brilliant torpedo tactics of the Japanese light forces sank two of Lee's escorting destroyers and crippled the other two before any of them could launch a single torpedo of their own. *South Dakota*, silhouetted by a burning destroyer, was then illuminated by searchlights from the three Japanese heavy ships and her superstructure badly damaged by forty-two 14-inch and 8-inch shells fired at the close range of 5,000 yards. At this point, *Washington* fired eight nine-gun salvos of 16-inch at the *Kirishima* and reduced her to a wreck in a matter of minutes.

Lee, by then left with only *Washington* in action, turned to the north. Kondo briefly paralleled his course while he digested the information that he faced two new American battleships with only two heavy cruisers and light forces. When this fact sank home, the Japanese turned sharply away and retired behind a smoke screen. Satisfied that he had successfully countered the troop landing, Lee then withdrew to the south. The shattered *Kirishima* was scuttled and abandoned by her crew at 0320, the second Japanese battleship lost in as many days.

Far distant, Tanaka had anxiously watched the progress of the night battle. Of the twenty-three ships with which he had left the Shortlands less than two days before, only *Hayashio* and four transports remained. The indomitable admiral ordered them to run full speed for Guadalcanal, realizing that his only hope of getting the remnants of the 38th Division ashore was to run his troopships aground. His recommendation to do so was first rejected by Mikawa and then approved by Kondo. So it was that, in the faint predawn light of November 15, *Kinugawa Maru, Yamatsuki Maru, Hirokawa Maru*, and *Yamaura Maru* ran up on the Guadalcanal beaches at Doma Cove and Tassafaronga Point. A few miles away, *Hayashio* fled northward to get out of aircraft range before dawn. The greatest of all the Cactus Expresses finally had arrived.

At 0555, eight SBDs led by Joe Sailer took off to attack

the beached ships, which were only fifteen miles away from the hornets' nest of Henderson Field. The Marines got three hits on two of the transports. Half an hour later, three aircraft of Scouting Ten went out, accompanied by Scoffer Coffin in a TBF armed with four 500-pounders. The three SBDs were attacked at 12,000 feet by eight float Zeros, avoided them, and scored two hits on another transport. Coffin stayed low to avoid the Japanese fighters and got a hit with one of his bombs. Two more of Scouting Ten's dive bombers went out at 0700 for a search of the beaches and to bomb the most favorable targets. One hit a transport and the other placed his 1,000-pound bomb directly in the center of a huge pile of salvaged supplies which had been landed from another of the ships.

The two iron Marine majors, Sailer and Richard, took nine SBDs off at 0730, including two from Scouting Ten; this group hit an already-damaged transport with four more 1,000-pounders and scored another on the supply dump alongside. Returning with this group at 0825, Bill Martin was ready to go again twenty minutes later with three other SBDs. This flight got three more hits on one of the shattered Japanese ships, and was the final mission for Scouting Ten in the battle for Guadalcanal.

Only three more attacks were made on this last day of the great battle, all by Navy squadrons. About 0920, Swede Larsen and Engel of Torpedo Eight—flying unofficially, since their sqadron had been relieved—with two from Torpedo Ten took off to attack four of Tanaka's transports, burning and abandoned but still afloat off the Russells. They found them a little after 1000, and Engel struck the final blow of the war for Torpedo Eight by hitting one of the hulks squarely amidships. Welles hit the stern of another and both were left to sink. Four other VT-10 TBFs led by Coffin sprayed incendiaries and 500-pounders on each of the beaches where Tanaka's four surviving ships had run up on the shore of Doma Cove. Finally, three of Bombing Ten's SBDs in an early afternoon strike scored hits on one of the ruined Japanese transports and on a nearby ammunition dump. The latter burned for hours, producing enormous clouds of black smoke, and the sight was hailed by Radio Guadalcanal, with cheerful hyperbole, as the greatest ever seen on the island.

At 1230 two divisions of Fighting Ten took off to fly a combat air patrol over the field and Ironbottom Sound. Down below, the destroyer *Meade* operated in lonely splendor and cruiser seaplanes skittered back and forth between Tulagi and the wreckage of the two naval battles, picking up survivors. The CAP was uneventful until 1500, when the Henderson Field radar picked up a flight of Japanese aircraft sixty-five miles out. In a flurry of roaring engines and clouds of dust, eight more F4Fs of Fighting Ten scrambled from the Fighter Strip in two divisions, led by Stan Ruehlow and Bobby Edwards. Jimmy Flatley took the CAP up to 20,000, keeping within gliding distance of the field because his eight planes were very short on fuel. Twenty minutes after the radar first located them, eleven Zekes were sighted over Savo Island and attacked by Ruehlow's and Edwards' divisions, closely followed by Flateley. It was a good fight. Stan Ruehlow, unsuccessful in his first experience of air combat at Santa Cruz, was absolutely determined that he was going to shoot down a Zeke. He singled out a loner, but his wingman evinced some interest too. Ruehlow's voice, clear and waspish, came over the radio: "Voris, that's *my* Zero. I saw him. Leave him alone!" A few seconds later the same voice, three octaves higher: "For Christ's sake, somebody get this guy off my tail!" The Fighting Ten pilots claimed six. Butch Voris was slightly wounded and Dave Pollack ditched in the sound, but was recovered unharmed.

So ended the five days of almost unrelieved combat called the Battle for Guadalcanal. It was the climax of eighty-seven desperate days during which the whole future course of the Pacific depended on what happened to a little airstrip on an obscure and disagreeable island. In his final lunge at Henderson Field, Yamamoto used four battleships, two carriers, eight cruisers, thirty-three destroyers, and eleven transports. He lost two of the battleships—the only two he committed to action—a cruiser, three destroyers, ten transports, and about 4,000 men. For this staggering cost, the result was the landing at Doma Cove of 2,000 soldiers, 260 cases of artillery ammunition, and 1,500 bags of rice.

Why did the Americans win? Certainly a large part of the answer was the sacrifice of Callaghan's ships and men in the early morning hours of the 13th. If they had not kept the Japanese battleships from bombarding Henderson Field, the whole Cactus Air Force might have been nearly wiped out as it had been a month before. In this case, the enemy troop convoy might have suffered far less damage, and the bulk of its troops and equipment could have survived the trip to the island.

Next in importance was the intervention of the *Enterprise* Air Group just when it was needed most badly. The Japanese cruiser bombardment, the weather, and the exhaustion of the ground crews reduced the Cactus Air Force to a critically low number of available aircraft by the 14th. The fresh and experienced Air Group Ten provided enough margin of strength to cripple the Eighth Fleet and destroy Tanaka's convoy. Finally, the endless work of the Henderson Field ground crews and the unflagging courage of the pilots and gunners of the Cactus Air Force and Air Group Ten owe much of their inspiration to the energy and aggressiveness of Louis Woods. Quick, decisive, seemingly everywhere, with a sharp order here, a word of encouragement there, the stocky Marine aviator was, in the words of one of his air group commanders, "the finest officer I ever saw in the Battle for Guadalcanal."

One factor that is still unexplained is the almost complete lack of Japanese air opposition. Certainly the execution wrought by the Cactus Air Force on November 11 and 12 must account for some of this passivity. Twenty of Kusaka's maximum of seventy available Bettys were lost in those two days. But the enemy's fighters were employed only on fruitless defensive missions covering the *Hiei* and Tanaka's convoy, instead of on the aggressive sweeps that might have chewed up Woods's air strength. It is equally unclear why Yamamoto never committed the *Hiyo* and *Junyo* to the battle. Probably they lacked enough aircraft to be effective, or perhaps by then he had come to realize what was likely to happen to any ship that got within aircraft range of Henderson Field during the daylight hours.

17

EIGHTY-SEVEN DAYS
August 20–November 15

So, after eighty-seven days, the trial of the Cactus Air Force ended. Although the battle for Guadalcanal went on until the 9th of February, 1943, exactly six months after the American landings, the days of desperation passed with the November crisis. The pilots and gunners kept on flying, the ground crews continued to work endlessly, and the dusty, mud-spattered, sun-faded fighters and dive bombers still taxied every day out to the take-off end of the airstrips and floated in over the palm trees at the end of the day. The dust clouds still blew across the field and rain fell day in and day out. The men of the Cactus Air Force—those who were still on the island—were too busy to realize that it was all over.

There still would be combat, although there was only one more major air attack on Guadalcanal before the Japanese abandoned it. And there still would be losses: the able Joe Sailer was shot down on December 1 in an attack on a group of destroyers and did not return. The war slowly moved up into the Northern Solomons in 1943. But before it did so there was one final act in the drama of Guadalcanal. On April 18, 1943, Army P-38s took off from Henderson Field and headed north toward Bougainville. The flight was commanded by Major John Mitchell, one-time flight leader in the 67th Fighter Squadron, and included several Guadalcanal veterans. Their mission was one of strategic assassination. Alerted by the Pacific Fleet's cryptographic wizardry, they had the precise itinerary of Admiral Isoroku Yamamoto, commander in chief of the Combined Fleet, on an inspection trip to forward air bases. They went out to shoot down his airplane, and they were successful. His plane plunged, burning, into the jungles of Bougainville. And so the great Yamamoto was killed by planes and men from the airfield he had tried so long and so fruitlessly to capture.

Eleven months after Pearl Harbor, Japan's offensive power was irreparably shattered. The pitiful beachhead at Doma Cove with its burned, twisted ships and its few bags of rice was the high-water mark for a valiant, stubborn warrior race. The long nightmare of Guadalcanal was decisive. From mid-November, 1942, until their empire came to its end on the quarterdeck of the *Missouri*, the Japanese were in bitter, reluctant, but constant retreat. Until Midway they might have won their war. Until the Battle for Guadalcanal, the United States might still have lost it. When the final lunge at Guadalcanal was turned back, the empire was doomed.

The Guadalcanal campaign was overwhelmingly an air campaign. It all turned around the battered air strip in its grassy square mile of plain, and the men and planes that flew from it. The Marines safeguarded the field with their lives. The Japanese Army lost thousands of men trying hopelessly to recapture it. The two navies lost dozens of ships and more thousands of sailors, all for the purpose of saving or capturing Henderson Field. From this field, always outnumbered but never outfought, flew the few dozen planes and few hundred men of the Cactus Air Force. In large part it was those men who beat back four successively more powerful attempts to seize their vital airfield. It was against the rock of their courage and skill that a numerically larger Japanese Air Force broke, and in its breaking took to their deaths the empire's best pilots. The air arm of the Japanese Navy never recovered from the savage attrition of those few weeks in late 1942.

There was a little more to this epic than just stubbornness and the inability of United States Marines to admit defeat. Mostly there was courage. Not just the highhearted bravery of swift air combat, but the kind of courage that can keep men going day and night under appalling living conditions, exhaustion, and the ever-present fear of death. Americans were not supposed to have the fortitude needed for the long pull. But the men of Henderson Field had it.

Tactical skill was perhaps of equal importance. It was this factor that allowed the Marine and Navy fighters, outnumbered in virtually every engagement they fought, consistently to shoot down more planes than they lost. The use of the two-plane section as the basic air fighting unit, the dive-and-run tactics of the F4F, and the marvelous ruggedness of that little fighter were all elements of tactical excellence. But all of them would have been unavailing without the coastwatchers. That handful of brave Australians living in primitive isolation far behind enemy lines, facing death every time they sent their vital radio messages, was an essential part of the team. Without the advance warning they provided, the American fighters would have been caught on the ground or at low altitude once too often, and that would have been the end of the Cactus Air Force—and of Guadalcanal.

It is too easy to dismiss the Japanese performance as totally inept. To be sure, the Eleventh Air Fleet never was able to defeat the American airmen, even though they usually outnumbered them two to one. To some extent this was because Japanese air tactics never evolved beyond World War I-style dogfighting, and their aircraft sacrificed all defensive qualities in order to excel in maneuverability. They could not cope very well with adversaries who declined to fight them on these terms. But the major Japanese problem was their lack of bulldozers, not fighter planes. They never appreciated the importance of rapid airstrip construction in an island war, nor had they the tradition and experience of large construction projects that gave the Americans endless varieties of earth-moving equipment and thousands of skilled operators. The slow pace of Japanese airstrip construction in the Solomons probably condemned their pilots to as many losses as did their tactical and material weaknesses. The distances involved in flying from Rabaul and Kavieng to Guadalcanal and back, as has been said, forced the Japanese fighters to accept combat laden with belly tanks they *couldn't* jettison. And the long flight back through the violent weather that so often overlay the Solomons meant eventual ditching for many a damaged aircraft that might have made it to a closer base.

It is difficult to be very precise about the relative losses of the Cactus Air Force and the Eleventh Air Fleet. Japanese records simply are incomplete; the few surviving action reports of the units involved mention no losses at all for virtually all of September, although other records show that thirty-six Zekes and twenty-four Bettys were lost in combat that month. The estimate of a Japanese staff officer, cited in

Sherrod's *History of Marine Corps Aviation in World War II,* that eighty-three fighters and fifty-three bombers were the total Japanese losses during the entire Guadalcanal campaign proves, on the most cursory examination of Japanese records, to be far too low. Records kept by the Japanese Navy on monthly aircraft losses show that its combat losses for the four months of August-November, 1942, were 344 fighters, 125 land-based medium bombers, and 198 carrier-based bombers and torpedo planes. Since Japanese Naval aviation was engaged in major combat only in the Solomons during these months, the bulk of the losses must have been the result of the struggle for Guadalcanal and the carrier battles of the Eastern Solomons and Santa Cruz. The best estimate of the losses inflicted directly by the Cactus Air Force in air combat and by Guadalcanal's antiaircraft from August 20 through November 15 is ninety-six fighters, ninety-two Bettys, and seventy-five other types, mainly float planes. The Cactus Air Force's own combat losses during the same period were 101 aircraft. In other words, the men of Henderson Field, outnumbered two to one, shot down two and one half times as many planes as they lost. Eighty-four Cactus pilots were killed from all causes, thirty-eight of them fighter pilots killed in combat.

Not too surprisingly, many of those who excelled in the Cactus Air Force went on to full and useful lives. Roy Geiger, that complete Marine, became a commander of ground forces, led the Corps that took Guam and Okinawa and, on the latter island, became the only Marine and the only aviator ever to command an American field army. Louis Woods rose to the rank of lieutenant general, retiring in 1950. Smith and Galer both left the Marine Corps as colonels, but Mangrum, Marion Carl, John Dobbin, George Dooley, and Paul Fontana all stayed on to become general officers. Dick Mangrum retired in 1967 as a lieutenant general and assistant commandant of the Corps. Carl led some of the first Marine units into Vietnam in 1965 and in 1969 was a Major General. Joe Foss returned to his native South Dakota after the war, became its governor for two terms, and has remained in the public eye in various capacities.

Among the Navy flyers, Don Felt went on to become a four-star admiral and eventually to command all Army, Navy, and Marine units in the Pacific in which he once fought as an air-group commander. Fighting Five's exec,

Dave Richardson, as a vice admiral in 1968 commanded the 6th Fleet in the Mediterranean. Bullet Lou Kirn too became a rear admiral, and Turner Caldwell, as a vice-admiral, is the Navy's senior antisubmarine-warfare officer. Gus Widhelm was killed in a jet crash in 1954 and Jimmy Flatley died tragically of cancer in 1958.

The legendary heroism of the First Marine Division and the Cactus Air Force on Guadalcanal helped to give that fierce, proud old Corps the spirit that was to carry it over the satanic beaches of Iwo Jima and, in a later war, on the long march back from the Chongjin Reservoir. Perhaps the legend still is remembered sometimes along the Seventeenth Parallel by men condemned to relive the trials of their fathers.

Guadalcanal is quiet now, bypassed by history. A new city was built on the island after the war, a little west of the perimeter. Henderson Field and Fighter One still are there, and the faint signs of the battles on the Ridge can be found just to the south of them. Of the desperate days, little now remains to be seen. Small clouds of butterflies now dance over the grassy plain where, twenty-five years ago, men were so frightened and so brave. In the depths of the South Pacific the shattered ships sleep forever. Here and there in the darkness of the jungles, little heaps of torn aluminum and rusting steel lie in the rain, all that is left of the beauty and power of the planes. And over the silent islands the clouds roll and moil endlessly in a sky empty of man.

APPENDIX A
The Flyers of the Cactus Air Force

MARINE FIGHTING SQUADRON 223 (VMF-223)
August 20–October 11

Pilots   *(arrival date, remarks)*

Maj JL Smith   (8/20, Evac 10/11),

Maj RJ Morrell, Jr.   (8/20, WIA 9/5, Evac 9/6)

Capt ME Carl   (8/20, Evac 10/11)

Capt HK Marvin   (9/24, Evac 10/11)

2/Lt ER Bailey   (8/20, KIA 8/24)

2/Lt CM Canfield (8/27, Evac 9/10)

2/Lt RA Corry (8/20, KIA 8/26)

2/Lt KD Frazier   (8/20, Evac 10/12)

2/Lt FE Gutt   (8/20, Evac 10/12)

2/Lt CS Hughes   (8/27, Evac 10/12)

2/Lt CR Jeans   (8/20, Evac 10/12)

2/Lt CH Kendrick   (8/20, KIA 10/2)

2/Lt WS Lees III   (8/26, KIA 10/2)

2/Lt N McLennan   (8/20, KIA 9/13)

2/Lt H Phillips   (8/20, Evac 9/24)

2/Lt ZA Pond   (8/20, KIA 9/10)

2/Lt OH Ramlo   (8/20, WIA & Evac 9/14)

2/Lt RR Read   (8/20, Evac 10/11)

2/Lt EA Trowbridge   (8/26, Injured in crash & Evac 9/14)

2/Lt CG Winter   (8/27, Evac 10/11)

T. Sgt JD Lindley   (8/20, Evac ?)

Pilots from other squadrons who served in VMF-223

Maj FR Payne   (VMF-212, 9/27–10/2)

Capt LD Everton   (VMF-212, 8/26–8/31)

2/Lt JE Conger   (VMF-212, 9/27–10/2)

2/Lt JSP Dean, Jr   (VMF-121, 9/28–)

2/Lt FC Drury   (VMF-212, 9/27–10/2)

2/Lt CM Freeman   (VMF-212, 8/20–8/26)

2/Lt RO Haring   (VMF-212, 8/27, KIA 9/13)

2/Lt JH King   (VMF-212, 8/20–)

2/Lt FA Lynch   (VMF-121, 9/27–)

2–Lt JM Massey   (VMF-212, 8/20–8/26)

2/Lt McLeod   (VMF-212, 8/20–8/26)

2/Lt Taylor   (VMF-212, 8/20–8/26)

MG HB Hamilton   (VMF-212, 8/20–8/26)

MARINE SCOUT BOMBING SQUADRON 232

(VMSB-232)

August 20–October 2

Pilots*   (*arrival date, remarks*)

LtCol RC Mangrum   (8/20, Evac 10/12)

Maj FL Brown, Jr.   (8/20, Lost in heavy weather 9/6)

Capt D Iverson, Jr.   (8/20, Wounted in bombardment of 9/12 & Evac 9/14)

2/Lt L Baldinus   (8/20, Killed in bombardment of 9/12)

2/Lt RB Fleener   (8/20, Evac 10/2)

2/Lt HW Hise   (8/20, Evac 9/3)

2/Lt CB McAllister   (8/20, Lost in heavy weather 9/6)

2/Lt DE McCafferty   (8/30, Evac 10/2)

2/Lt O Mitchell, Jr.   (8/20, Shot down by destroyer AA 8/28)

2/Lt TF Moore, Jr.   (8/20, Injured in crash & Evac 9/3)

2/Lt AF O'Keefe   (8/28, Evac 9/16)

2/Lt DV Rose   (8/20, Killed in bombardment of 9/12)

2/Lt LE Thomas (8/20, Shot down accidentally & killed by US Navy AA 9/18)

Aircrewmen†

Corp DE Byrd

PFC EL Eades

Pvt FL Fraley

PFC AS Gilbert

Corp CB Hallyburton   (Injured in crash and Evac 9/3)

Corp JK Humphreys

Pvt LP Macias

Pvt TL Mahan

Corp WR Proffit   (Lost in heavy weather 9/6)

Corp RS Russell   (Lost in heavy weather 9/6)

Pvt PO Schackman   (Shot down by destroyer AA 8/28)

Sgt DE Sewell

Sgt JN Stanner

---

*All pilots, with the exception of 2/Lt McCafferty, flew into Henderson Field from USS *Long Island* 8/20. All gunners but one flew in on the same day.

†Dates of evacuation of gunners not in available records.

67TH PURSUIT SQUADRON, USAAF

August 22–February 8, 1943

Pilots* (*arrival date, remarks*)

Maj DD Brannon (8/22, Injured in air raid & Evac 9/14)

Maj Hubbard (10/6, Evac 10/15)

Capt TJJ Christian (Evac 9/11)

Capt JW Mitchell (10/7)

Capt Sharpstein (10/7)

Capt JA Thompson (8/27, Evac 9/25)

1/Lt Barr

1/Lt BW Brown

1/Lt DS Canning (10/3)

1/Lt PM Childress (Injured in air raid & Evac 9/14)

1/Lt RE Chilson (KIA 8/30)

1/Lt GG Dewey (10/3)

1/Lt WL Dinn (10/7, Shot down 10/28. Walked in 11/4)

1/Lt AH Dutton

1/Lt WHB Erwin (Evac 9/11)

1/Lt Farron (10/7, KIA 10/14)

1/Lt KS Fjelstad (10/3)

1/Lt Gillon (10/7)

1/Lt MW Haedtler (10/4)

1/Lt VL Head

1/Lt BF Holmes (10/3)

1/Lt J Jacobson (10/7)

1/Lt JT Jarman

1/Lt BB Johnston (Evac 9/16)

1/Lt Kaiser

1/Lt RW Kerstetter (10/4)

1/Lt JK Morton (9/21, MIA 10/15)

1/Lt DP Miller, Jr. (9/21)

1/Lt AM Patterson (10/4)

1/Lt FV Purnell (10/7)

1/Lt LH Ramp (10/3)

1/Lt JR Sawyer (9/21)

1/Lt WS Shaw (10/7)

1/Lt Stern (10/7)

1/Lt KW Wyethes (KIA 8/30)

2/Lt KC Banfield (10/7, KIA 10/10)

2/Lt EE Brzuska (Evac 9/11)

2/Lt JF Campbell (10/3)

2/Lt BE Davis (Evac 9/16)

2/Lt EL Dews (10/7)

2/Lt BH Dillon

2/Lt EH Farnam (Shot down 9/22. Walked in & Evac 10/5)

2/Lt A Farquharson (9/22)

2/Lt RE Ferguson (9/22)

2/Lt DH Fincher (Injured in air raid & Evac 9/14)

2/Lt ZD Fountain (Evac 9/16)

2/Lt F Franz (10/4)

2/Lt LM Glazier (Evac 9/14)

2/Lt DC Goerke (Evac 10/15)

ENTERPRISE FLIGHT 300

August 24–September 27

Pilots (*arrival date, remarks*)

Lt TF Caldwell (8/24, Evac 9/27)

Lt RB Woodhull (8/24, Evac 9/17)

---

*Two pilots KIA 11/12 not identified in records of this squadron, which are fragmentary.

Ens JT Barker   (8/24, Evac
9/27)
Ens WE Brown   (8/24, Evac
9/27)
Ens HL Buell   (8/24, Evac
9/19)
Ens ER Conzett   (8/24, Evac
9/27)
Ens WW Coolbaugh   (8/24,
Evac 9/27)
Ens C Fink   (8/24, Evac
9/27)
Ens TT Guillory   (8/24, Evac
9/19)
Ens HW Liffner   (8/24, Evac
9/19)
Ens HC Manford   (8/24, Evac
9/17)
Aircrewmen
ARM 3/c EK Braun   (8/24,
Evac 9/21)

ARM 1/c JH Coles   (8/24,
Evac 9/27)
ARM 2/c NA Fives   (8/24,
Evac 9/27)
ARM 1/c AW Garlow   (8/24,
Evac 9/27)
ACRM WE Glidewell   (8/24,
Evac 9/27)
ARM 1/c CA Jaeger   (8/24,
Evac 9/27)
ARM 3/c HL Joselyn   (8/24,
Evac 9/27)
ARM 2/c ML Kimberlin
(8/24, Evac 9/27)
ARM 1/c SJ Mason, Jr.
(8/24, Evac 9/27)
ARM 3/c EJ Monahan (8/24,
Evac 9/27)
ARM 3/c JL Villareal (8/24,
Evac 9/27)

MARINE FIGHTING SQUADRON 224 (VMF-224)

August 30–October 16

Pilots   (arrival date, remarks)
Maj RE Galer   (8/30, Evac ?)
Maj K. Armistead   (8/30,
Evac 10/16)
Maj JF Dobbin   (8/30, Evac
10/16)
Capt DD Irwin   (8/30, Evac
10/16)
Capt SS Nicolay   (8/30, Evac
10/13)
2/Lt RR Amerine   (8/30,
Bailed out 8/31. Walked in
& Evac 9/9)
2/Lt WV Brooks   (8/30, Evac
10/16)
2/Lt CE Bryan   (8/30, MIA
8/31)
2/Lt RM D'Arcy   (8/30, Evac
10/16)
2/Lt DS Hartley   (8/30, Evac
10/16)

2/Lt GL Hollowell   (8/30,
Evac 10/16)
2/Lt R Jefferies, Jr.   (8/30,
KIA 9/5)
2/Lt AJ Johnson   (8/30, Evac
10/16)
2/Lt JM Jones   (8/30, KIA
9/9)
2/Lt MH Kennedy   (9/3,
Evac 10/16)
2/Lt CM Kunz (8/30, Evac
10/16)
2/Lt CH Moore   (8/30, WIA
9/9 & Evac)
2/Lt JC Musselman   (8/30,
Evac 10/16)
2/Lt GE Thompson   (8/30,
MIA 8/31)
2/Lt HL Walter   (9/3, Evac
10/16)
S.Sgt CD Garrabrant   (8/30,
KIA 9/5)

Pilots from other squadrons who flew with VMF-224

2/Lt CC Chamberlain (VMF-212, 9/13, Evac 9/18)

2/Lt LM Faulkner (VMF-212)

2/Lt RF Flaherty (VMF-212)

2/Lt TH Mann (VMF-121, 9/25)

2/Lt CJ Quilter (VMF-212)

2/Lt RF Stout (VMF-212)

2/Lt JAO Stub (VMF-121, 9/25, Evac 10/3)

2/Lt GA Treptow (VMF-121, 9/25, KIA 10/2)

2/Lt WM Watkins (VMF-212)

2/Lt RO White (VMF-212)

MARINE SCOUT BOMBING SQUADRON 231

(VMSB-231)

August 30–October 16

Pilots (arrival date, remarks)

Maj LR Smith (8/30, Evac 9/19)

Capt EA Glidden, Jr. (8/30, Evac 10/16)

Capt R Iden (8/30, Ditched out of gas & drowned 9/20)

Capt B Prosser (8/30, Evac 9/19)

2/Lt RJ Bear (8/30, Evac 10/11)

2/Lt HV Cook (8/30, Evac 10/15)

2/Lt YW Kaufman (8/30, Killed in crash while on search 9/14)

2/Lt OD Johnson (8/30, KIA 9/13)

2/Lt DL Leslie (8/30, Shot down 9/28. Rescued by coastwatchers, returned 11/3)

2/Lt GB Loeffel (8/30, Evac 10/16)

2/Lt VG Rubincam (8/30, Evac 10/13)

2/Lt AM Smith (8/30, Evac 10/7)

2/Lt RW Vaupel (8/30, WIA 10/7, evac 10/9)

2/Lt JW Weintraub (8/30, Killed during bombardment of 9/12)

2LLt JW Zuber (8/30, Evac 10/13)

S. Sgt LF Blass (8/30, Evac 10/16)

S. Sgt. WW Witherspoon (8/30, Evac 10–16)

*Aircrewmen**

Pvt BJ Arnold (Killed in crash while on search 9/14)

Pfc VS Byrd

Pfc TA Costello

S. Sgt CT Hickman

Sgt MT Johnston

Sgt JB McDougall

Pfc RT Ramsay

Pfc WJ Reid

Corp DL Rhodes

Corp RS Russell

Sgt TL Sidebottom (Wounded & Evac 9/12)

Pfc HE Smith

Pfc JB Strange

Pfc FW Thiessen

Pfc HB Thomas (KIA 9/13)

Pfc WH Tubbs

Pfc WH Van Kirk

Pfc DM Winters

*All aircrewmen arrived 8/30. Dates evacuated not available.

SCOUTING SQUADRON THREE (VS-3)

September 6–October 17

Pilots   (arrival date, remarks)

Lcdr LJ Kirn   (9/13, Evac 10/17)

Lt MP McNair   (9/13, Evac 10/17)

Lt RM Milner   (9/6, Evac 10/17)

Lt FJ Schroeder   (9/13, Evac 9/20)

Lt R Weymouth

Ltjg RP Balenti   (9/28, Evac 10/17)

Ltjg JJ Davidson   (9/28, Evac 10/17)

Ltjg WJ Foley, Jr.   (9/28, Evac 10/17)

Ltjg AS Frank   (9/6, Evac 10/17)

Ltjg WE Henry   (9/13), Evac 10/17)

Ltjg EC Mildahn   (9/13, Evac 10/17)

Ens DW Byerly   (9/13, Evac 10/17)

Ens LR Comer   (9/13, Evac 10/17)

Ens RC Crow   (9/16, Evac 10/6)

Ens O Newton   (9/6, KIA 9/16)

Ens RE Pellissier   (9/6, Evac 9/16)

Ens RC Purdum   (9/13, Evac 10/17)

Ens AG Russell   (9/13, Evac)

Ens FJ Sauer   (9/13, Evac 10/17)

Ens ES Wages, Jr.   (9/6, MIA 9/13)

Ens NS Weary   (9/13, Evac 10/17)

Ens A Wright   (9/13, Evac 10/17

Aircrewmen

ARM 2/c DH Beaman   (9/6, Evac 10/17)

ARM 3/c GD Bradberry   (9/13, Evac 10/17)

ARM 3/c MM Bryson   (9/13, Evac 10/17)

ARM 2/c AW Dobson   (9/13, Evac 10/17)

ARM 2/c GJ Farrell   (9/6, Evac 10/17)

ARM 3/c CM Gunter   (9/28, Evac 10/17)

ARM 3/c R Hanson   (9/13, Evac 10/17)

S.2/c V Henry   (9/6, MIA 9/13)

ARM 3/c KL Johnson   (9/28, Evac 10/17)

ARM 3/c M Lachowitz   (9/13, Evac 10/17)

ARM 3/c E Ladwick   (9/13, Evac 10/17)

ARM 3/c TH Liever   (9/6, Evac 10/17)

ARM 2/c WM Rambur   (9/13, Evac 10/17)

ACRM CE Russ   (9/13, Evac 10/17)

ARM 1/c JW Schliekelman,   (9/28, Evac 10/17)

ARM 2/c CR Simpson   (9/13, Evac 10/17)

ARM 3/c WT Stafford   (9/6, Evac 10/17)

ARM 2/c BA Sumner   (9/13, Evac 10/17)

ARM 3/c MK Taylor   (9/13, Evac 10/17)

ARM 3/c RS Thornton   (9/6, KIA 9/16)

ARM 3/c WL Wright   (9/13, Evac 10/17)

FIGHTING SQUADRON FIVE (VF-5)

September 11–October 16

Pilots (arrival date, remarks)

Ledr LC Simpler (9/11, Evac 10/16)

Lt WE Clarke (9/11, Evac 10/15)

Lt HW Crews (9/11, Evac 10/5)

Lt HM Jensen (9/27, Evac 10/16)

Lt DC Richardson (9/11, WIA & evac 9/12. Returned 10/12, Evac 10/16)

Ltjg FO Green (9/11, Evac 10/15)

Ltjg HL Grimmell, Jr. 9/11, Evac 10/15)

Ltjg ET Stover (9/11, Evac 10/15)

Ens FJ Blair (9/27, Evac 10/16)

Ens MK Bright (9/11, Evac 10/6)

Ens BF Currie (9/11, Evac 10/5)

Ens CE Eichenberger (9/11, Killed in crash after combat 9/12)

Ens JA Halford (9/11, Evac 10/14)

Ens DA Innis (9/11, WIA & evac 9/13. Returned 10/11, evac 10/16)

Ens JM Kleinman (9/27, Evac 10/15)

Ens MV Kleinmann, Jr. (9/11, Evac 10/14)

Ens RL Loesch (9/11, WIA & evac 9/13)

Ens HA March (9/11, Evac 10/6)

Ens JB McDonald (9/27, Evac 10/14)

Ens GJ Morgan (9/11, MIA 10/2)

Ens FR Register (9/11, Evac 10/14)

Ens MC Roach (9/11, Evac 10/14)

Ens WM Rouse 9/11, WIA & Evac 10/15. Missing on ferry flight 10/21)

Ens JD Shoemaker (9/11, KIA 9/29)

Ens JM Wesolowski (9/11, Evac 10/14)

Ens WW Wileman (9/11, KIA 9/13)

NAP RM Nesbitt (9/11, Evac 10/15)

NAP LP Mankin (9/11, Evac 10/14)

Pilots from other Squadrons who flew with VF-5

Lt CW Rooney (VF-71, 10/5)*

Ltjg RH Kenton VF-71, 10/5)*

Ltjg RH Myers (VF-71, 10/5, Evac 10/16)

Ltjg CW Tucker (VF-71, 10/5, MIA 10/9)

---

*Remained after 10/16 to fly with VMF-121. Date of evacuation not in records.

TORPEDO SQUADRON EIGHT (VT-8)

September 13–November 16

Pilots (arrival date, remarks)

Lt HH Larsen (9/13, Evac 11/16)

Lt BL Harwood (9/28, Evac 10/16)

Ltjg JP Barnum (9/13, Evac 10/16)

Ltjg RA Divine (9/28, Evac 11/14)

Ltjg AK Earnest (9/13, Evac 10/27)

Ltjg LS Engel (9/18, Evac 11/16)

Ltjg RS Evarts (10/1, Evac 11/14)

Ens Grady (9/13, Injured & evac 9/14)

Ltjg ER Hanson (9/13, Evac 10/27)

Ltjg A Katz (9/28, Evac 10/27)

Ltjg F Mears (10/1, Evac 10/27)

Ltjg RE Ries (9/28, Evac 10/16)

Ltjg J Taurman (10/3, Ditched 10/5 and never located)

Ens WG Esders (10/3, Evac 10/16)

CAP BM Doggett (9/13, Killed in crash during night bombing attack 10/5)

CAP WH Dye (9/18, Ditched 10/1 and evac)

Aircrewmen

ARM 3/c JE Aube (9/13)

ARM 1/c A Aulick (9/13)

ARM 2/c J Bachlotte (10/1)

AMM 2/c FW Balsley (9/13)

AOM 3/c WW Bartlett

ARM 3/c RJ Bradley (10/3, Ditched with Ltjg Taurman 10/5, rescued 10/8)

AOM 3/c B Bragg

AOM 3/c FB Carniero (9/28)

AOM 3/c NE Delchamps 9/28)

AM 2/c AC DeWeber (9/28)

AMM 2/c WA Dietsch (10/1)

AOM 1/c BC Edmonds (9/28)

S 1/c HA Fortson (9/28)

Ptr 1/c RM Francis (9/13)

AM 3/c EL Hawkins (10/1)

ARM 3/c JD Hayes (9/13, Killed in crash during night bombing attack 10/5)

ARM 3/c GL Hicks (9/13)

ARM 2/c JW King (9/28)

ARM 2/c ZW Kowaleski (10/1)

AM 2/c CH Lawrence (9/13, Killed in crash during night bombing attack 10/5)

ARM 3/c RW Liccioni (9/28)

ARM 3/c J McNamara (9/28)

S 1/c JP Miller (9/13)

ARM 2/c CE Monroe (9/28)

AOM 1/c BM Rich (9/12)

S 1/c J Robak (10/3, Lost in ditching 10/5)

AOM 3/c RL Shively

S 1/c RC Smyth (9/13)

ARM 1/c CM Sparks (9/13)

AOM 3/c RJ Steele

AOM 3/c EC Struble

ACRM JG Sullivan (9/28)

AOM 1/c EF Wendt (9/13)

AOM 2/c GP Wirick (10/3)

ARM 2/c JW Wright (9/13)

MARINE SCOUT BOMBING SQUADRON 141
(VMSB-141)

September 23–November 19

Pilots (arrival date, remarks)

Maj GA Bell (10/5–6, Killed during bombardment of 10/14)

Capt RA Abbott (10/5–6, Killed during bombardment of 10/14)

Capt EF Miller (10/5–6, Killed during bombardment of 10/14)

1/Lt LR Norman (9/30, KIA 10/8)

2/Lt WS Ashcraft (9/23, KIA 11/8)

2/Lt WE Ayres (9/30, Shot down 10/2)

2/Lt WR Bartosh (9/30)

2/Lt W Baumet, Jr. (10/7, Killed in crash 10/26)

2/Lt D Benedetti (10/5–6, KIA 10/15)

2/ Lt JA Blumenstein (9/23, WIA 10/7, Evac 10/9)

2/Lt WB Campbell (10/5–6)

2/Lt HA Chaney, Jr. (9/30, Killed during bombardment of 10/14)

2/Lt DA Daglish (10/5–6)

2/Lt JL Dexter (10/5–6)

2/Lt GH Elliott (Lost on catapulting from *Copahee*, 9/29)

2/Lt JF Fogarty (10/5–6, Killed in crash 10/22)

2/Lt WH Fuller (9/30,

2/Lt SJ Gillespie (10/5–6, Missing on patrol 10/17)

2/Lt RF Graham (10/5–6)

2/Lt CF Hahn (10/5–6)

2/Lt JW Hanna (9/30)

2/Lt JO Hull (10/2)

2/Lt RW Johannessen (10/5–6)

2/Lt JR Kennedy (10/5–6)

2/Lt WJ Knapp (9/30, KIA 11/13)

2/Lt RC LeBlanc (10/5–6, KIA 10/15)

2/Lt RK Meents (10/5–6, KIA 10/31)

2/Lt WP Parrish (10/5–6)

2/Lt RM Patterson (9/23)

2/Lt A Sandretto (10/5–6, KIA 11/13)

2/Lt JE Shepard (10/5–6)

2/Lt SA Shute (10/5–6)

2/Lt LS Smith III (9/23, KIA 11/12)

2/Lt FB Sullivan (?)

2/Lt AJ Turtora (9/26, Killed in crash 10/15)

2/Lt JM Waterman, Jr. (9/23, KIA 10/16)

S. Sgt HK Bruce (10/5–6)

S. Sgt JD Cook (9/30, KIA 10/9)

S. Sgt FW Lescher (10/5–6)

Aircrewmen

Aldridge

Sgt J Astronskas

S. Sgt DA Barwick

Pvt FE Bensnyder

Sgt EJ Burman

Sgt WT Campbell (KIA 10/9)

Pfc JR Carey

Sgt JM Conn

Sgt SB D'Armond

Corp LR Dixon

T. Sgt JF Fazendin

Pvt NH Frank

Corp XL Fulton (KIA 11/13)

Corp HW Hamilton

S. Sgt TB Haynes, Jr. (KIA 11/12)

Sgt RH Kerr (KIC 10/15)

S. Sgt LJ Kniffle (KIC 10/22)

Pfc FF Lamons

Corp RE LeBlanc (MIA 10/15)

S. Sgt LM Manning (KIA 11/13)

Corp RJ Martin

S. Sgt EL McClelland

Sgt BB McVicker

Pvt SER Nelson (KIA 10/8)

Pvt EJ O'Connor (KIC 10/26)

Corp NG Perez

Pfc HA Peterson

Pfrc ER Priest (KIA 10/15)

Corp SD Preston (KIA 11/8) Reid

Sgt PH Rivers (KIA 10/15)

Pfc SF Smith (Missing on patrol 10/17)

Pvt LS Sopuch

Corp CA Strauss

Corp JL Vallee

Pfc LA Van Belle

Pfc JE Walsh

Pfc EJ Witkowski (MIA 10/31)

Corp GA Wood

Arrival dates of aircrewmen not in available records.

SCOUTING SQUADRON 71 (VS-71)*

September 28–November 7

Pilots (arrival date, remarks)
Ledr J Eldridge, Jr. (9/28, Killed in crash on Santa Isabel in storm 11/2)
Lt PW Maxwell (10/3)
Lt WP Kephart (10/3, Killed during bombardment of 10/14
Ltjg P Coit (?)
Ltjg CH Chester (?)
Ltjg RH Perritte (9/28, Missing on patrol 10/2)
Ens WR Garrett (9/28)
Ens GR Lerman (10/3, Missing on patrol 11/2)
Ens RJ Mohler (10/3)

Ens HN Murphy (10/3)
Ens CV Zalewski (10/3)
Aircrewmen
ARM 2/c EH Faast (10/3)
ARM 3/c IE Newsome, Jr. (9/28, Missing on patrol 10/2)
S 1/c T Panno (10/3)
ARM 3/c JW Phillips (10/3)
ACRM LA Powers, Jr. (9/28)
ARM 3/c CE Spires (9/28)
ARM 3/c JC Swann (10/3, Missing on patrol 11/2)
ARM 3/c TJ Turner, Jr. (10/3)
ARM 3/ FE Wise (10/3)

MARINE FIGHTING SQUADRON 121 (VMF-121)†

October 9–December

Pilots (Remarks)
Maj LK Davis
Capt JJ Foss
1/Lt OH Brueggeman
1/Lt EC Fry

2/Lt DK Allen
2/Lt Andrews
2/Lt OM Bate (MIA 11/7)
2/Lt KC Brandon (KIA 11/14)

*Most surviving pilots and aircrewmen evacuated by 11/7.
†Most of VMF-121's pilots were flown off the *Copahee* into Guadalcanal 10/9. A few arrived later by transport plane.

224   THE CACTUS AIR FORCE

2/Lt CC Chamberlain (Evac 10/19)
2/Lt DL Clark
2/Lt JH Clark
2/Lt WH Craft
2/Lt D Doyle (KIA 11/7)
2/Lt M Folsom
2/Lt WB Freeman
2/Lt Furlow
2/Lt LD Grow (Shot down 10/18. Rescued by coast watchers & returned 11/3)
2/Lt RG Haberman
2/Lt GK Loesch

2/Lt WE Marontate
2/Lt JL Narr
2/Lt AL Nehf
2/Lt AA Nuwer (KIA 10/20)
2/Lt RMA Ruddell
2/Lt Rutledge (KIA 10/15)
2/Lt Schuler
2/Lt RF Simpson
2/Lt WG Wethe
S. Sgt JA Feliton
M. Sgt JJ Palko
T. Sgt A Thompson (KIA 10/15)

Pilots of other squadrons who flew with VMF-121

Lt CW Rooney (VF–71)
Ltjg RH Kenton (VF–71)
Ltjg HH Reese (VF–71)
Ltjg MC Thrash (VF–71)

BOMBING SQUADRON SIX (VB-6)*

October 14–November 3

Pilots

Ledr R Davis
Lt RP Kline
Ltjg VL Michael
Ltjg RH Mills
Ltjg WR Pittman
Ltjg GS Richey
Ltjg EE Rodenberg
Ltjg RF Wolfe

Aircrewmen

AMM 1/c HH Carruthers
AMM 2/c SL Duncan
ARM 1/c ES Gerandy
ARM 1/c JF Heard
AOM 2/c HL Jones
AMM 1/c JV Lawless
ACMM WE Schwarz
ACRM JW Tratt

MARINE FIGHTING SQUADRON 212 (VMF-212)

October 16–into 1943

Pilots (arrival date, remarks)
Lt Col HF Bauer (10/16, KIA 11/14)
Maj FR Payne, Jr.† (10/16)
Capt LD Everton† (10/16)
1/Lt RR Baker (10/16)

1/Lt SF Bastian (10/16)
1/Lt CC Chamberlain (10/16, Evac 10/19)
1/Lt JE Congert† (10/16)
1/Lt LM Faulkner (10/16)
1/Lt JH King† (10/16, Shot

*All pilots and aircrewmen arrived October 14. Most were evacuated Nov. 3.
†Served temporarily with VMF-223 or VMF-224 prior to arrival of squadron as a unit.

down 10/25. Walked in
  10/29)
1/Lt JM Massey† (10/16)
1/Lt JF Rogers (10/16)
1/Lt JP Sigman (10/16)
1/Lt RF Stout (10/16)
2/Lt FC Drury† (10/16)
2/Lt RF Flaherty (10/16)

2/Lt CM Freeman† (10/16)
2/Lt CJ Quilter (10/16)
2/Lt WM Watkins (10/16)
2/Lt RO White (10/16)
MG HB Hamilton† (10/16),
  KIA 10/21)

MARINE SCOUT BOMBING SQUADRON 132*

(VMSB-132)

November 1–into 1943

Pilots (arrival date, remarks)
Maj LB Robertshaw (11/7)
Maj J Sailer, Jr. (11/1)
1/Lt CL Bright (11/1)
2/Lt HC Haum, Jr. (11/7)
2/Lt WA Eck (11/1)
2/Lt WR Gentry (11/1,
  Killed in crash during storm,
  night 11/2)
2/Lt GB Herlihy (11/7)
2/Lt WH Hronek (11/1)
2/Lt RL Janson (11/7)

2/Lt RE Kelly (11/1)
2/Lt CE Kollman (11/7)
2/Lt JH McEniry (11/7)
2/Lt MR Nawman (11/1,
  Killed in crash during storm,
  night 11/2)
2/Lt AD Simpson (11/7)
2/Lt J Skinner, Jr. (11/1)
2/Lt JE Sperzel (11/7)
M. Sgt KL Gordon (11/1)
S. Sgt FJ Wallof (11/7)
Aircrewmen

VMSB—132 Aircrewmen are identified in the squadron War Diary.

MARINE FIGHTING SQUADRON 112 (VMF-112)

November 2–into 1943

Pilots (arrival date, remarks)
Maj PJ Fontana (11/2)
Cap RB Fraser (11/10)
2/Lt HW Bollman (11/2)
2/Lt AA Case (11/10)
2/Lt LL Clark (11/2)
2/Lt HG Cleveland III
  (11/2, Evac 11/15)
2/Lt JJ DeBlanc (11/10)
2/Lt AG Donahue (11/7)

2/Lt F Green (11/10)
2/Lt TH Hughes, Jr. (11/10)
2/Lt JE Johnson (11/2)
2/Lt WW Laird (11/7)
2/Lt JB Maas (11/2)
2/Lt EK Pedersen (11/2)
2/Lt G Percy (11/10)
2/Lt JL Secrest (11/2)
2/Lt FE Sedlacek (11/10,
  Evac 11/15)

*Another six pilots arrived on the island after the Battle for Guadal-
canal. They are not listed because they were not present during the
period covered by this book.
†Served temporarily with VMF-223 or VMF 224 prior to arrival of
squadron as a unit.

2/Lt JR Stack (11/10)
2/Lt FC Thomas (11/2)
2/Lt EV Wagner (11/10)
2/Lt JF Wagner (11/10)
2/Lt WW Wamel (11/7)

S. Sgt WH Cochran, Jr. (11/10. MIA 11/11)
S. Sgt. GJ Conti (11/10)
S. Sgt. TC Hurst (11/2, Shot down 11/14. Walked in 11/30)

MARINE SCOUT BOMBING SQUADRON 131

(VMSB-131)

November 12–into 1943

Pilots   (*arrival date*)
Lt. Col P Moret (11/12)
Capt JC Aggerbeck (11/14)
Capt GE Dooley (11/12)
1/Lt DA Bangert (11/12)
1/Lt WW Dean (11/12)
2/Lt JJ Conrad (11/12)
2/Lt EM Hatfield (11/12)

2/Lt Hayter (11/12)
2/Lt T Levandowski (11/12)
2/Lt McGuire (11/12)
2/Lt McShane (11/14)
2/Lt AT Molvik (11/14)
2/Lt MB Roush (11/12)
2/Lt Smyth (11/14)
2/Lt JL Warren (11/14)

The War Diary of this squadron is very sketchy, not listing any of the aircrewmen and including only the last names of some pilots.

MARINE SCOUT BOMBING SQUADRON 142

(VMSB-142*)

November 12–into 1943

Pilots   (*arrival date*)
Maj RH Richard (11/12)
2/Lt GL Allen (11/12)
2/Lt AL Clark (11/12)
2–Lt MK Cohenour (11/12)
2/Lt RR Finch (11/12)
2/Lt AO Hellerude (11/12)
2/Lt JS Henderson (11/12)
2/Lt A Wiggins (11/12)
M.Sgt DS Thornbury (11/12)
S. Sgt AC Beneke (11/12)

Aircrewmen
Sgt EJ Bober (11/12)
Pvt GC Armstrong (11/12
Pvt JD Audas (11/12)
Pvt JC Charter (11/12)
Pvt JE Connor (11/12)
Pvt JJ Denny (11/12)
Pvt JT Grant (11/12)
Pvt TL Huddleston (11/12)
Pvt TB Johnson (11/12)
Pvt JA Keith (11/12)

*The remainder of the squadron came up following the period covered by this book.

APPENDIX B
*Officers and Aircrewmen of Carrier Air Group Ten**
CAG CDR R. K. Gaines

FIGHTING SQUADRON TEN (VF-10)

Pilots   (*remarks*)
Ledr JH Flatley
Ledr WR Kane
Lt JC Eckhardt
Lt RE Edwards
Lt FE Faulkner
Lt CE Harris
Lt McG Kilpatrick
Lt AD Pollock
Lt SG Ruehlow
Lt JF Sutherland
Lt SW Vejtasa
Ltjg JD Billo
Ltjg WK Blair
Ltjg HA Carey
Ltjg JA Leppla   (KIA) 10/26)
Ltjg RE Reiserer
Ens GF Barnes   (KIA 10/26)
Ens AG Boren
Ens Boydston
Ens JE Caldwell   (KIA 10/26)
Ens JD Coalson
Ens GV Davis   (KIA 10/26)

Ens F Donahoe
Ens J Dowden
Ens EL Feightner
Ens LJ Fulton
Ens D Gordon
Ens Harmon
Ens Hendrick
Ens Heinston
Ens Kanzie
Ens SG Kona
Ens WH Leder
Ens MP Long
Ens AE Mead   (POW 10/26)
Ens McClougherty
Ens WB Reding
Ens RE Rhodes   (Pow 10/26)
Ens Schonk
Ens LE Slagle
Ens PE Souza
Ens RM Voris
Ens MN Wickendoll
Ens RR Witte

---

*This air group, in addition to operating from U.S.S. *Enterprise* in the battles of Santa Cruz and Guadalcanal, was based at Henderson Field, November 13–16.

BOMBING SQUADRON TEN (VB-10)

Pilots   (*remarks*)

Ledr JA Thomas
Ltjg RD Gibson
Ltjg RH Goddard
Ltjg JL Griffith
Ltjg JG Leonard
Ltjg BA McGraw
Ltjg JD Wakeham   (KIA 11/14)
Ltjg FR West
Ens RN Buchanan
Ens JH Carroum   (Shot down 11/14. Recovered 11/28)
Ens DH Frissell
Ens PM Halloran   (KIA 11/14)
Ens RA Hoogerwerf
Ens GC Nelson
Ens L Robinson
Ens EJ Stevens
Ens NE Wiggins

Aircrewmen

ARM 1/c HC Ansley   (KIA 11/14

Lt VW Welch   (KIA 11/14)
Ltjg HL Buell
ARM 3/c JC Bennett
ARM 3/c E Gallagher
ACRM GC Gardner
ARM 3/c RJ Haas
ARM 2/c CHO Hamilton
ARM 3/c DO Herget
ARM 3/c RH Horton
ARM 3/c RC Hynson   (Shot down 11/14)
ARM 3/c CV Mayer
ARM 3/c Lt McAdams
ARM 3/c JW Nelson
ARM 2/c HS Nobis
ARM 3/c CH Otterstetter
ARM 2/c CE Schindele
ARM 1/c FG Stanley   (KIA 11/14)
ARM 3/c JG Teyshak

SCOUTING SQUADRON TEN (VS-10)

Pilots   (*remarks*)

Lcdr JR Lee
Lt WI Martin
Lt SB Strong
Ltjg HR Burnett
Ltjg Bloch
Ltjg MD Carmody
Ltjg RF Edmondson
Ltjg WC Edwards
Ltjg HN Ervin
Ltjg CG Estes
Ltjg JH Finrow
Ltjg WE Johnson   (KIA 11/14)
Ltjg TW Ramsay
Ltjg JF Richey
Ltjg LJ Ward
Ens CB Irvine

Ens L Lucier
Ens MD Mohr

Aircrewmen

ARM 3/c N Baumgartner, Jr.
ARM 3/c DuB Bevier, Jr.
ARM 3/c HC Blalock
ARM 2/c WC Colley
ARM 2/c LS Craft
ARM 3/c JE Criswell
ARM 1/c CH Garlow
ARM 2/c RA Gowling
ARM 3/c HP Hughes, Jr. (KIA 11/14)
ARM 2/c J Liska
ARM 3/c JA Moore
ARM 3/c JB Pugh
ARM 2/c RE Reames

ACRM IA Sanders
ACRM FJ Sugar
ARM 2/c LM Wheeler

ARM 3/c EP Williams
ARM 3/c RP Wynn

TORPEDO SQUADRON TEN (VT-10)

Pilots   (*remarks*)
Lcdr JA Collett   (KIA 10/26)
Lt AP Coffin
Lt JW McConnaughay
Lt MD Norton
Lt MD Thompson
Ltjg RK Batten
Ltjg JE Boudreaux
Ltjg GL Welles
Ltjg RL Wyllie
Ens RE Oscar
Ens JM Reed   (KIA 10/26)
Aircrewmen
ARM 3/c RW Ackley
AM 2/c EB Bjerke
AMM 3/c Bjorklund
ARM 1/c DK Coffey
          Courtney
          Dahl
AMM 3/c HC Ehemann

ARM 3/c MC Emberson
          Frissell
AMM 3/c M Glasser   (KIA 10/26)
AMM 3/c RW Grueble
ARM 3/c MG Harrison   (KIA 10/26)
ARM 3/c LE Hollingsworth
AM 2/c RS Holgrim
          Kraft
AMM 3/c Langworthy
ARM 2/c JF McMullen
ARM 1/c   Mitchell
AM 1/c S Nadison   (KIA 10/26)
ARM 1/c TC Nelson   (KIA 10/26)
AMM 3/c TA Powell
AMM 1/c   Richards
ARM 3/c WM Schmeckle
          Shinneman

APPENDIX C
Organization of Japanese Naval Aviation in the South Pacific, August 7–November 15, 1942

August 7

25 Air Flotilla	Rear Admiral Sadayoshi Yamada		Rabaul
Tainan Air Group	24 Zeke		
2nd Air Group	15 Hamp, 16 Val		
Yokohama Air Group	7 Mavis, 9 Rufe	Tulagia	
	2 Mavis, 2 Rufe	Rabaul	
4th Air Group	32 Betty	Vunakunau airfield	

9 Bettys of the Misawa Air Group flew down from Tinian on the morning of August 7 and the remaining 17 arrived the next day.

September 2

11th Air Fleet	Vice Admiral Nishizo Tsukahara	Rabaul
25th Air Flotilla	Rear Admiral Sadayoshi Yamada	Rabaul
Tainan Air Group	10 Zeke	Rabaul
2nd Air Group	16 Hamp	
	6 Val	Rabaul
4th Air Group	12 Betty	Rabaul
Toko Air Group	10 Emily	Shortlands, Rabaul

26th Air Flotilla	Vice Admiral Jinichi Kusaka	Kavieng
Kisarazu Group	12 Betty	Kavieng
Misawa Air Group	12 Betty	Rabaul
6th Air Group	20 Zeke	Rabaul

September 30

| 11th Air Fleet | Vice Admiral Nishizo Tsukahara | Rabaul |
| 25th Air Flotilla | Rear Admiral Sadayoshi Yamada | Rabaul |

Tainan Air Group	8 Zeke	Rabaul
2nd Air Group	16 Hamp	Rabaul
6th Air Group	12 Zeke, 13 Hamp	Rabaul
3rd Air Group	20 Zeke	Rabaul
Kanoya Air Group*	8 Zeke	Rabaul

| 26th Air Flotilla | Vice Admiral Jinichi Kusaka | Kavieng |

Kisarazu Air Group	15 Betty	Kavieng
Misawa Air Group	12 Betty	Kavieng
Takao Air Group	19 Betty	Kavieng
Kanoya Air Group*	16 Betty	Kavieng

October 15

| 11th Air Fleet | Vice Admiral Jinichi Kusaka | Rabaul |
| 25th Air Flotilla | | Rabaul |

Tainan Air Group
6th Air Group*
3rd Air Group
Kanoya Air Group

| 26th Air Flotilla | | Kavieng |

Kisarazu Air Group
Misawa Air Group
6th Air Group*
2nd Air Group
31st Air Group

| 21st Air Flotilla | | Rabaul |

Hq only (no operational units at this time)
Total operational strength of the 11th Air Fleet in this period averaged 50 Bettys, 40 Zekes, 40 Hamps, 20 Vals, 8 Mavis and Emilys.

November 1

| 11th Air Fleet | Vice Admiral Jinichi Kusaka | Rabaul |
| 21st Air Flotilla | | Kavieng |

---

*This group split, fighters at Rabaul, bombers at Kavieng.

253rd Air Group	20 Zeke	Kavieng
751st Air Group (formerly Kanoya A. G.)	30 Betty	Kavieng

25 Air Flotilla (returned to Japan November 10) | | *Rabaul*

251st Air Group (formerly Tainan A.G.)		Rabaul
582nd Air Group (formerly 2nd A. G.)	Average of 30	Rabaul
253rd Air Group	Zeke	Rabaul
202nd Air Group (detachment)	Opera-	Lae
24th Air Flotilla (detachment)	tional	Lae

26th Air Flotilla | | *Rabaul*

204th Air Group (formerly 6th A. G.)	20 Zeke	Rabaul
705th Air Group (formerly Misawa A. G.)	20 Betty	Rabaul
707th Air Group (formerly Kisarazu A. G.)	20 Betty	Buin

Flying Boat Unit

851st Air Group (formerly Toko Air Group)	Rabaul
14th Air Group (detachment)	

November 15

11th Air Fleet		*Rabaul*
21st Air Flotilla		*Kavieng*

253rd Air Group		Rabaul, Kavieng
751st Air Group		Kavieng

26th Air Flotilla | | *Rabaul*

204th Air Group	Buin
582nd Air Group	Rabaul
705th Air Group	Rabaul

Flying Boat Unit | *Rabaul*

851st Air Group

APPENDIX D
U.S. Navy and Marine Corps Squadron Designations

As in most air forces in the world, the basic aviation unit in naval and Marine aviation was the squadron. These varied in size depending on the particular mission of the unit. The principal combat missions in naval aviation in mid-1942 were fighting, scouting, dive-bombing, torpedo-bombing and patrol. These missions were indicated by the letters F, S, B, T, and P respectively. A squadron designation was made up of the prefix "V," which was a generic symbol standing for aircraft, followed by the mission letter, followed by a number. Thus Fighting Squadron Five was abbreviated VF-5 (and referred to in conversation as "Fighting Five"). A 1942 carrier air group consisted of one fighter squadron, which increased in size from 18 to 38 aircraft during that year; one 18-plane scouting squadron; one 18-plane dive-bombing squadron (the scouts and the dive bombers flew the same type of aircraft and, as a practical matter, were completely interchangeable. The distinction vanished in 1943); and one 12-plane torpedo squadron. Carrier squadrons were given the hull number of the carrier to which they were assigned. Thus *Enterprise* which bore the hull number 6 would normally have had based on board VF-6, VS-6, VB-6 and VT-6.

Marine squadrons used essentially the same system except that they combined the scouting and dive-bomber missions in one squadron, and their designations included the letter "M" following the "V" to indicate Marine Corps. However their squadron numerals, rather than being sequential as they were in the Navy, followed a 3-digit system. The first two digits established the Marine Air Group (abbreviated MAG) to which the squadron belonged. The third digit was 1, 2, 3 or 4, since each MAG had four squadrons assigned. Thus VMF-121 was a fighter squadron assigned to Marine Air Group 12.

As always happens in wars, peacetime affiliations are broken and units assigned wherever they are most urgently needed. By the late summer of 1942, some carriers had on board squadrons nominally assigned to two or three other carriers, and Marine Air Groups went into combat with their attached squadrons assigned on the basis of availability.

APPENDIX E
Sources

The outstanding single piece of primary source material on the Cactus Air Force is the war diary of Marine Air Group 23. That of MAG-14, which succeeded MAG-23 in operational control on Guadalcanal in mid-October is unfortunately short and sketchy. The war diary of Commander Air Force South Pacific is indispensable for its account of the concerns of higher command and the varied relief measures undertaken to keep the Cactus Air Force flying. The squadron war diaries vary greatly in quality and amount of detail. Those of MF-223 and -224 were particularly good, as were those of Torpedo Eight and Fighting Five. VMF-212, on the other hand, appears to have left no written record of its important service on Guadalcanal; the history of the 67th Pursuit Squadron was recreated from the memories of a few of its surviving pilots almost a year after the great events in which it played such a part. The diaries of VMSB-131 and 132 are very fragmentary for this period. For the carrier air groups, the post-battle reports of *Saratoga*, *Enterprise* and *Hornet* were done carefully and in great detail.

On the Japanese side the primary sources are very few. The most useful are translations of the Eleventh Air Fleet's war diary, the Daily War Report of the 25th Air Flotilla and Summary of Information, 26th Air Flotilla. Although not primary sources in the strict sense, two histories written by Japanese staff officers for General MacArthur's headquarters after the war are invaluable. These are the *Outline of Southeast Area Naval Operations* and *Southeast Area Naval Air Operations*. Although both have some gaps and numerous

235

errors, the authors evidently had access to all the pertinent Japanese records that survived the war. Two reports of the U.S. Strategic Bombing Survey that were particularly concerned with naval operations, *Interrogations of Japanese Officials* and *Campaigns of the Pacific War*, are most useful.

Among secondary sources, John Miller, Jr's *Guadalcanal: The First Offensive* (Department of the Army, 1949) is the best account of the background of the invasion. Volume 5 of Rear Admiral Samuel Eliot Morison's monumental *History of U.S. Naval Operations in World War II* (Little Brown, 1949) is the standard account of the naval battles of the Guadalcanal campaign. Robert Sherrod's classic *Marine Corps Aviation in World War II* summarizes the Guadalcanal air fighting very well, and J. A. DeChant *Devil Birds* (Harper, 1947) includes many anecdotes of interest. Commander E. P. Stafford's *The Big E* (Random House, 1962) besides being one of the best ship histories ever written has much material of interest to a historian of Guadalcanal's air battles. General A. A. Vandegrift's *Once a Marine* (Norton, 1964) is a solid narrative, useful for its statement of his feelings and reactions to the campaign's many crises. Richard Tregaskis' famous *Guadalcanal Diary* (Random House, 1943) contains interesting accounts of the earlier air fighting. Other wartime books worth reading are H. L. Merillat *The Island* (Houghton Mifflin, 1944); Eugene Burns' *Then There Was One* (Harcourt Brace, 1944); *Joe Foss, Flying Marine*, as told to Walter Simmons (Dutton, 1943); and Ira Wolfert, *Torpedo Eight* (Houghton Mifflin, 1943).

Rear Admiral Raizo Tanaka's two articles on Guadalcanal in the *United States Naval Institute Proceedings* (July and August, 1956) are essential to an understanding of the Japanese strategy and tactics during their attempts to recapture the island. *Zero!* by Jiro Hirokoshi and Masatake Okumiya, with Martin Caidin (Dutton, 1956) despite its peculiar title is a useful summary of Japanese naval aviation organization and operations. *Samurai!* by Saburo Sakai with Caidin and Fred Saito (Dutton, 1957) contains a most valuable account of the training of Japanese naval aviators, as well as the first major air combat over Guadalcanal.

INDEX

RELAX!
SIT DOWN
and Catch Up On Your Reading!

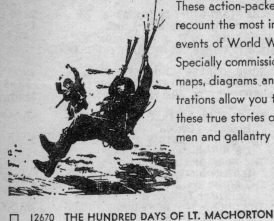

We Deliver!

And So Do These Bestsellers.

Join the Allies on the Road to Victory

BANTAM WAR BOOKS

These action-packed books recount the most important events of World War II. Specially commissioned maps, diagrams and illustrations allow you to follow these true stories of brave men and gallantry in action.

Bantam Book Catalog

Here's your up-to-the-minute listing of over 1,400 titles by your favorite authors.

This illustrated, large format catalog gives a description of each title. For your convenience, it is divided into categories in fiction and non-fiction—gothics, science fiction, westerns, mysteries, cookbooks, mysticism and occult, biographies, history, family living, health, psychology, art.

So don't delay—take advantage of this special opportunity to increase your reading pleasure.

Just send us your name and address and 50¢ (to help defray postage and handling costs).